Gender Politics

Gender Politics

Surya Monro

Pluto Press
LONDON • ANN ARBOR, MI

First published 2005 by Pluto Press
345 Archway Road, London N6 5AA
and 839 Greene Street, Ann Arbor, MI 48106

www.plutobooks.com

British Library Cataloguing in Publication Data
A catalogue record for this book is available from the British Library

ISBN 0–7453–1969–6 hardback
ISBN 0–7453–1968–8 paperback

Library of Congress Cataloging in Publication Data applied for

10 9 8 7 6 5 4 3 2 1

Designed and produced for Pluto Press by
Chase Publishing Services, Fortescue, Sidmouth, EX10 9QG, England
Typeset from disk by Newgen Imaging Systems (P) Ltd, India
Printed and bound in the European Union by
Antony Rowe Ltd, Chippenham and Eastbourne, England

Contents

Acknowledgements

Although this book is written by myself, I can hardly claim sole ownership. Of course, I do not seek to lay the blame for its limitations at anyone else's door; rather, I wish to thank and acknowledge the many people who have helped, influenced, stimulated and challenged me over the years. Those who have particularly supported this work (although they may not agree with all my arguments) include Stephen Whittle, Alice Purnell, Kate More, Roz Kaveney, Salmacis, Zoe Jane Playdon, Kate N'Ysabet, Christie Elan Cane and Simon Dessloch. The contributors to the project on Lesbian and Gay Equality in Local Government were too numerous to list by name. A number of members of the bisexual community have also supported my work or contributed significantly to the book, including Jennifer Moore, Grant Denkinson, and Kerry. Organisations that have been particularly helpful with the research include Press For Change, GENDYS, the Gender Trust, the Gender and Sexuality Alliance, the Beaumont Society, BiCon and Biphoria, Stonewall, and the LGB Consortium.

This book started life at the Department of Sociological Studies, Sheffield University, and I would particularly like to thank Diane Richardson, Lorna Warren, Nick Stevenson and Lena Dominelli for their support with the first research project. My time at the Law Department, Keele University, working with Davina Cooper and Jean Carabine (Open University) provoked an expansion in my understandings of gender and sexuality. The Gender, Sexuality and the Law network and colleagues such as Sally Sheldon and Ruth Fletcher provided a conducive environment for developing this work, and students on the Gender and Sexuality modules I taught also stimulated my thinking. More recent colleagues, including Philip Tovey at the University of Leeds and Brinda Bose at the Centre for Feminist Legal Research, Delhi University, have also supported my interest in gender diversity. Several people read and provided useful comments on the draft: Roz Kaveney, Tracey Lee, Lewis Turner, Sally Sheldon, Davina Cooper, Chris Creegan and Julian Cohen.

It is rather hard to do justice to the other friends – and family members – who have helped with this project. Afron Monro, Paul Wood, Christine Moon, Sunil Nandi, Gordon Maclellan, Jenny Daff,

J.L. Dakin, Dominic Davies, Elizabeth and Ivor Perry, William Bloom, Toni, Lisa Halse, Sue Wardell and Bob White were particularly supportive.

I would also like to acknowledge colleagues at Pluto Press, who have been a pleasure to work with. And, lastly, the Economic and Social Research Council provided funding for most of the empirical research, and the Leverhulme Foundation funded the small project on sexual and gender diversity in India.

List of Acronyms and Abbreviations

FTM: Female-to-Male transsexual
GRS: Gender Reassignment Surgery
LGB: Lesbian, Gay, Bisexual
LGBT: Lesbian, Gay, Bisexual, Transgender
LGT: Lesbian, Gay, Transgender
MTF: Male-to-Female Transsexual
MUD: Moral Underclass Discourse
NSM: New Social Movement
PPM: Political Process Model
RED: Redistributionist Discourse
SID: Social Integrationist Discourse
SM: Sadomasochism

1
Introduction

We inhabit a culture which seems to revolve around fixed categories, opposites, and which seems much less comfortable with ambiguity, change, blurs ... on the issue of gender and sexual binaries, a great deal of cultural, political, and emotional effort and energy has been vested in constructing, reproducing, and sustaining certain opposing categories.

Dunphy 2000: 3

Is it possible to move beyond the male–female gender binary system? What happens to gender theory when we consider sex and gender identities as more than just 'male' or 'female'? In what ways are the sexual orientation categories that we take for granted in the West – heterosexual, lesbian, and gay – destabilised by sexual and gender fluidity? And, crucially, what are the implications of gender and sexual fluidity and multiplicity for social policy, citizenship, new social movements, and democracy?

This book explores the territory that is opened up when gender, and sexual orientation, binaries are disrupted or displaced. The gender binary system is continually problematised, by women and men who transgress gender stereotypes, by sissy boys and tomboys, by butch dykes and camp men, and by many others. Sexual orientation binaries are destabilised when people move between or beyond gay and straight identities. Gender and sexual dimorphism are also continually reinscribed, and people who move beyond – or exist outside of – the binary system are systematically socially excluded via the operation of social institutions and discourses that privilege non-trans[1] and non-intersex[2] people, and heterosexuals, in a wide range of ways.

This book reads from the margins, taking the standpoints of gender and sexual minorities who are socially excluded[3] as its starting point. It reverses the privileging of non-trans men and women, foregrounding issues of relevance to transsexuals, intersex people, cross-dressers, androgynes and people with multiple gender identities, whilst recognising that their interests are shared by anyone who is concerned with creating a society that is more equal and tolerant of difference. It marginalises heterosexuals and addresses the interests of lesbians, gay men, and, in particular, bisexuals and other people with fluid or multiple sexualities. In doing this, it broadens under-standings of gender and sexuality, provoking a more complex and finely grained way of looking at gender and sexual politics, and contributing to the cultural enrichment envisaged by authors such as Parekh (1994). The book paints a temporary picture of a complex, ongoing set of processes. My objective is to provide some tools for analysing this messiness. The book has a limited remit. Whilst emphasising the diversity of gender and sexual minority people's experiences and views, I cannot hope to fully represent them/us in a text of this nature, or to provide any kind of 'expert' view. In addi-tion, I have focussed on the Western, specifically UK, situation, whilst providing some acknowledgement of the situation in other parts of the world, and I have – as noted above – foregrounded trans people, whilst including sexual minorities (especially bisexuals), and, also, non-trans women, in some parts of the book.

I have drawn on empirical material whilst writing this book, enabling me to inform arguments and provide illustrative case studies. My data has been drawn from four main studies (see the method-ological note for more details about these projects and the identities of the contributors). First, I draw on an in-depth exploration of trans politics, which I conducted during the 1990s, and which included transsexuals, intersex people, cross-dressers, drag kings and queens and others. Second, I have used material from a large study of lesbian and gay equalities work in local government (this included bisexu-als and trans people to an extent) which took place in 2001–03. Third, I have included data from a small study of gender and sexual diversity in India, which I conducted in 2003. Lastly, I conducted interviews with a number of bisexual, lesbian and gay, and trans peo-ple during 2003, as a way of updating the earlier study on trans-gender, and gaining more material on bisexuality. In keeping with the usual norms (see Kirsch 2000), I shall identify myself at this stage as a female-bodied bisexual, who does not identify as trans in any substantial way at present, but who has explored some trans identities in the past. I have identified the people who took part in the research projects as research contributors, and their contributions can be distinguished from the literature by the absence of dates in the text.

They are quoted by name unless a preference for anonymity was expressed. The projects that contributors took part in are identified in some cases by the following: (a) Transgender Politics; (b) Lesbian and Gay Equality in Local Government; (c) Gender and Sexual Diversity in India; and (d) LGBT research.

KEY THEMES

This book is underpinned by a number of key debates, which are reflected in varying ways in the literature on gender theory, sexuality, and political economy. The fundamental issue for work in the field of gender and sexual diversity concerns the tensions between fluid, liminal (existing outside of duality) identities, and concrete identities that fit into fixed binary categories. Discrete forms of categorisation form the basis for social identification, identity politics, and social policy initiatives, yet this rigidly binaried categorisation stifles diversity. Post-structuralism reveals the gender and sexual binary system as socially constructed, and lacking an inherent reality. However, post-structuralist approaches are also problematic in a number of ways. I therefore argue for the combination of post-structuralist and other forms of analysis, and I begin to map out different conceptual approaches to gender and sexual diversity.

Another theme, which runs through the book, concerns the tensions between universalism and particularist forms of politics and policy initiatives. Should we aim for 'one size fits all', or universalist, forms of equalities politics, or do we need particularist, diversity oriented approaches, that address the varied needs and interests of the different groups? Universalist approaches are better suited to those types of identity that are fluid or not categorised, as particularist politics requires people to identify with certain categories and identities. Universalism is inclusive, not only of marginalised minorities but also of dominant majorities. However, although it has a number of advantages, it risks glossing over differences and reinforcing the dominant order, because the loudest voices tend to get heard if particular attention is not paid to the quieter ones. Particularism, on the other hand, is useful in foregrounding the interests of minority groups, but is problematic where it 'freezes' identities in a restrictive way, and can also lend itself to factionalism between groups. I argue, following the work of feminist theorists and others, that a combination of universalist and particularist approaches is necessary for gender politics.

A further issue concerns the implications of complex, fluid identities for identity politics. What is the basis for alliances when identities are deconstructed or multiple? The issue is not only that people with deconstructed identities are difficult to organise into movements. The groups that I am concerned with in the book sometimes straddle different, oppositional identity categories – for example some bisexuals have alliances both with heterosexuals and with lesbians and gays, who may build their identities in opposition to heterosexuality. In addition, there are huge tensions between assimilationist politics, where marginalised groups aim to fit into (and become part of) the heterosexual, gender binaried mainstream, and radical, oppositional politics, where people seek to challenge this. These different aspects of the sexual and gender minority communities can lead to a considerable amount of conflict, both within communities, and between them – conflict that is fuelled by the effects of forces such as patriarchy and homophobia. Alliances can, however, be formed, based on notions of respect, self-determination, equality[4] and care. The notion of 'rainbow alliances' is perhaps particularly helpful, as it is inclusive, and covers both universalism (the rainbow) and particularism (the different colours). However, issues will remain concerning differences of interest, and the operation of processes of stigmatisation, problems with achieving representation of all members of communities, and the way in which movements get defused when members access mainstream culture and the associated privilege.

Another key theme for this book is the way in which mainstream citizenship, social policy, and democracy, can – or cannot – be changed to reflect the needs of marginalised groups. These institutions are currently dominated by the interests of white, male, heterosexual, middle-class people, although these interests are hidden because they are generally embedded in these institutions, via hidden assumptions and normalised procedures. For example, mainstream models of citizenship and democracy embody the idea that politics takes place in the public sphere, which disadvantages women, who tend to have less access to the public sphere than men, as well as sexual minorities, because sexuality is framed as a private matter and heterosexuality is privileged by default. Arguably, the recognition of the rights of gender and sexual minorities broadens ideas of equal rights, and the related social institutions, but there are also related dangers in that, by engaging with the mainstream, minorities lose their identities and power base. The debate concerning whether it is possible to extend mainstream institutions is reflected more widely in gender and sexual politics, with ongoing tensions between the creation of separate social spaces and communities, and attempts to integrate and alter the mainstream to make it more equitable. Some forms of politics, for example queer politics and lesbian separatism, are formed in opposition to the mainstream, but this is problematic for people whose identities shift between mainstream and marginalised social spaces.

A further issue is intersectionality, or the relationship between different social structuring factors, such as 'race', class, nationality, disability, gender, and sexuality. This book focuses on gender, and to a lesser extent, sexuality, but I have attempted to locate my discussions of these in the context of the other structuring forces where possible, as gender and sexuality are constructed in relation to them. These forces operate in complex, contextualised ways, and are hierarchical, so that some groups gain power and control over others because people with certain characteristics (such as being white) are privileged over others, and processes of normalisation mask discrimination. Obviously, the way in which these power dynamics operate differs depending on geographical and social location. From a post-structuralist perspective, the power relations are internalised by individuals so that they become seen as natural, although there are sites of resistance to this.

THE ORGANISATION OF THIS BOOK

This book begins by providing the theoretical and empirical foundations for later discussions, before moving on to address the areas of social policy, social movements and activism. Lastly, I explore gender and sexual diversity in relation to the fields of citizenship and democracy.

The second chapter, 'Gender Theory', explores different ways of theorising gender and sexuality beyond the gender binary system. I start by demonstrating the ways in which gender and sexual orientation binaries are exploded by some types of trans and intersex. The destabilisation of the gender binary system also involves the problematisation of the sexual orientation binaries that rely on discrete male–female genders for their meaning. How can this diversity and complexity be theorised? First, gender and sexuality must be understood in relation to other social factors, so I begin by contextualising them via a discussion of intersectionality. I then outline a range of theories concerning gender and critically evaluate these in relation to gender pluralism. Although aspects of second-wave feminisms and masculinity studies are conceptually useful, they are flawed because they rely ontologically on discrete male–female categorisation. Post-structuralist approaches provide crucial tools for conceptualising gender diversity, as does queer theory, but these bodies of theory have some limitations, such as a tendency to overlook bodily realities and to valorise transgression. I therefore explore a number of alternatives that draw on post-structuralism but combine this with recognition of its limitations. These alternatives can be separated into three ideal types: the broadening of the gender binary system, degendering, and gender pluralism. I argue that degendering is useful but limited because it erodes the basis for gender politics, and that broadening the gender binary system, whilst important, fails to include people of all genders. Gender pluralism, whilst problematic in some ways, is the most fully inclusive approach.

In the third chapter, 'Gender, Sexuality, and Social Exclusion', I describe the social exclusion of gender diverse people (transsexuals, cross-dressers, intersex people, gender fluid people, and gender plural people), framing it in relation to theories of social exclusion. Trans and intersex people have varied experiences of social inclusion and exclusion. However, there are some general trends, concerning not only areas traditional to discourses of social exclusion (poverty and employment), but also social institutions such as language, bureaucracy, healthcare, and the family. Trans and intersex people provoke a broadening out of concepts of social exclusion to include cultural and identity factors more fully. This is because the sources of their exclusion are deeply embedded, taking place, in many cases, at earlier stages than those identified by social exclusion theorists. The processes of erasure take place at discursive as well as institutional levels. The discourses that contribute to the social exclusion of gender minorities include ethnocentrism, patriarchy, and homophobia. The stigmatisation of gender diversity reinforces, and is reinforced by, the social exclusion of other groups, especially women and sexual minorities.

The fourth chapter, 'Social Policy Implications', provides a critique of mainstream and some other approaches to social policy, documenting the processes by which gender and sexual minorities are overlooked. I begin by evaluating some of the traditional models of social policy in relation to gender and sexual diversity, concluding that they are usefully pragmatic, but limited in scope. I then explore the work of post-structuralist Carol Bacchi (1999) and apply some of Bacchi's concepts to gender and sexual diversity. I argue that whilst post-structuralist approaches are valuable in foregrounding the processes by which gender and sexual minorities are excluded from policy processes, they need to be combined with the implementation oriented mainstream approaches in order to impact on the social policy arena. I then move on to explore ways of implementing equalities initiatives via equal opportunities policies, arguing that liberal and radical approaches both have positive aspects, but that a strong liberal approach may be most useful for the inclusion of gender and sexual minorities, because it is incrementalist and pragmatic. Lastly, I outline some of the social policy implications of the three theoretical models of gender diversity that I developed in the theory chapter. The broadening gender binaries, and degendering, approaches support measures that are held within strong liberal frameworks. The gender pluralism model is mostly compatible with the former approaches, but goes beyond them, providing greater support for gender diversity. All of these approaches entail support for gender and sexual minorities to engage in policy-making and political processes.

The fifth chapter, 'Activism: Tensions and Alliances', provides an overview and analysis of some of the tensions between, and within, the lesbian, gay, bisexual, trans (LGBT) and feminist communities.[5] I begin by demonstrating the close historical identity overlaps between these different groups, and then describe the ways in which the early gay and lesbian liberation movement became fragmented along gender lines. I outline the ways in which trans and bisexual people are ostracised and excluded by the lesbian, gay, and feminist communities, arguing that although the recognition of difference is necessary, prejudice against trans people and bisexuals – and the resulting exclusion of these groups from lesbian, feminist, and gay organisations – is unjustifiable for a range of reasons. The chapter then moves on to explore the possibility of 'rainbow alliances' – alliances that recognise and support diversity across the range of gender identities and sexual orientations. Alliances across the LGBT communities have developed considerably over the last few years, and are seen by many contributors as being crucial to the development of a progressive and effective movement, but there are ongoing challenges concerning the formation of these alliances.

The sixth chapter, 'Gender, Sexuality, and the New Social Movements', provides an overview of the development of a number of key movements concerning gender and sexuality – the women's liberation movement, the men's movements, the gay and lesbian movement, the bisexual movement, and the trans and intersex movements – analysing them in relation to new social movement (NSM) theory. I argue that NSMs concerning gender and sexuality share many characteristics. They tend overall to move from a period of collective insurgency through to more stable, institutionalised forms – although some have not attained the latter stage. The movements associated with trans, and intersex people are less well developed than some of the others, for various reasons, including the small numbers[6] of people, diversity within the communities, and tensions concerning aims. The bisexual movement is similarly underdeveloped. Its membership is diverse, and the identity fluidity associated with bisexuality means that bisexuals easily become politically assimilated into either heterosexual or lesbian/gay cultures. All of the movements can be analysed using NSM theories to some degree, although some of them highlighted points for further exploration, such as the importance of cyberspace in providing political opportunities, the influence and role of non-political subcultures in the formation of NSMs, and the complex nature of the relationships between NSMs and mainstream organisations.

The seventh chapter, 'Citizenship', outlines some aspects of mainstream models of citizenship and analyses them in relation to feminist, sexual minority, and trans citizenships. Feminist and sexual models of citizenship have developed in response to the inadequacies of mainstream models of citizenship, however, feminist models of citizenship are themselves limited, in that they serve to erase subjects with identities that do not fit into male or female, or gay and straight, categories. Although there is a wide range of approaches to sexual citizenship, there has been little analysis of bisexual citizenship, and existing work on trans, fetish and Sadomasochism (SM) citizenships is limited. Bisexual citizenship focuses on concerns such as increasing bisexual visibility, creating support for same-sex relationships in a way that does not produce rigid categories, and polyamory. SM and fetish citizenships are concerned with equal rights for adults to participate in consensual fetish and SM activities, including group activities in semi-public places. Central concerns for trans citizenship are with rights claims and managing the destabilisation of gender and sexual orientation binaries that trans and intersex involve. I demonstrate the way in which mainstream as well as alternative notions of citizenship can be used in developing notions of citizenship in these areas, and the way in which the citizenship of gender and sexual minorities highlights some of the flaws of the different approaches.

In the eighth and final chapter, 'Gender and Democracy', I expand on earlier discussions and integrate them with existing scholarship concerning democracy. I begin by outlining some of the key aspects of liberal and representative, and participative models of democracy, and I also discuss queer and anarchist trans political stances. These different approaches have a number of advantages and disadvantages for trans politics. Liberal democracy provides central concepts, such as autonomy, justice, and self-determination – concepts that are widely evident in transgender politics – and representative democracy goes some way to including gender minorities. However, these approaches are limited, and prone to the difficulties associated with universalism. Participatory, and strong, models of democracy usefully emphasise citizen engagement in politics, but there is a lack of capacity to support this amongst the gender and sexual minority communities. Queer and anarchist positions helpfully assert the independence of gender minorities, but are arguably lacking in political clout unless combined with other approaches. After evaluating these different types of democracy in relation to trans, I explore a number of relevant debates in the feminist literature concerning democracy. Feminist discussions about universalism and diversity provide a basis for theorising trans and democracy. I argue that a fusion of approaches, in which particularism and universalism are balanced, seems to be the best approach, and that radical pluralism also provides interesting possibilities.

2
Gender Theory

The ultimate thing is to have the option of being fluid ... the thing is we're moving to a much softer and more loose, but finely grained, gendered system.

Kate N' Ha Ysabet

We live in a world that is deeply structured by sex and gender. The categorisation of people as 'male' or 'female' permeates our society on every level, including our language, relationships, social institutions, and academic debates. On a social level, biological determinism, or the belief that we act in certain ways because of our physical make-up, is rife. This is the case despite the changes that have occurred over the past century in the way that gender and sexuality are constructed, and high levels of cross-cultural gender and sexual variance. The development of constructionist, or 'nurture', approaches, and, more recently, post-structuralist (and postmodernist) theories, has disrupted biologically determinist approaches to gender and sexuality, but at the same time, evidence to support the existence of some biological basis for gender differences continues to emerge (see for example Swaab 1995).

This chapter provides a critical overview of some of the key issues and bodies of theory concerning gender, in order to provide a basis for theorising gender and sexual diversity, and begins an exploration of different ways of conceptualising gender pluralism. The chapter is divided into four separate, but related, sections: the first is titled 'Trans and Gender/Sexual Orientation Complexity'; the second, titled, 'Intersectionality', focuses on the intersections between social characteristics such as 'race',[1] class, and sexuality. This part of the chapter provides a foundation for the later focus on gender, and includes an illustrative case study of gender and sexual diversity in India. The third section is titled 'Overview of Existing Theories' and the fourth, 'Gender Pluralist Theory'. It is important to point out that some authors conceptualise gender as being determined by processes concerning sexual orientation, others see sexuality as resulting from gender, whilst still others see gender and sexuality as being interwoven, so that our gender identities are shaped by our sexual orientation and vice versa (see Richardson 2000d). Whilst holding ultimately to the latter viewpoint, I focus this discussion on gender, because the process of gender ascription in infancy seems to precede the ascription of sexual identities, serving in practice as a foundation for later categorisation. I would also like to note that although I provide an indication of the importance of intersectionality, dealing in any depth with cross-cultural variations in gender and sexual categorisation is outside of the scope of this book. Interested readers can refer to Feinberg (1996), Herdt (1994), Bullough and Bullough (1993), Ramet (1997) and Prieur (1998). Similarly, analysis of disability and gender/sexual fluidity and multiplicity is an important area, which I do not deal with here (see for example Blackburn 2002). I also do not address some of the other relevant issues, such as challenges to gender norms amongst non-trans people, which are widely discussed in the feminist and masculinities literature.

TRANS AND GENDER/SEXUAL ORIENTATION COMPLEXITY

This section explores the ways in which gender and sexual diversity challenges rigid gender and sexual orientation binaries in the West. Most Western people are brought up to think that being 'male' or 'female' is a crucial aspect of identity – and that 'female' and 'male' are the only options available. Transgender and intersex challenge this normalisation of gender binaries. Sexual orientation categories are also disrupted when people have non male/female genders, or experience gender fluidity, because the notions of 'lesbian', 'gay', 'heterosexual/straight', and 'bisexual' are based on male and female categorisation.

Gender Diversity

Gender diversity provides a challenge to the gender binary system in a number of ways – via intersex, third or other genders, gender fluidity, positions outside of gender, gender fuck and gender queer. Whilst the majority of trans people and cross-dressers exist within a gender binary system, identifying as either male or female, there are a range of other people who are gender diverse. Gender diversity which challenges the gender binary system includes:

1. Intersex, which disrupts the binary system on two levels: on a physical level, as the various conditions subsumed under the umbrella term of intersex involve physiological characteristics (for example chromosomal, hormonal and gonadal) which are other than (or a mixture of) those conventionally associated with males and females; and in terms of identity, as research contributions showed that in some cases intersex people wish to have an identity that is other, or in addition to, male or female (projects (a) and (d)).

2. People who are born as male or female but seek to identify as androgynous, third, fourth, or other sexes or genders, or as non-gendered. Some of my research contributors (projects (a) and (d)) identified as other than male or female. For example, Simon Dessloch, a female-to-male (FTM) trans person, said that he felt himself to be in between, or neither, or both, or third sex. Similarly, Christie Elan Cane, who started life as female, said in 1998:

   > I don't feel male or female, and I say that I'm basically third gender because I can't identify as male or female ... I mean I'm still trying to unravel how I wanted to be. I wondered whether maybe I could be part of both, which is not how I feel any longer but I sort of went through several stages along, trying to express and figure out how I felt, but now I feel I'm neither. I can't relate to male and female.

3. 'Third space' as opposed to 'third sex or gender' (see Bornstein 1994, Nataf 1996, Garber 1992). 'Third space' allows for the articulation of various gendered identities, without these identities being solidified into clear categories.

4. Gender fluidity amongst trans people during the period that they are changing sex (and in some cases, later). For example contributor Zach Nataf described the way that, during the early stages of his transition from female to male, he felt more like a man on some days and more transgendered on others, and that this depended to an extent on who he was with (see also Bornstein 1994).

5. Fluidity amongst other gender diverse people, including drag kings and queens, cross-dressers and transvestites. Butch dyke Hamish described gender fluidity as a state in itself, whilst gender

transient Phaedra Kelly said:

> It's about a discipline of duality with an open mind, without changing sex with hormones, with pills, with injections or surgery, living one's dualism as much as possible. If I am Phaedra, I allow elements of Bruce through, and there is no self-hating or loathing going on. If I am Bruce I allow elements of Phaedra – it's horses for courses, but like the transvestite, and to some degree the trans person living full-time, I live with a separate identity. I have accepted my separate identity as well.

6. Transsexuality as a space beyond gender binarisms. Cameron (1996) sees transsexuality as an in-between place outside of gender duality, while Stone argues that 'a trans person currently occupies a position which is nowhere, which is outside of the binaried oppositions of gendered discourse' (1991: 295). Some contributors mirrored this, for example Christie Elan Cane discussed moving beyond the gender system and being non-gendered.

7. 'Gender fuck', which refers to conflicting sex/gender signals. In some cases these are consciously taken on as part of identity (see Halberstam 2002).[2] Kate N'Ha Ysabet explained that:

> if I have a penis and big tits that's gender fuck, if I wore makeup and butch clothing that's gender fuck. And what's quite interesting is that androgyny is acceptable because there's a reason for that, but gender fuck isn't, because people go 'oh, OK' but with gender fuck its this thing of 'shit, I'm getting two sets of signals' and it feels like you're having a drum and bass mix on one side and classical music on the other and you're going 'Oh my God which am I going to listen to?'

8. 'Gender queer': this is any type of trans identity that is not always male or female. It is where people feel they are a mixture of male and female.

9. Non-gendered people – people who refuse to be defined in a gendered way.

10. Intentional eunuchs (see for example <http://bmeworld.com/smooth/>), who may or may not have sexual reasons for their castration.

11. Multiple genders (sometimes called 'gender pluralism'). This is where an individual has a number of differently gendered personalities, and is non-pathological.

12. Gender variant people's reproduction. This includes FTM trans people who have had babies after starting their gender transition (stopping hormone treatment in order to conceive and deliver, but continuing to identify as male) (More 1998), male-to-female (MTF) trans people who store sperm in order to be able to parent after transition, and trans people who parent in alternative ways, for example in a lesbian relationship after one partner has had gender reassignment surgery.

13. Unintentional gender variance following surgical removal of gonads or genitals due to illness (see for example <http://prostrate-help.org/caeunuc.htm> which documents a survivor of prostate cancer identifying as a eunuch). Of course, many people who have had this type of surgery will continue to identify as male or female.

The gender pluralism and multiplicity, which are evident amongst some trans and intersex people, disrupt culturally entrenched notions of gender binarism. They provoke discussions of a society in which there are more than two types of gender, and in which for some people, gender is fluid or multiple. Gender pluralism has important implications for systems of sexual orientation, as well as for theory concerning gender and sexuality.

Sexual Orientation

The sexual orientation categories that are used in the West – lesbian and gay, heterosexual, and bisexual, are based on the gender binary system. In other words, being heterosexual means being attracted to people of the opposite sex, whereas being lesbian or gay entails same-sex attraction, and bisexuality involves attraction to both males and females. Our system of sexual orientation categorisation is problematised by gender diversity (see Rothblatt 1995) physically, in terms of sexual expression, and socially, in terms of identity. Gay, lesbian, and heterosexual sexualities rely on the notion that people are only attracted to people of one sex (this can also be termed 'monosexual'), that there are only two sexes and genders, and that people can be identified as clearly falling within one of them. The term 'bisexuality', whilst allowing for polysexual attraction (desire for people of more that one sex) also implies two sexes and genders. As I have shown above, gender diversity sometimes involves gender fluidity and non-male/female genders. Whilst the majority of people can relate to notions of same-sex or opposite-sex attraction, the categories of LGB (lesbian, gay, and bisexual) and heterosexual are insufficient in describing, for example, attraction between an androgyne and someone who identifies as gender transient. Sexual orientation categories based on the gender binary system are disrupted by gender diversity. The genitals of some gender diverse people are physiologically 'other' than those usually associated with women and men, although, of course, these people may identify as male or female. For example at the 1998 Transgender Film Festival Del LaGrace Volcano (an initially female bodied person who took testosterone) displayed photographs of his and other people's phalloclits, which resemble small penises enwreathed in labial lips. Sex between people with non-standard genitals is unlikely to fit heterosexual, gay, or lesbian sexual norms. As FTM trans person James Green told me: 'First of all I never had sex as a woman, and I will never have sex as a man. You know, I will always in that sense be other. And I cannot pretend that I'm not a transgender male.'

The destabilisation of sexual orientation categorisation that gender diversity can provoke may elicit a number of different types of (often overlapping) response. I will list these briefly here, before exploring them in more depth:

- alternative types of sexual orientation are developed, for example 'polysexual';
- individuals and groups continue to use existing definitions, whilst acknowledging their limitations;
- there is overlap of categories when people move around different gender subject positions;
- the signals associated with gender diverse and LGB images conflict, causing tensions between different groups;
- gender diversity and the tensions it provokes are channelled into sexual expression, for instance, contributor Zach Nataf said 'Once you've realised how unfixed gender is already, then sex, then sexuality, you know, gets thrown up [for questioning], you know it's just open.'

Alternative types of sexual orientation include those documented by Queen (1997): 'omnisexual', (attracted to multiple genders), and 'pansexual', a term coined by Firestone (1970) to mean diverse, unbounded desire. Other alternatives include for instance 'trannie lover'. These terms are not widely used, even in the sexual fringes where people are conversant with sexual orientation fluidity.

Individuals and groups continue on the whole to use existing definitions, even when they do not fit very well. For example, Annie Cox,
a MTF trans person, defined herself as a 'woman who loved woman'
although she has a penis, whilst Rosario (1996) describes a study of
the partners of gay FTM trans people who were happy with their
partners having vaginas, despite identifying as gay. These issues also
apply to the category of bisexual:

John: Some bisexuals are aware of the way in which gender diver-
                 sity problematises the category of bisexual ... I am careful
                 to say I am attracted to more than one gender. We need
                 strategically to use 'bisexual' as it's known – I am uncomfort-
                 able with pansexual and omnisexual. Bisexual is sufficient to
                 freak people out, if we go further, it is even more alienating
                 than with bisexuality.
Interviewer: *You don't see 'bisexual' as binaried?*
John: No – I am uncomfortable about the 'bi' aspect and the 'sex-
                 uality' aspect. I want an equivalent to 'lesbian' or 'gay' [in
                 which lifestyle and political aspects are acknowledged].
Interviewer: *What are the implications of this for third or intersex people?*
John: There's an option of being monosexual – you could only be
                 attracted to one type ... I think sexual identity comes from
                 gender identity, and if you identify as male or female you can
                 slot into gay and lesbian categories. It's much easier.

Overlap of categories occurs when people move through a number
of different spaces or identities. For example contributor Kate More
said 'the only space I don't occupy, I think, is bisexual. And yet, in
every way taking gay, lesbian, straight, whatever into consideration.
Taking all three roles, that would make me bisexual I suppose.' This
kind of statement is confusing for people who use mainstream
sexual orientation categories, which tend to assume a single sexual
identity being taken over a period of months or years – people do
not generally think of someone being 'gay' for a couple of hours,
then 'heterosexual' for the next couple of hours. People who are
fluid about their desires might identify as bisexual. However, it is
also possible to be bisexual and in a monogamous relationship for
years, perhaps 'freezing' someone to an extent in an identity as
'heterosexual' or 'gay' or 'lesbian' – but also illustrating the way
in which desire and sexuality mean more than physical sexual
expression.

Gender and sexual orientation fluidity or multiplicity may cause conflicts within the cultures associated with sexual minorities. This is because signals that challenge gender stereotypes have historically been used by gay men and lesbians as a way of identifying themselves – butch and camp are important aspects of lesbian and gay culture. For example More (1996) described how MTF trans person and camp gay signifiers conflict, disrupting the delicately cross-gendered discourses of the lesbian and gay communities. She discussed the way in which transgender implodes the established divide between gender and sexuality, in which femininity and masculinity, can, for example, be associated with heterosexuality, and cross-gender identities associated with the lesbian and gay cultures.

Another, very different way of dealing with gender and sexual orientation fluidity and contradiction is found in various fringe sexual scenes. Some of the people involved in trans, fetish, or sex work worlds eroticise gender and sexual orientation dissonance and multiplicity (see Nataf 1996). This takes place amongst some gender diverse people, for example:

> If you open something up on the other person about their own gender position where they've not actually had that kind of question about themselves before, that gives them access to more material for desire and different ways of being sexual ... they can then take that into a situation with a non-transgender person and open that up for everyone, so that it becomes, in fact it can become a gift. (Zach Nataf)

The fetish scenes provide a space where erotic transgression can take place within semi-public, rather than private, settings. Cross-dressing is an established part of the fetish and sadomasochistic scenes, as is 'gender play' (where different gender identities are enacted in a sexual context). Some of the contributors to research project (a) discussed gender play – for example I met a lesbian who dragged (cross-dressed) as a man and had sex with women as a man, and another lesbian who had several male sub-personalities that she used for sexual purposes. Gender play is also part of some transvestite identities – for example contributor Yvonne Sinclair described auto-erotic activity: 'to see an erect penis poking out from very pretty knickers, a frilly petticoat, and there it is, this woman who's got a prick and bollocks'. Gender diversity is also evident on the sex work scene, where certain types of transgender sex workers (usually 'she males' or preoperative MTF trans people) attract the interest of (usually male) clients – again, this is segregated away from mainstream society (see Evans 1993). Transgender categories are sexualised in unequal ways, reflecting unequal social relations. For instance, sex work primarily revolves around the eroticisation of the she male as gender ambiguous, enabling heterosexual male expression of what is possibly, in some cases same-sex attraction, without disruption of the gender binaried, patriarchal system.

Overall, the complexity that is apparent when gender and sexual orientation categories become fluid and multiple is managed in a number of ways, including continuing with the current, inadequate system, creating alternatives, and eroticising dissonance within certain subcultures that are segregated away from the mainstream.

INTERSECTIONALITY

This section aims to contextualise gender and sexuality, indicating the way in which they are related to other structuring forces. Historically, many of the characteristics that are now routinely seen by social scientists as being social constructs, such as 'race', class, and gender, were once thought to have a biological basis. Praxis (theory and politics) that has moved on from this position has tended to focus on one or two social structuring mechanisms, such as class, sexuality and gender, or 'race', sometimes obscuring or reinforcing other systems of domination.[3] Authors such as McClinton (1995) have explored the ways in which different social characteristics interact. McClinton argues that race, gender and class are related realms of experience, but that they cannot simply be yoked together. They come into existence in, and through, relationship to each other, 'if in contradictory and conflictual ways' (1995: 5). These complex relationships were demonstrated in research project (b), where some contributors discussed 'race', class and gender as 'adding onto' each other, whilst others saw them as combining in specific ways. For example, a black lesbian community member noted that a middle-class black gay man is likely to have very different experiences to those of a working-class black gay man.

Some authors have attempted to produce integrated models of social inequalities. For instance, Weber (2001) provides an analysis of the ways in which social characteristics structure US society. She outlines the way in which 'every social situation is affected by society wide historical patterns of race, class, gender, and sexuality that are not necessarily apparent to the participants and that are experienced differently depending on the race, class, gender and sexuality of the people involved' (Weber 2001: 19). According to Weber these social characteristics are structured in a hierarchical way, forming systems of oppression, in which certain groups have historically gained power and control over assets and other people, so that some groups become dependent on other groups and are exploited by them. This dynamic is masked by ideologies,[4] so that inequalities are seen as being the result of a group's traits rather than social inequities. Structural inequality continues because members of privileged groups benefit from arrangements, and this is supported by a lack of wider awareness of the experiences of subordinated groups. The dynamics are not uniform – some people's experiences are different from the general pattern – and they are malleable to an extent.

Analysis of power and social inequality can utilise a number of theoretical bases, for example group-based approaches (including Marxism and radical feminism), in which certain groups (middle- and upper-class people, men) are seen to have power and to exploit others in a systematic way, and post-structuralism, in which power is seen as fluid and located in multiple places. I will draw primarily on post-structuralist approaches. For the post-structuralist author Foucault, power operates productively through the heterogeneous micro-relations that form social life (Sawicki 1991) – in other words, everything we do is part of wider power relations, challenging or reinforcing social norms. The mechanism of hegemonic (dominant) power is 'the construction of the subject by a discourse that weaves knowledge and power into a coercive structure that "forces the individual back on himself [sic] and ties him to his own identity in a constraining way" ' (Alcoff 1995: 415). This means that people internalise dominant ideologies and end up thinking that their own position in society is justified, and that society is fair and equal. So, if they are in a subordinate position, it must be 'their own fault', or if in a privileged position, they think they are 'naturally' better or more deserving. For post-structuralists, power is constantly disputed via competing discourses (sets of ideas), so that subjectivity (a person's experience of themselves) is a site of conflict (Weedon 1994). The various discourses associated with race, class, gender, sexuality, age, ability and other characteristics interact in different ways for different people – and these people resist them in varied ways, for instance someone might challenge sexism but perpetrate racism.

The interrelationship of different discourses may be particularly complex for people with fluid genders or sexualities, as they are likely to experience marked changes in social context, meaning that they are affected by very different, sometimes conflicting, sets of discourses at different times. For instance, a MTF trans person may have learnt 'masculine' skills (such as car mechanics) whilst living as a man, but when she goes through GRS (Gender Reassignment Surgery) she may feel under pressure to abandon these due to social pressure to conform to feminine norms – but may also be influenced by feminist critiques of gender stereotyping.

Case Study: Gender and Sexual Diversity in India

What does intersectionality mean in practice? In this case study, which uses material from research project (c), I provide a snapshot of gender and sexuality categorisation in India, highlighting the ways that gender, sexuality, caste/class and processes of globalisation interact. Gender variance in India has ancient, even prehistoric, roots. According to one text, 'The Hijra communities in India have a recorded history of more than 4000 years' (PUCL-K 2003: 17). Hijras, who are born as intersex or as male (some undergo castration), trace their origins to the myths in the ancient Hindu scriptures of the Ramayana and Mahabharata. Hijras belonged to the 'Eunuch' culture that was common across the Middle East and India, where Eunuchs worked as guards, advisers, and entertainers (PUCL-K 2003). Other forms of gender pluralism in ancient India were also socially accepted. Gender variant women took roles as mercenaries, advisers, and religious people, and same-sex sexual expression is also documented, often taking place alongside opposite-sex relationships (Penrose 2001); 'traditionally, sexuality has always been more fluid, less rigidly categorised [than in the West]. Western naming, for many Indians, does not correspond to the amorphous nature of sexual experience' (Seabrook 1997).[5] With the advent of British colonialism, the established social position of gender variant people was undermined, for example the British removed the land rights of the Hijra communities. Indigenous sexualities were also suppressed by the British, and to some extent by Islam (Seabrook 1997).

Current exploratory research in India (project (c)) shows that there are different systems of gender and sexuality classification operating simultaneously, set against the backdrop of ancient systems of gender variance, dominant patriarchal norms, and post-colonialism. These systems are being integrated to some extent by the growing LGBT communities, which bridge indigenous and Western systems of categorization,[6] and are reportedly inclusive of Hijras and Kothis (effeminate gay trans people). Gender or sexually variant Indians who are born female have fewer options than those born as male. They can identify as lesbian or transsexual, but these possibilities are often only available to the middle and upper classes. In theory, people born as male, on the other hand, can identify as gay, transgender, cross-dresser, Kothi or Hijra. In practice, these choices are heavily structured by caste/class and location. As Seabrook (1997) says, 'there are men who call themselves gay in India, but they are overwhelmingly middle class, English speaking, and privileged'.[7]

According to Seabrook (1997), the undefined same-sex expression that was present prior to British rule still takes place to an extent in the slums and villages, whilst amongst the less affluent urban dwellers, a heavily gendered system of male classification has emerged. Men who have sex with men are divided into two categories – the 'karte hain' (those who do) and the 'karvate hain' (those who are done to). Same-sex sexual expression is not linked with gay identification. For instance, one Kothi contributor told me that 'some heterosexual men like anal sex. If I do sex with a straight man, fucking him, he gets some pleasure from anal sex. Homosexuality is about attraction, it's not physical.' Heterosexual identification is usual amongst the giriyas, or active partners. Kothis seem to identify more with transgender than gay identities – although some of the Kothis I met identified as gay. Kothis are further subdivided into feminine and masculine Kothis, reflecting the gender binaried nature of Indian society.

The Kothi and Hijra systems seem to exist side by side, overlapping to some degree. The extent to which Hijras do, or do not, identify as third sex is debatable:

> Hijras are akwas [not castrated] and nirvana [castrated] – some Hijras are akwas, so biologically they are men. They are mostly homosexual though they may be married with kids, but this is due to convenience, they are not bisexual. These are the Kothis, who cross over into the Hijra communities. Less than 1 per cent are intersex and 5 per cent have been castrated … they would not speak about this to most people because it is not in their interest. (Sexual health organisation worker)

This contributor pointed out that Hijras occupy a position in society that is simultaneously revered and stigmatised, and that they cultivate the mystique associated with this. They are seen as having the power to curse or bless people, due to their spiritual heritage, and they are also seen as having a huge potential for embarrassment because they threaten to expose themselves physically if they are not paid. The Hijras utilise these sources of power, retaining a somewhat secure position in society. This means that they can beg, and are less harassed by the police than other gender and sexual minorities.[8] In addition, there are some designated political seats for Hijras, and Hijra involvement in party politics is well documented in the newspapers. Hijras are using their third-sex status to advantage, marketing themselves as 'incorruptible Eunuchs' (Chakraborty 2002). As one contributor said, 'they are seen as not being part of the mainstream, which then allows them to have a place in the mainstream'. However, most Hijras belong to the poorer castes and classes, and economic marginalisation structures their experiences very heavily. As Gupta says, 'Hijras might have an accepted place in Indian society, but it is a place pretty much at the bottom of the heap – making them not only a sexual but also a highly deprived social minority' (2002: 21).

Overall, therefore, it appeared that three main types of gender and sexual classification are current in India – unclassified sexual activity, the Hijra and Kothi systems (where transgender and same-sex expression are merged but are heavily structured by the gender binary system), and Western systems. These three forms of categorisation illustrate intersectionality because their operation is a product of caste, class, and colonialism-related inequalities, as well as the gender and sexuality inequalities that permeate Indian society. The Hijras, by occupying a social position in opposition to the binary system, have carved out a social space in which mainstream norms are rejected or revised, perhaps challenging, but not escaping, other structuring factors.

The sex/gender classification system in India provides an illustration of intersectionality. Intersectionality, or the way in which different social structuring factors interact, forms a crucial backdrop for discussions concerning gender and sexuality, as people's gender and sexual identities, as well as their positions in society, are formed in relation to factors such as class, ethnicity, and nationality.

OVERVIEW OF EXISTING THEORIES

As I have shown, gender and sexuality are constructed in relation to other social characteristics, such as class and nationality. These processes of intersectionality frame the normalisation of the gender binary system, something that is disrupted in the West by people with a range of non-binaried gender identities. What conceptual tools do existing theories of gender and sexuality provide for theorising these types of gender and sexual diversity? This section aims to provide a brief overview of a number of established bodies of theory, examining them in relation to gender, and to a lesser extent, sexuality categorisation. I will begin by very briefly outlining the feminist theories and theories of masculinity that tend to assume the existence of a gender binary system. I will then provide a short introduction to post-structuralist theories, before addressing post-structuralist feminist and masculinities theories and queer theory. I will explore the ways in which these less rigidly binaried approaches can be applied to gender pluralism, and the limitations to post-structuralist approaches that are highlighted by gender pluralism.

Feminisms

It is impossible, within the constraints of this book, to do justice to the range of feminist theories and approaches. I will therefore only briefly outline some of the general characteristics of some of the various feminisms, analysing them in relation to gender categorisation. Detailed accounts of feminisms are provided by authors such as Tong (1998).

Liberal feminism stems from eighteenth- and nineteenth-century thinking concerning individual equal rights (see Tong 1998: 10). As the 'mainstream' face of feminism, it involves a focus on achieving equal rights via reform, particularly in the public sphere – legal, institutional and political struggles for equality (Beasley 1999: 51–2). There is an emphasis on the rights of individuals, limited state intervention in order to redress inequalities, and freedom from prejudice (Beasley 1999: 52). Some liberal feminists recommend androgyny as a means of liberating both women and men – some arguing for monoandrogyny, where individuals combine traditional female and traditional male characteristics (Bem 1976). Others advocate polyandrogyny, where some personality types are totally masculine, some are totally feminine, and others are a mixture of femininity and masculinity (Tong 1998). Liberal feminism can be used as a basis for developing a politics of sexual and gender diversity. The emphasis on individual rights is useful for supporting diversity, and the models of androgyny developed by some liberal feminists are echoed in more recent discussions concerning gender. There are, however, some difficulties with the liberal approach. The liberal emphasis on individual rights overlooks the collective nature of politics, the rationalism associated with liberal models of the self is problematic because rationalism is linked with masculine subjectivities, and liberal feminism serves primarily the interests of middle-class white women (Tong 1998). Also, importantly, liberal notions of androgyny do not extend to physiological gender diversity.

Whilst liberal feminism had its history in movements for social reform, radical feminism developed in relation to the radical civil rights movements of the 1960s.

Radical feminism describes sexual oppression as the primary oppression for women, and other forms of power are often seen as stemming from patriarchy (social systems of male domination). Men as a group are considered to be *the* beneficiaries of this systematic and systemic form of power. (Beasley 1999: 55)

Women are seen as having more in common with each other than any woman has with any man, and various degrees of woman centeredness and separatism are encouraged, ranging from support for other women to the political rejection of heterosexuality (see Beasley 1999: 54–6). These types of approach, like conservative, biologically determinist positions, model women and men as inherently different, with no middle ground or alternative to gender binaries. People who are gender diverse, unless they identify strongly as being female (and 'pass' as female), are excluded by radical feminisms. Although the aim is women's equality, radical feminisms may act to reinforce gender categorisation, for example progressive men are framed as unable to contribute to a more equal society. However, like some liberal feminists, some early radical feminists aimed for androgyny. For example, Millet (1970) discussed an androgynous future in which individuals evaluate and integrate masculine and feminine traits, whilst Firestone (1970) envisaged the development of technology enabling the end of male–female gender differences based on biology. In this scenario, gender roles will have vanished and 'Androgynous persons will find themselves living in an androgynous culture in which the categories of "the technological" and "the feminine" will have disappeared' (Tong 1998: 53).[9] These strands of theory are clearly relevant to gender and sexual diversity, although, as with liberal feminisms, they do not extend to physiological gender pluralism.

Marxist feminists modelled sexual oppression as an aspect of class power. They focused on labour relations and the economic base of society, and a revolutionary approach in which the overthrow of capitalism was seen as necessary to the dismantling of male privilege (Beasley 1999: 60–1). Socialist feminism evolved at the intersections between radical and Marxist feminisms, and involved various approaches which combined both strands of thinking, and which sometimes incorporated insights from psychoanalytic feminisms. Beasley (1999) discusses the demise of Marxist and socialist feminisms following the collapse of socialism in Eastern Europe, although some aspects are being utilised for post-colonial feminist analysis. Marxist and socialist feminisms are problematic for theorising gender and sexual diversity. They risk reinforcing gender binaries, because they model women and men as belonging to discrete gender categories. However, notions of a materialist (economic, social institutional) basis for inequality are important for gender politics because people of non-mainstream genders and sexualities are likely to experience economic disadvantage (see Chapter 3).

Psychoanalytic feminists are concerned with the psychological processes that lead to the formation of women as different from men. There is a range of different psychoanalytic feminisms. French feminists such as Kristeva (1982), and Irigaray (1985) draw on Lacan, linking unconscious mental phenomena with the construction of femininity on both psychological and social levels. For Lacan, the self and sexuality are socially constructed via language. There is no gender or sexuality prior to a child learning language, and language/culture is seen as masculine, with femininity being seen as the negative pole to this. Post-Lacanian feminists reframed this analysis, arguing that the feminine offers a site for cultural creativity that has the potential for disrupting the dominant masculine order (Beasley 1999). The usual critique of feminisms – the way in which they may inadvertently reinforce gender binaries – applies to psychoanalytic feminisms. However, psychoanalytic feminisms could be useful for theorising gender and sexual diversity. For example, insights concerning the way that femininity is erased could be adapted in theorising the erasure of genders that fall outside of the categories of 'female' and 'male'; these latter identities could be reclaimed and celebrated just as 'the feminine' has been reconceptualised by the French feminists. Prosser (1998) and More (1999) provide accounts of transgender that draw on psychoanalysis; Hemmings' (2002) book on bisexuality also utilises psychoanalytic theory.

Black feminisms (including those developed by hooks (1984), Davis (1981) and Hill Collins (1990)) form a variety of positions, and share an underlying critique of white feminism's lack of attention to race and ethnicity. White feminism is seen as marginalising or repressing differences between women, and any idea of a universal female identity is deemed problematic (see Beasley 1999: 104). The anti-assimilationist approaches that developed after the 1970s took two trajectories. First, an identity politics stance emerged, in which identities are seen in terms of common struggle within the black/ethnic communities, and the differences between black/ ethnic and white communities. Second, a social constructivist position evolved, in which assumptions about commonalities between different black and minority ethnic groups are deconstructed, the essential foundation for these identities is rejected, and categories are seen as unstable and fluid. Post-colonial feminisms also involve critiques of the ethnocentricity of white feminist thinking (for example Mohanty et al. 1991). Post-colonial theorists such as Spivak (1987), for instance, examine how racism operates to construct racial boundaries, which continue to organise both the colonalisation of indigenous peoples and the black/ethnic 'diaspora communities'.[10]

There are a number of aspects of black and post-colonial thought that are important in understanding gender and sexual diversity. First, many people who are non-stereotypical in terms of gender and sexuality are black or minority ethnic, yet the Western transgender and LGB movements are predominantly, although not exclusively, white. Black and minority ethnic trans and LGB people in the UK may face different issues. These include exclusion by their own communities in some cases – for example, I met a British Kashmiri gay drag queen who had been forced to leave his community because of his sexual identity. Second, there are a number of parallels between black feminisms, and movements for gender and sexual diversity, including concerns with the paradox concerning identity deconstruction and the need for identity as a basis for activism. Post-colonial feminisms are also relevant, for instance the way that race/ethnic categorisation constructs difference and inequalities on a structural level is mirrored by the ongoing categorisation of people into male, female, gay, lesbian, and heterosexual categories, which perpetuates the marginalisation of people who do not fit these categories.

Masculinity Studies

Masculinities studies encompass a number of perspectives, ranging from conservative and mythopoetic perspectives, and those concerning men's rights through to pro-feminist and postmodern perspectives (see below). As Dunphy (2000: 87) says, the conservative perspective is rooted in (gender binaried) essentialism, in which traditional ideologies of masculinity and femininity are seen as natural expressions of male and female biological, and other, differences. The men's rights movement, which is an extension of this (see Young 1993: 319), reinforces male–female binaries and denigrates women. The mythopoetic movement (Bly 1990), which naturalises a supposedly male spirituality or essence, is also problematic for theorising gender diversity, because it reinforces essentialist notions of masculinity (see Chapter 6). Pro-feminist male theorists, who vary in approach, have developed alternatives. Radical pro-feminists mainly mirror radical feminism in framing masculine privilege as created within a patriarchal system, upheld by violence against women and misogyny. Liberal pro-feminist men see masculinity as a set of constraints that can be reformed, whilst socialist pro-feminists frame masculinity in material terms, grounded in class and economic inequalities (Dunphy 2000). These types of pro-feminist approaches to masculinity studies are useful for theorising gender and sexual diversity insofar as they support the equality of women and men, forming discourses that can be utilised in understanding gender diversity which are particularly relevant to people who identify as male. However, like feminisms, they tend to reinforce gender divisions by framing women and men as distinct groups.

Post-structuralist Approaches

The theories that I have described so far tend to assume that men and women are the only types of sexed/gendered people, and that categories are discrete – even where there is fluidity of gender roles. Post-structuralism goes beyond these approaches, deconstructing not only rigid gender roles, but also the notions of 'male' and 'female' themselves. In this section, I shall provide a short overview of post-structuralism, before outlining some of the core elements of post-structuralist feminist and masculinities studies. I shall then discuss and critique post-structuralist trans theory, before reviewing and critiquing queer theory in relation to gender diversity.

Post-structuralism is an influential body of theory that emerged in the West in the latter parts of the twentieth century. It developed as critiques of mainstream theory and the radical thinking of the 1960s and 1970s (Beasley 1999). Prior to its development, theorists (with the exception of psychoanalysts) tended to assume that people were rational, autonomous beings, with coherent identities, and that there was a foundational essence, or reality, to the world. This approach was called Enlightenment, or modernist, thinking. Post-structuralists, who take a range of different approaches, share a critique of the idea that we make decisions rationally on the basis of a unified sense of self, and that there is an essential truth. Instead, they see subjectivity as socially constructed, often contradictory, and fragile, and reject the notion that there is an underlying reality in our world – instead, 'reality', including gender binaries, is seen as constructed via the exclusion of other options (Beasley 1999). For example, the development of a 'male' identity involves the rejection of supposedly 'female' characteristics, such as the 'caring' involved in playing with dolls, and identification with supposedly 'masculine' traits, such as being competitive. Post-structuralists view subjects as discursively constituted (see below). Some authors, such as Beasley (1999), see post-structuralism and postmodernism as overlapping and interchangeable. However, I will use the term 'post-structuralism', following the work of Smart, who argues that

> although we can construct postmodernism and poststructuralism on a philosophical continuum, so to speak, there remains for me one very important distinction. Postmodernism is a critique of epistemology. It makes us rethink and reconsider what we know. But poststructuralism is more intimately connected with the production of local knowledge ... when I think of poststructuralism I conjure up intellectual work which theorizes about discourses, relationships, subjects. (1995: 8)

The work of Judith Butler (1990, 1991, 1993) is a crucial contribution to post-structuralist gender theory. Her work forms a starting point in discussing post-structuralist approaches to gender pluralism.[11] Butler develops her analysis of gender via Foucault, Freud, Derrida, Lacan and the French feminists. She sees physiological sex, as well as gender, as socially constructed phenomena (1990). Although we tend to think that our bodies are a 'given', actually our experience of them is formed by discourses. Discourse and discursive formations are produced via repetition of ideas and acts (Lechte 1994), which become naturalised (or seen as normal) at both micro and macro levels. While the experience of identity is a reality, this is due to the power exercised on the subject via discourse: we have no separate consciousness (Weeks 1995, Plummer 1995). Therefore, there is no gender identity behind the expressions of gender; 'that identity is performatively constituted by the very "expressions" that are said to be its results' (Butler 1990: 25). For Butler (1997), the repression of same-sex desire forms not only an individual's sexual identity but also their sex and gender. The representation of heterosexuality as foundational or natural (Prosser 1998) means that alternatives become constructed as abnormal or deviant. Butler argues for gender identities that are freed up from any 'given' sex – so that:

> It does not follow that the construction of 'men' will accrue exclusively to the bodies of males or that 'women' will interpret only female bodies ... When the constructed status of gender is theorized as radically independent of sex, gender itself becomes a free-floating artifice, with the consequence that *man* and *masculine* might just as easily signify a female body as a male one, and *woman* and *feminine* a male body as a female one. (Butler 1990: 6)

Post-structuralism has had a profound effect on ways of conceptualising gender diversity, with a number of trans authors drawing on the work of post-structuralists such as Butler (for instance Prosser 1998, Wilchins 1997, More and Whittle 1999). Trans theorists draw on, and develop, post-structuralist accounts in a number of ways, initially following Stone, who saw transsexuality as 'a genre, a set of embodied texts whose potential for productive disruption of structured sexualities has yet to be explored' (1991: 296). Post-structuralist transgender theory has a number of key characteristics: it describes sex and gender as performative rather than fixed; the body as a technologised commodity; the disruption of sex as well as gender; and the plurality of gender binaries. Some transgender theorists see identities as performative and as processual – for example, contributor Kate More, following Butler, described sex and gender as constructed and as occurring through signification. Kate's views are echoed in the work of other trans people, for instance 'Gender is not what culture created out of my body's sex; rather, sex is what culture makes when it genders my body' (Wilchins 1997: 51). Because these attributes are discursively constituted, it is possible to disrupt them. As Shapiro (1991) argues, trans makes the processes of gender explicit and exposes the way in which we are all 'passing' as sexed and gendered subjects and exposing discrepancies between biological sex and gender. Another aspect of post-structuralist trans theory concerns commodification of the body. For Cameron (1996), transsexual bodies are the realisation of the body as image and commodity, and transsexuality is one practice among others, which offers the means for reconfiguring subjectivity. Thus, 'sex reassignment surgery could be seen as just another form of body modification along with piercing, branding and tattooing' (Nataf 1996: 55). Some trans theorists further extend this. For example Nataf (1996) draws on notions of shifting, hybridised, monstrous bodies as envisaged by Haraway (1991), and morphing, which involves changing gender and changing species when in internet virtual reality (see for example Wakeford 2000).

Post-structuralism provides important tools for understanding gender diversity. Notions such as the discursive construction of subjectivity are crucial in unpicking ways in which people are normatively conditioned into binaried sexual and gender identities. The conceptual disassociation of gender identities and bodies also allows theorisation of more complex forms of gender. However, there are a number of limitations to post-structuralist approaches, including:

- post-structuralist transgender and other theories tend to overlook the importance of the body. Contributors mentioned the limits of surgery and the high rates of complications, the effects of hormones and the impact of stature, age and appearance on 'passing'. Research by authors such as Zhou, Hofman, Gooren and Swaab (1995) provides evidence for biological determinism;
- feminist arguments about technologisation as a feature simply of male power (see Wajcman 1991) collapse in the face of trans. For example, Wilchins (1997) documents the use of surgery by one person to retain the head of their penis as well as having a vagina created. However, issues concerning unequal access to, and control over, technology remain pertinent;
- some transgender and other people experience themselves as having an essential self, or gender identity, that is 'other' than their body or social conditioning. Whilst this may, ultimately,

also be constructed, denial of people's lived experience can be oppressive;
- deconstruction can be dangerous if an ethical basis is not developed to shape this in progressive, non-harmful ways (see Weeks 1995). For example sexual fluidity is fine providing it is consensual and between adults;
- post-structuralism (and postmodernism) undermines the unitary nature of identity, because everything is seen as constructed. This is problematic for identity politics:

> What is left to organise around if we don't use identities? While postmodernism has been largely unable and unwilling to apply itself to the nitty-gritty of social change, you and I don't have that luxury. We have a movement against gender oppression to mount. (Wilchins 1997: 85)

Theorists such as Butler (1992) argue that seeing the subject as constructed does not mean that it is predetermined, and that it is the individual's ability to reformulate discourses, and to exploit the contradictions between the different discourses that are imposed on them, that enables agency. Identities can certainly be used and reformulated for political purposes[12] – for example contributor Kerry said that 'I'd look at bisexuality as a tool to be used on the way to gender and sexual cultural subgroups being more fluid and diversifying – bisexuality might not last for ever.' However, arguably, there are still difficulties with the destabilisation of identity that post-structuralism provokes.

Queer Theory

Queer theory emerged during the late 1980s and 1990s, at the intersections between (mostly) lesbian and gay academic work in the areas of literary and cultural studies, and LGB activism concerning issues such as HIV (see Dunphy 2000). It has its roots in post-structuralism, drawing heavily on the work of Foucault (1979). One of the hallmarks of queer theory is the destabilisation and subversion of existing categories. Key theorists (Foucault 1979, Sedgewick 1991) explore the way in which sexual desire is constituted via dualistic discourses, so that people are conditioned to think that heterosexuality and homosexuality are the only options. Queer theory deconstructs gender and sexual identities, primarily via interpretations of cultural texts (see Butler 1990, Sedgewick 1991). For instance, Butler (1990) interprets drag and cross-dressing as queer and as challenging heteropatriarchal norms because they expose the ways in which gender is constructed. Thus, gender identities are enacted with the aim of destabilising the normalisation of certain types of gender and sexuality, so that we are made aware of how *all* genders and sexualities are fictitious. Queer theory also creates space for imagining alternatives to the rigid gender binary system. As Dunphy says:

> It also invites us to investigate the possibilities of a plurality of masculinities and femininities, of a range of ways of living our lives. In so far as this tends towards an implosion of gender as a useful category of analysis, disentangling sex, gender and desire, queer theory also encourages us to focus on the utopia of a gender-free world. (2000: 32)

Queer theory is useful to exploring gender and sexual diversity, and its influence is apparent in the post-structuralist trans theory outlined above. Findings from research project (a) showed that queer praxis can be used to support fluidity and multiplicity. For example, contributor Hamish said

> people can be fluid with their sexualities and their gender by using the definition 'queer'. If someone who has been having relationships with women for 25 years has a one-night stand with a man, it doesn't mean she has to stop being a dyke.

Performativity and gender parody are apparent amongst some trans people, for example:

Joanna/Dave:	I don't come across as your archetypal trannie. I would say I come across as more sort of like, it's a performance, it's all my way of acting, it's sort of like, you're going out you're putting on a show, you know?
Interviewer:	*Yeah, yeah but it's not like drag either?*
Joanna/Dave:	No, no. It's not like that. I am the show.
Interviewer:	*I'm interested in the sort of bit in between the two (transvestite and drag queen). I mean how do you switch, is it just the clothing or is there a mind-switch that goes with it?*
Joanna/Dave:	It's one of those things. As soon as, it's not, once the makeup's on, and then the wig goes on, then it's a complete character change, or can be. Um … It's quite scary actually.

Interviewer: *It's like a different person, is that what you mean?*

Joanna/Dave: Yeah. Cause it's sort of like [Joanna's] taking over … all of a sudden you're switching from one to the other.

Although the term 'queer' is useful for understanding gender and sexual pluralism in some ways, there are difficulties with queer theory. First, Butler (1990) argues that it is only possible to subvert the gender binary system from within the processes of repetitive signifying (i.e. the performance of gender via appearance), which for her does not include surgical alteration. She therefore sees cross-dressing as radical and, in her later work (1993), transsexuality as reactionary. Transsexuality is, in fact, understood by Butler as reinforcing heteronormative constructions of gender (Prosser 1998), and in this respect Butler's work is similar to the transphobic work of Raymond (1980, 1994) (see Chapter 5). Second, there are difficulties with the way in which 'The newly emerging "Queer Theory" is an attempt to get beyond the gendered and sexual practices of the social world, yet it continually harks back to those categories which it seeks to undo; male, female, straight, bisexual' (Plummer 1995: xvi). So, although queer theory seeks to destabilise gender and sexual binaries, it fails perhaps to move beyond them. Transgender disrupts the gender and sexual orientation binaries on which queer theory is based (see Whittle 1996) to the extent that the term 'queer' becomes destabilised and loses cohesiveness. As I have shown, terms such as 'gay' and 'heterosexual' are problematic in the context of shifting, fluid or multiple gender identities. If queer praxis goes full circle (i.e. gender and sexuality binaries are completely deconstructed) it becomes either fluid, or encompassing of heterosexuality. Third, while transgender is defined in some circles as the transgression of gender norms (Bornstein 1994), it is also an umbrella term covering transsexual people and others, some of whom seek to assimilate within the mainstream. The notion of transgression excludes, or is resisted by, trans people who identify as heterosexual and assume conventional gender roles (see Prosser 1998). The term 'queer' has been reclaimed and valorised by the LGB communities, but to some people the term 'queer' is still experienced as oppressive. For instance, contributor Salmacis, who was termed a 'freak' during the course of sexual and emotional abuse, rejected the term 'queer'. A further difficulty concerns the way in which identity politics is rejected and political strategies are underdeveloped. These difficulties can be understood in relation to the way that queer theory developed – amongst an elite group of academics, who were perhaps out of touch with the lived realities of marginalised LGBT people, as well as the importance of political activism (see Dunphy 2000).

Feminism, masculinity studies, post-structuralism, and queer theories provide a number of tools with which to theorise gender diversity. Second-wave feminisms, including liberal, radical, and Marxist theories, provide important insights into some aspects of gender. However, these approaches, like the early forms of masculinity studies, tend to reinforce gender binaries via their reference to 'male' and 'female' as separate categories. The later developments, including black feminisms, post-structuralism, and queer theory, provide means of conceptualising gender and sexuality as constructed, diverse, and malleable – and post-structuralist trans theory has drawn on some of these theories. However, there are difficulties with post-structuralist approaches to gender diversity, including a tendency to overlook bodily limitations and the importance of categorisation as a basis for identity politics. Therefore, I will draw on post-structuralism when I begin to conceptualise gender pluralism, but will also splice in some other elements.

GENDER PLURALIST THEORY

Why have we not begun to count and name the genders that are clearly emerging at this time? One could answer this question in two ways: On the one hand, we do not name and notice new genders because as a society we are committed to maintaining the gender system. On the other hand, we could also say that the failure of 'male' and 'female' to exhaust the field of gender variation actually ensures the continued dominance of these terms ... the very flexibility and elasticity of the terms 'male' and 'female' ensures their longevity.

Halberstam 2002: 370

This section aims to explore different ways of conceptualising gender and sexual pluralism. Theorising the spaces that are opened up when rigid gender binaries are destabilised provokes a number of questions: Is gender diversity likely to be contained within male/female categories, by expanding these categories? Is it possible to move beyond gender altogether? Or, is a gender plural system emerging, in which male/female categories are complemented by other identities, and if so, how can this be theorised? These questions are addressed by different theoretical approaches, which I outline below. Whichever approach is taken, key concepts concern:

- intersectionality: as shown above, gender and sexuality operate *in complex, contextualised, and changing* interaction with other forms of social stratification such as nationality, age, ability, 'race' and ethnicity, and class/socio-economic variables;
- gender and sexuality as made up of a number of different biological, psychological and social factors;
- gender and sexuality as the result of a combination of essentialist and constructed processes (see Bullough and Bullough 1993). These processes are ultimately contingent and temporary (we are born, we age and we die; we can change our bodies, personalities and social situations to an extent);
- the importance of political context and implications: degendering and having plural sexes/genders are strategies that are rejected by many transgender and intersex people. For example, the Intersex Society of North America (<http://www.isna.org/drupal/index.php>) warns academics and others not to claim that it is in favour of three sexes, no sexes or eliminating gender.

The Expansion of Male and Female Categories

As Halberstam (2002) suggests, the elasticity of gender binary categories allows gender diversity to be subsumed into 'male' and 'female' – at least to an extent. This is why, for example, David Beckham can wear earrings and effeminate clothing without his masculinity being disputed. Expanding the gender binary categories involves theorising femininities and masculinities as diverse, including people who have bodies or social roles that are different to those traditionally associated with women and men, for example, intersex people living as male or female (see Dreger 2000). The expansion of binary categories is conceptually related to notions drawn from masculinity studies. The notion of masculinities as plural involves moving away from an understanding of masculinity as white, middle class, heterosexual and able-bodied, towards thinking about masculinities as multiple, and the notion that some masculinities are hegemonic, whilst others are subordinated (see Hearn and Morgan 1990: 11). Hearn and Collinson discuss 'distinctions between gay, nonheirarchic heterosexual, and hierarchic heterosexual; between white and black, between nonfathers and fathers; unpaid careers, paid careers, and non-careers; and non-violent, violent, and militant masculinities' (1994: 107).[13] This understanding of femininities and masculinities as plural is helpful in theorising gender and sexual diversity, because it includes people such as camp gay men, butch women, and trans people who have undergone full sex reassignment.

There are limitations to the 'expanded gender binaries' model, which can be illustrated by looking at the notion of female masculinities. Halberstam (2002) describes a range of female masculinities, for example tomboys, butch dykes, and masculine heterosexual women. This interpretation of gender problematically erases non-binaried trans identities. It also risks co-option of what can be seen as transgressive and positive identities that are arguably female, not male (for example butch). In addition, if masculinity is de-essentialised and unlinked from male bodies, it becomes slippery and hard to characterise, relying on ideas that reinvoke social inequalities, such as rationality and aggression. If, as Halberstam says, 'Masculinity in this [US] society inevitably conjures up notions of power and legitimacy' (2002: 356), then the *delinking of these characteristics from masculinity*, and the construction of female and transgender notions of power and legitimacy, would be a worthwhile project. Another problem with the expanded binaries model is that it fails to include those people who fall more fully outside of the gender binary system, and perhaps defuses the potential for gender pluralism because some alternative identities are subsumed into 'male' and 'female'. However, it is a pragmatic strategy, enabling many people with diverse sexualities and genders to gain social rights and acceptance, as well as perhaps broadening out options for others.

Moving Beyond Gender

Feminist authors such as Lorber (1994) argue for the 'degendering' of society. The notion of gender liminality can be linked with degendering. As shown above, authors such as Stone (1991), Bornstein (1994) and Cameron (1996) describe transsexuality as a place outside of duality. Notions of moving beyond gender, and gender liminality, are useful for conceptualising gender diversity. A number of contributors discussed the need for a less heavily gendered society – for example, the use of 'male' and 'female' on forms when sex/gender is irrelevant to the matter at hand. In a society where there was less concern with gender, androgynous and gender ambiguous people would face fewer barriers to social inclusion, and gender norms overall would be less heavily enforced. A certain amount of degendering is clearly helpful in achieving a more equal, inclusive society. As contributor Jennifer Moore argued, 'I think if the whole world could simultaneously reduce the amount of society and convention that rests on gender divisions and sexuality divisions, that would work.' Similarly, decategorising sexuality can be seen as a useful strategy. For example contributor Grant Denkinson said that 'what I'd like to see is more of a connection with not having binaries, so that rather than having another box that says "bisexual", it's saying it's complicated, fuzzy, but also sometimes you don't need to know the category', and another contributor to project (d) argued that 'people need to start thinking and stop putting other people in boxes'.

Despite the advantages of decategorisation, there are some difficulties with the 'degendering' approaches. First, once fluidity is named, it becomes a space which people can inhabit (see Prosser 1998), and is therefore arguably no longer a non-category. Second, identity categories seem to be necessary as a basis for cultural and political organization – for example, it is important for some trans people to be 'out' in order to gain civil rights for all trans people. If a strategy focused on erasing gender is pursued, the minority gender groups – and those who have less power, including non-trans women – are likely to be disadvantaged because the default dominance of men and non-transgender people will remain unchallenged. Third, degendering, if pursued in a prescriptive manner, would deny people the choice to identify in a gendered way. As contributors to the research argued:

> Abolishing gender is preposterous, as it goes against people's rights for self-determination.

> There is no way to get rid of gender – it's like saying 'let's turn the world into an anarchy'. People are brought up in capitalism, so people will be selfish ... anyone wanting to get rid of the gender system is selfish – they should let people have their fun, so long as it doesn't stop me doing what I want to do. (BiCon conference, project (d))

Gender Pluralism

A further theoretical strategy concerns conceptualising gender as plural, and as a spectrum, a field, or intersecting spectra or continua (see Fig. 1). Gender is seen as being more finely grained than is the case with the binary system, and as being formed via the interplay of different characteristics associated with gender and sexuality.

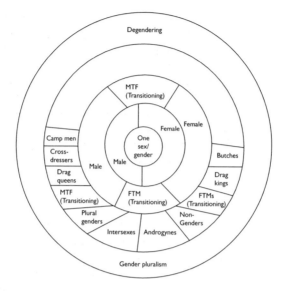

Figure 1   Revised Gender System

Gender pluralism involves 'calls for new and self-conscious affirmations of different gender taxonomies' (Halberstam 2002: 360). It involves conceptualising gender as 'fields' or 'groupings' of – in some cases overlapping – masculinities, femininities, and gender diverse identities. It could entail the more widespread use of pronouns such as 'ze' and 'hir' (see Feinberg 1996) for people who chose them as alternatives to male/female pronouns. The recognition of more gender possibilities also means that the categories of 'lesbian', 'gay', 'bisexual' and 'heterosexual' cannot encompass all sexual orientation options, and complementary terms are likely to become more widespread. Gender pluralism could also mean the extension of categorisation beyond the term 'trans'. As one contributor (project (c)) said: 'to what extent Hijras occupy the category of transgender is questioned, as transgender is mostly about Kothis [in India]. Those who identify as a third sex wouldn't identify as transgender, because transgender is a binary concept.'

There was support for gender pluralism amongst some of the research contributors to projects (a) and (d). Some said that they would prefer to identify as something other than female or male if this was socially possible. Sex and gender as a continuum or as a spectrum was discussed by contributor Ann Goodley:

Ann: I see the main problems being that society and indeed children, in other words all of us, are programmed to only see in black and white, in monochrome. A concept I actually see as a rainbow, or many shades of grey. I prefer to see it as a rainbow, that's more positive. The grey areas are actually the technicolor colours between black and white. I believe that there are elements of all the colours in everybody, but that people knee-jerk into one column or the other quite often in Western patriarchal society. And I think that's damaging.

Interviewer: *I'd like to ask a bit further into that if that's OK.*

Ann: Surely.

Interviewer: *Um, it sounds as if you're saying that it's not a rigidly gendered binary system?*

Ann: No I'm certain this division isn't on behavioural, biological or spiritual levels, if there is such a thing, but on all levels. In terms of personal identity it's one of the ways in which each of us defines ourselves, and is defined by other people. It forms a portion of a very complex mosaic that makes a person.

Some of the literature supports the spectrum model of sex and gender. Rothblatt (1995) discusses what she terms 'gender continuum theory', a shift away from bipolar sex/gender categories towards a multiplicity of genders. The notion of a gender and sex continuum may be expanded. For example one (non-trans) bisexual contributor described genders as places in space rather than a continuum. Debates about the viability and advisability of a plural gender system will continue, with contributors remarking that 'third gender – I resist that phrase, because all it does is rigidify, codify stuff' (James Green), that 'it's [third gender] got a sort of dustbin sense to it, even though I know people would use it for themselves' (Hamish) and that the time is not right for a movement for third and other sexed/gendered people's rights, given existing social conservatism and bigotry and the need to fight other battles first (Ann Goodley). Moreover, there are difficulties with spectrum identity politics – for example one intersex contributor said that intersex people feel as uncomfortable about intersex and do not want to wear that identity on their sleeves (project (d)). At the same time, a number of people do identify as third or other genders. Overall, blocking the possibility of a sex and gender spectrum (or universe) necessitates the exclusion of intersex, androgynous and multiple sexes/genders as socially viable identities.[14]

CONCLUSION

This chapter explored different means of theorising gender and sexuality beyond the gender binary system. First, I demonstrated the way in which Western gender and sexual orientation binary systems are blown apart by some types of transgender and intersex in a number of different ways. Intersex, androgyny, multiple genders and gender queer are just some of the identities that disrupt discrete male/female categorisation. This disruption extends to the Western sexual orientation system, as the categories of 'lesbian', 'gay', 'bisexual', and 'heterosexual' are all based on either same-sex or opposite-sex attraction, or both of these. People who are gender fluid, multiple, or other than male or female, may inhabit these sexual orientations, but they may also move between them, straddle different orientations, or identify in other ways entirely. I then began to develop foundations for building gender pluralist theory, by discussing intersectionality, or the intersections between different social characteristics such as 'race', ability and class. Gender and sexuality cannot be understood in isolation from other social factors, although looking at them separately is a useful temporary strategy. I described the way in which gender and sexuality are historically and culturally specific as well as intersectional, by providing a brief case study of gender and sexuality categorisation in India.

The problematisation of gender and sexual orientation binaries provokes an evaluation of gender theories, including feminisms, masculinity studies, and post-structuralist and queer approaches. Although aspects of second-wave feminist and most masculinity studies approaches to gender and sexuality are conceptually useful, these bodies of theory are flawed in relation to gender pluralism because they rely ontologically on discrete male–female categorisation. Discrete categorisation became broken down to an extent by black feminist and post-colonial critiques of white Western feminisms, and post-structuralist feminist and masculinities studies extended this problematisation. Post-structuralist approaches provide crucial tools for conceptualising gender and sexual diversity, including understandings of the body and subjectivity as discursively constructed and notions concerning the dislocation of gender and physical sex. Queer theory, which shares similar territory to post-structuralism, offers important insights into the transgression of gender and sexual orientation binaries and the creation of inclusive social space. These approaches are, however, limited in some key ways, which include overlooking the importance of the body and bodily limitations, valorising transgression, and undermining the basis for identity politics by denying the importance of categorisation on a social and political level. These limitations lead into an exploration of conceptual alternatives to the gender binary system that draw on, but move beyond, post-structuralist theory.

There appear to be three different ways of thinking about and managing gender and sexuality diversity. These approaches share the same aim – of creating a more egalitarian, inclusive society with respect to gender and sexual diversity. The first approach is the expansion of the existing system, so that the categories of 'female' and 'male' become inclusive of intersex people, transsexual people, and other gender diverse people. In practice, this is the strategy that is generally adopted, and it provides a means of destigmatising and normalising gender diversity. However, there are obvious limitations to this approach. Whilst the expansion of the binary system enables more people (including those who do not identify as trans or intersex) to 'do' gender in different ways, those people who either do not wish to, or cannot, fit into the binary system will remain excluded. The broadening of the binary system, whilst supporting diversity in some ways, perpetuates binary categorisation by absorbing and defusing difference and dissent, so that people who do not assimilate will remain a very small minority.

The second approach, degendering, is useful in some ways. There are many aspects of social existence that could be less heavily gendered, ranging from official forms through to sexual behaviour. However, in itself it is an inadequate approach, because of the power of existing systems of categorisation and the related structural inequalities. Faced with a gender vacuum, existing hegemonic norms are likely to be reasserted, and marginalisation of people with different genders and sexualities will be perpetuated.

The last option, gender pluralism, is perhaps the most contentious, involving a broadening out of gender categorisation to include intersex, third and multiple sex, and androgynous identities as socially viable. The difficulties with this stance include the level of social opposition that it could face and the related ghettoisation of people who choose to identify as other than male and female. Perhaps such an approach is utopian, given the levels of change it would require and the other forms of social inequality that require attention, including inequities concerning women and LGB people. This approach could also be seen to perpetuate categorisation, although as I have argued, categorisation seems to be necessary on a temporary basis for identity politics. Gender pluralism does have a number of advantages. Politically, the development/recognition of identities that are intersex, androgynous, third and other sex, or gender diverse in other ways is powerful because it enables calls for justice and social change. It moves beyond the post-structuralist deconstruction of gender and sexuality binaries towards reconstruction – of a more diverse and potentially tolerant society. Theoretically, gender pluralism allows for the inclusion of both biological and constructionist approaches to gender and sexuality – and it moves gender theory beyond the binary system.

3
Gender, Sexuality and
Social Exclusion

People who have identities that do not fit with mainstream conceptions of gender and sexuality face disadvantage in a wide range of ways. Linguistic, legislative, and other institutional structures support the institutions of heterosexuality and gender binarism, limiting the extent to which moving outside of mainstream genders and sexualities is possible. A range of intersecting discourses, including patriarchy, homophobia, sexphobia, and ethnocentrism, underpin the inequalities that trans and LGB people face. Whilst each person's position in this complex web of structuring forces is unique, some underlying trends can be discerned. These concern the ways in which certain types of people tend to be privileged (those people who, for instance, fit gender binaries, or who are heterosexual, male, white, healthy, or able-bodied), and others (those who are gender diverse, not heterosexual, female, minority ethnic, challenged in terms of health, or disabled) may face discrimination.

The processes by which people with non-binaried genders and minority sexualities are marginalised can be understood using notions of social exclusion. Social exclusion refers to the way in which certain groups lack the resources to participate in wider society and face barriers to participation at institutional and cultural levels. There are different models of social inclusion. Those that focus on poverty will be of limited use for understanding the marginalisation of gender and sexual minorities, but the broader models also address factors such as cultural norms. Notions of social inclusion tend to highlight individual choice, and to model social exclusion and inclusion as processes. This means that people may be seen as moving in and out of mainstream society, depending on levels of access to factors such as education and employment. Social exclusion approaches therefore allow for some flexibility – people are not seen as necessarily being 'frozen' into identities that doom them to a life of social marginalisation.

This chapter documents and analyses the social exclusion of trans and intersex people. Although some work has been done on gender and social exclusion (see for example Levitas 1998), there is an absence of literature concerning gender minorities and social exclusion. The chapter will frame the marginalisation of trans people in social exclusion terms, including not only a discussion of the material and structural barriers to inclusion, but also an analysis of the discursive construction of inequalities concerning gender and sexuality. My research findings suggested that discourses and ideologies play an important and complex role in the perpetuation of gender and sexual inequality (all projects). It is worth pointing out that the analysis of oppressive ideologies may be useful not only in academic terms, but also as a tool for activism. This is because systems of inequality rely on the normalisation of certain ideas about the way things 'should be', and assumptions that, if unchallenged, support the status quo.

The chapter begins by outlining some of the key concepts associated with the field of social exclusion. I then provide an overview of the material and structural ways in which trans and intersex people face social exclusion, including in relation to language, legislation, employment, relationships and families, violence and abuse, and the medical establishment. The chapter then describes some of the key processes and discourses underlying the exclusion of sexual and gender minorities, including ethnocentrism, patriarchy, homophobia, sexphobia, and body fascism. The chapter foregrounds gender minorities, given the way in which the exclusion of women and sexual minorities is documented elsewhere (see for example Dunphy 2000, MacInnes 1998, Plant et al. 1999, Count Me In 2001).

SOCIAL EXCLUSION

The modern notion of 'social exclusion' developed in France in the 1970s, and then spread across Europe (Burchardt et al. 2002). In 2000 the Amsterdam Treaty introduced the fight against social exclusion into its policy provisions (Articles 136 and 137), and the European Council of Lisbon (March 2000) framed the eradication of poverty and social exclusion as an essential aspect of the Union's ten-year strategies. In the UK, the predominant approach is similar to that taken in Europe: there is a focus on poverty (Burchardt et al. 2002). The United Nations Development programme has taken a somewhat different approach to social exclusion, in which 'Social exclusion was ... conceptualised as a lack of recognition of basic rights, or where the recognition existed, lack of access to political and legal systems necessary to make those rights a reality' (Burchardt et al. 2002: 3).

'Social exclusion' is a contested term (Burchardt et al. 2002). The main ways in which the concept is used concern, first, exclusion from the labour market, and, second, the vicious circle that people get into when they are poor, so that for example alcoholism relating to despair at being unemployed can make someone unemployable (Mayes et al. 2001: 5). Thus, 'social exclusion is not just a description of the adverse consequences of disadvantage, but of the process by which people become distanced from the benefits of participating in modern society' (Mayes et al. 2001: 1). The notion of social exclusion goes beyond earlier social policy concerns with poverty, as it addresses other types of blocks to participation in society, such as ill health, discrimination, geographical location, and cultural identification. Social inclusion and exclusion take place via the interaction of different factors – individual capital (such as childhood circumstances and financial resources), external influences (including constraints affecting people and communities), and agency (Burchardt et al. 2002). Some factors contributing to disadvantage cannot be changed, some tend to lead to an accumulation of the characteristics of exclusion, and others are more fluid or transitional. Sources of exclusion can be directly created, for example legislation stopping foreigners from working in the public sector (Mayes et al. 2001), whilst in other cases they stem from less concrete factors, such as cultural norms and discourses (see Burchardt et al. 2002).

Levitas (1998) identifies three ideal types of discourse that underpin notions of social exclusion, pointing out that a lot of public discourse shifts between these:

1. The Redistributionist Discourse (RED) developed from British critical social policy, which focuses on poverty. The RED discourse highlights poverty as the main cause of social exclusion, and 'implies a radical reduction of inequalities, and a redistribution of resources and power' (Levitas 1998: 14). Although it focuses on the economic aspects of inclusion, it broadens out debates on exclusion by addressing social, political and cultural inclusion.

2. The Moral Underclass Discourse (MUD), which differs considerably from the RED discourse, in that it is individualistic, focusing on the behaviour of the poor, rather than social structures and inequalities. It frames socially excluded people as culturally distinct from others. It links social exclusion with notions of the underclass, and welfare dependency, where socially excluded people are seen as developing 'morally undesirable attitudes and behaviours, characterised by various types of parasitism, crime, and immorality' (Levitas 1998: 20).

3. The Social Integrationist Discourse (SID), which focuses on paid work. Paid employment is viewed as central to social and cultural integration, and because of this focus SID narrows the definition of social exclusion.

THE SOCIAL EXCLUSION OF GENDER AND SEXUAL MINORITIES

The social exclusion of trans and intersex people stems initially from complex cultural and social processes of inequality concerning gender and sexuality, rather than economic exclusion. Therefore, as suggested above, a broad model of social exclusion, one that addresses a range of blocks to participation in society, is needed for understanding the exclusion of gender minorities. Two of the discourses discussed by Levitas (1998) are also relevant: RED, because it provides a critical interpretation that addresses social structures and supports social change, and SID, because access to employment is important for trans and intersex people. In this section I will describe some of the ways in which trans (and to a much lesser extent LGB) people are excluded from social institutions via structural processes of inequality. Language, bureaucratic structures, and legislative inequalities are central to the exclusion of trans people. Economic exclusion is another important factor, whilst violence and exclusion from certain social spaces is crucial. Other contexts where trans, intersex, and LGB people experience exclusion include relationships and the family, the medical establishment, the media, the educational system and the penal system.

Language
English and many other languages automatically erase non-binaried trans and intersex people. English has no non-male or non-female prefixes or titles, and no currently acceptable nouns for people of

fluid or non-male or non-female gender. Gender categorisations in language tend to create trans and intersex people as 'other', or subsume them into male and female identities, preventing them from having the option of exploring and living middle-ground identities. Zach Nataf and Christie Elan Cane, as well as several other contributors, saw the lack of language as a major problem – it is hard to discuss alternatives to male and female when there are no words – whilst Salmacis saw the categorisation of gender through language itself as causing the oppression of trans and intersex people:

Interviewer: *Can you say a bit about what you think about gender categorisation?*

Salmacis: Yeah, I call it heterofascism. Gender categorisation can be best described as a large machine with lots of pins that dig into the sense of self and tear the mind to pieces. And in my situation, having been 'surgically treated' as a child, to me I see it as a more malicious act than most people in a [intersexed] condition would. I see a lot of malice behind it.

Interviewer: *Can you explain a bit more about that?*

Salmacis: This desperate element on the part of normals, that's men and women in an absolute anatomical sense, to try and define people almost exclusively against their will.

The lack of language for non-male and non-female states can be seen as part of the entrenched cultural resistance to non-male and non-female identities (see Chase 1998, Kessler 1998). Oppression and exclusion occurs via erasure: the complete denial by men and women of the existence of people of other genders, which means that these people and processes are rendered socially non-existent. Some authors, such as Feinberg (1996), discuss the creation of third-sex pronouns, but these have yet to be adopted within wider society, and the possibility of such change is contentious even amongst intersex and trans people (see the chapters on theory and on activism).

Bureaucracy

Bureaucracy is another major area where the exclusion of non-binaried trans and intersex people is evident. Most forms and official documents, including those produced by businesses when, for example, providing credit, require people to define their gender as either male or female. This is obviously problematic for people who are gender ambiguous, who identify as other than male or female, or whose gender identity is fluid. The importance of bureaucracy in structuring gender is indicated by this quote:

> So what happens if we get rid of gender, completely? You cannot tell the differences between genders. Therefore how can you discriminate against people if you don't know what gender they are? So therefore it all disappears. For example if you removed sex information off birth certificates, or sex information off anything, all the forms have male/female, male/female. (Kate N' Ha Ysabet)

The bureaucratic exclusion that non-male/female people experience has very real effects. For example, Christie Elan Cane described the difficulties they had had with their passport and with all other official forms, which demand categorisation as male or female. Christie was refused access to vital services unless they compromised and accepted categorisation as a woman. These findings are echoed by newspaper reports of Zoltar, another androgyne, whose name 'panicked the DSS computer' when they refused to accept Ms/Mr as a title (Wheelwright 1995). Although the situation concerning bureaucracy may be changing in some areas, such as passports, the vast majority of forms still ask people whether they are male or female, and provide no alternatives. Even where people fit into the gender binary system, they may still face social exclusion – for example some government departments fail to alter their records to fully reflect people's gender changes, meaning that they risk harassment <http://www.pfc.org.uk/>.

Economic Exclusion

Employment patterns vary widely among trans and intersex people. Some people pass as men or women, and, when their status is known, various instances of supportive or tolerant employers have been reported in the press (for example, Pink Paper 2000). However, economic exclusion is an issue for many trans and intersex people. Unemployment is a major problem, particularly for transsexuals, intersexuals and androgynes when they subsist on disability or other benefits because they are unable to find work. Where trans people do get jobs, they are regularly forced into lower-paid jobs <http://www.pfc.org.uk/>. There have been recent cases of harassment and discrimination, including the British Transport Police's refusal to give trans woman Lyndsay Watson permission to transition whilst at work <http://www.pfc.org.uk/>. Several of the contributors experienced sackings and job discrimination because of their gender status. For example Christie Elan Cane lost their job and cannot now get a job because of their gender status. Kaveney (1999) discussed the 'glass ceiling' that those transsexuals who are professionally successful frequently seem to hit – a ceiling that is lower than that faced by many others (for example women), because of the high levels of stigmatisation of transgender. Crucially, the Sex Discrimination (Gender Reassignment) Regulations 1999 make discrimination in employment or training against anyone who has had, is undergoing, or intends to undergo, gender reassignment illegal, and there have been successful cases brought against errant employers <http://www.pfc.org.uk/>. Since the introduction of the new legislation, the main employment problem may be empowering trans people to take up the right to work, as cultural exclusion is so heavy:

> Simon: The functional life is almost not within my grasp, whatever that means.
>
> Interviewer: *Whatever that means, yeah.*
>
> Simon: Well basically making a living and having that, the independence that comes from that.
>
> Interviewer: *I mean it does, clearly an issue for a lot of transsexual people not working, and I'm wondering just how much the labour market excludes people who are transsexual?*
>
> Simon: I think it depends on as usual 'who we know' and stuff like that. I think if we have certain kinds of connections or certain kinds of qualifications, or experience or knowledge or something like that, you can get around. But if you don't then you're basically just kind of excluded in a way. (Simon Dessloch)

Findings suggest that transvestites and cross-dressers usually remain unaffected by economic exclusion, because their form of trans usually takes place in private and remains hidden. There are, however, some situations in which transvestites face heavy discrimination. One contributor, for example, noted that legislation prevents transvestites from working in positions of governmental sensitivity because of the dangers of blackmail.

The economic exclusion of trans people affects many aspects of their lives. For example, Israel and Tarver (1997) link the exclusion of transgender people to increased rates of homelessness. Economic exclusion impacts on power relations within the trans communities as well as those in wider society. There appears to be a hierarchy within the community concerning surgery – post-operative trans-sexuals are at the top of this hierarchy, but access to private surgery, which is hugely expensive, is structured by economic position. Contributor Roz Kaveney noted that many working-class transsexuals have to resort to prostitution in order to fund surgery. Trans people risk exploitation by professionals who take advantage of their need to fit into mainstream society. Contributor MKP argues that 'there is a transsexual empire', while Stephen Whittle discusses the way in which trans people have been commercially exploited:

> There are people who hang on the community who do some real weird things and, you know, a lot of the therapists or supposed therapists, a lot of the shrinks, some of the lawyers who hang in, not many lawyers hang in on the community actually because I don't think they've got as much money, surgeons as well, hang in on this community they're not part of the community they're literally hangers on making money, making money, that's all it's about.

As I have shown, poverty and economic exclusion are important to the perpetuation of social exclusion, especially for analysts using mainstream and SID and RED models of social exclusion. Those trans and intersex people who have access to financial resources will be cushioned from the effects of other types of exclusion that they may face, and may override the structural forces of inequality in some ways. However, those intersex and trans people who are not particularly privileged economically are more likely than many other people to become trapped in a cycle of poverty and disadvantage, given the types of exclusion which they face.

Social Space, Violence and Abuse

Access to social space is problematic for intersex and trans people when they are visibly different from conventional heterosexual women and men, and in particular if they are gender ambiguous.[1] For example, contributor Salmacis found it impossible to walk around in public areas whilst looking gender ambiguous, due to harassment. Salmacis was forced to adopt a female identity in a similar way to the male identity Feinberg took on when ze found ze could not survive as a transgendered person (1996). Similarly, Christie Elan Cane described how their movements are severely restricted due to lack of social acceptance of androgynous people.

For many trans people, being in public space is linked with experience of violence and abuse. For instance, contributor Zach Nataf described instances of the murder of trans people, including the well-known case of Brandon Teena in the US. John Marshall stated the need to keep his transvestism hidden because of the danger of violence and vandalisation of property, while Alex Whinnom noted that the problem with coming out as transsexual was that 'all the local kids come around and put a fire bomb though your letter box'. Evidence of violence against trans people is found in the literature, including a groundbreaking study of violence in the US (Wilchins et al. 1997), which includes many accounts of murder and rape. Other literature, including newspaper reports, documents intersex people and trans people suffering abuse from neighbours (Wheelwright 1995), being spat on, stoned, and seriously beaten up (Hugill 1998), receiving death threats (Whittle 2002), and hate mail <http://www.pfc.org.uk/>, and experiencing many other forms of abuse (Wilchins 1997). There appear to be a range of associated factors that contribute to risk of abuse, including family breakdown (see below), and lack of access to appropriate welfare provision. For example, intersex contributor Salmacis described being sexually abused whilst in care, whilst Israel and Tarver (1997) describe the high incidence of drug abuse amongst young trans people in the US, leaving them at risk of violence and exploitation. Prostitution rates are high amongst trans people, again meaning vulnerability, while trans people in prisons (Bloomfield 1996, see below) and mental hospitals are frequently sexually harassed and raped (Israel and Tarver 1997).

Legislation

Until recently, trans people in the UK were legally excluded from citizenship in a number of ways. The majority legal opinion was that transsexuality is 'not a reality', as chromosomal sex change is impossible. Hence, people who were diagnosed as transsexual lost a substantial part of their civil liberties (McMullen and Whittle 1994), including the right to marry and to parent or adopt. Changes in the British legislation following the case of *P* v. *Cornwall County Council* in 1995 allow some legal protection against employment discrimination. Transsexual people's rights are now in the process of being extended via a Gender Recognition Bill, which enables people who are living in the opposite gender or who are recognised as having changed gender to obtain new birth certificates, as they already can in most of the Council of Europe states <http://www.pfc.org.uk/> – providing they can satisfy certain tests.[2] However, the new bill provides no new protection against discrimination on the grounds of being transsexual <http://www.gendertrust.org.uk/index/.htm>. Following Evans (1993) it is possible to identify a conservative policing of the morals of the population at the root of such discriminating legislation. This is particularly obvious in relation to the limitations of the Gender Recognition Bill, which in effect prohibits anything that could be construed as same-sex marriage. Sharpe (2002) provides an excellent cross-cultural exposé of the ways in which the 'spectre' of homosexuality is kept at bay by legislators eager to uphold heterosexist partnership norms, and the extent to which addressing transsexual people's rights threatens to unravel these norms.[3]

Whilst the gains made by transsexuals are significant, there are other sections of the trans communities that remain excluded from legal recognition and protection. Legislation is particularly problematic with reference to third-sex, multiple-sex, fluid and androgynous identities. For example, contributor Pamela Summers noted that there is no legal state of androgyne. She describes the paradox which legislators are faced with: the period of transsexual transition from one sex to the other means that there must be a third state; however, transsexuals are not permanently in this third state. Kate More argued that transsexuality and third sex force the authorities to deal with legislative realities they would prefer to ignore. For example once surgery is undergone, the government cannot make people go back to how they were before simply because equal opportunities legislation is not working.

Medicine

The medical system is an important force shaping the lives of intersex and trans people, who will probably have medical interventions at a number of stages. The medical system plays a crucial role in perpetuating the social exclusion of trans people, at the same time as paradoxically enabling the development of provision of treatment for transsexuals. Access to treatment is crucial to transsexuals. Press For Change <http://www.pfc.org.uk/> reports the difficulties with long queues, neglect, and in some cases denial of treatment, and other difficulties are reviewed by Whittle (2002). I will focus here on the problems facing a broader range of trans and intersex people concerning, first, the pathologisation of intersex conditions and transsexuality and then, more broadly, issues concerning gender stereotyping and homophobia. However, it is worth pointing out that trans people can be excluded from the healthcare system in a number of ways. As one contributor noted:

> trans people will inevitably have to deal with the healthcare system for a variety of reasons during the course of their lives. An issue that immediately comes to mind for me is the issue of gynaecological care ... Most of the FTMs I have spoken to over the years say they have reservations about going for such examinations (especially smear tests) ... obviously, in going for such a check the individual concerned would have to 'out' themselves, and moreover, also deal with the attitudes, expectations, prejudices etc of receptionists, nurses, and other patients. (Tracey Lee)

Intersex people face a particularly difficult set of issues concerning the pathologisation of gender diversity, and the medical system plays a crucial role in perpetuating these difficulties. Various authors (Chase 1998, Feinberg 1996, Kessler 1998) describe how the Western medical system treats the birth of an intersex infant as an emergency. The baby may have surgical and hormonal intervention, with infants usually being assigned as girls and having their clitorises cut off (Kaldera 1998). This is because intersex is viewed by the medical profession as a pathology, as it is socially threatening, even though many of the conditions are not in themselves harmful to the infant (Kessler 1998). For example, there have been cases of parents being advised to terminate pregnancies if the foetus has Klinefelter's syndrome (an intersex condition). Whilst Klinefelter's syndrome can be associated with some medical complications, this advice seems to be primarily the result of fears about the social problems such a child would encounter (Somers and Haynes 2001). The literature (Chase 1998, Holmes 1998, Kaldera 1998, Dreger 2000) documents the wider existence of serious problems with infant intersex surgery, including sexual dysfunction and mental health difficulties resulting from surgical trauma. There have been suggestions amongst medics that practitioners who carry out such 'treatments' have considerable exposure to litigation based on a failure to obtain informed consent (Beh and Diamond 2000). Whilst there is diversity within the intersex population concerning attitudes to surgery, with some people wishing to exist within the gender binary system, there is a strong critique of early surgical intervention, which has been reframed as intersex genital mutilation (see for example Morris 2004). Chase (1998) argues that surgery does not erase intersex but simply produces severely traumatised and dysfunctional individuals who need long-term medical treatment. Kessler suggests that:

> Rather than admit to their role in perpetuating gender, physicians 'psychologise' the issue by talking about the parent's anxieties and humiliation on being confronted with an anomalous infant. They talk as though they have no choice but to respond to the parent's pressure for a resolution of psychological discomfort and as though they had no choice but to use medical technology in the service of a two-gender culture. (1998: 32)

Other issues concern the psychiatric pathologisation of transsexuality. Debates between medics who see transsexuality as a physiological condition and those who frame it as a psychiatric pathology, linked with childhood trauma or disorder, have raged ever since the 1960s. The psychiatric pathologisation of transgender is generally rejected by the trans communities (for example at the TrAnsgender AGENDA Conference, 1998, and at the International Congress on Transgender Law and Employment (1993); see also Israel and Tarver 1997). Research contributor James Green argued that the characterisation of transsexuality as due to childhood trauma is wrong: trauma frequently occurs specifically because people are trans, not vice versa. However, as Purnell says, psychiatrists are pivotal decision-makers concerning access to treatment – this is inhumane, but is a situation which will continue until trans people stop being subject to psychiatric diagnosis (1998). It is clear that some trans people do experience mental health problems, although how much this is the result of the social exclusion of transgender is unknown. Research findings from project (a) suggest that direct and indirect social discrimination seems linked to the incidence of psychological problems among trans people, ranging from poor self-image and low self-esteem through to depression and suicide (Monro 2000a).

More broadly, some trans people face social exclusion from the medical system due to gender stereotyping.[4] Research findings from project (a) suggest that transsexuals who do not adopt stereotypical gender roles may still experience discrimination by medics. For example, contributor Meredith Malek had considerable difficulties getting hormone treatment and surgery because she did not fit femininity stereotypes. Medical stereotyping has led to transsexual people lying about their gender roles in order to gain treatment, and contributor Kate N' Ha Ysabet pointed out that this is destructive for both psychiatrists and patients. Evidence from research projects (a) and (d) and from informal discussions with practitioners suggests that practice is quite varied.

Heterosexism and homophobia within the medical system affect LGB and trans people's social inclusion. Trans has historically been subsumed under the category of homosexuality (Rosario 1996) with psychiatrists such as Socarides (1970, 1991) failing to distinguish between trans and homosexuality, and heavily pathologising both. This has impacted on treatment methods and is reflected in trans (and LGB) people's experience of the medical system. Trans people began to challenge medicine's heterosexism in the 1970s in the US (MacKenzie 1994), but findings show that in the UK heterosexism is still fairly entrenched. For example, Ann Goodley noted that gender identity clinics have tended to assume that clients will be heterosexual in their gender of identification. Professionals may ask MTFs whether they have a boyfriend, with the underlying presumption that the only reason that people want GRS (gender reassignment surgery) is to get a vagina in order to have sexual intercourse. Homophobia is also related to gender stereotyping – for example young female preference for 'tomboyish' activity and male company is seen as a precursor to FTM transsexuality (see Rosario 1996), which negates butch lesbian and nonconformist heterosexual female development. However, it is important to note that support for lesbian, gay and bisexual identities is increasing among medics, partly because of pressure from critics. For example, Watson and Hitchcock (2000) explicitly argue in response to my (2000a) paper for professionals to support sexual diversity.

Relationships and the Family

Trans people face a range of challenges concerning relationships and families. Transsexual people are often rejected by their relatives, and may lose custody of, or access to, their children, despite the absence of any evidence that transsexuality could cause difficulties <http://www.pfc.org.uk/>. Transsexuals are currently unable to legally adopt or foster in the UK (Young 1996), although the forthcoming Gender Reassignment Bill <http://www.gendertrust.org.uk/index/.htm> will support transsexual men as fathers if they are seeking treatment under the Human Fertilisation and Embryology Act when they are in a relationship with a woman.[5] Even where trans people have children and do not lose access to them, they can still face certain exclusions from the discourses and practices of 'parenting'. For example, naming can be an issue – does the parent shift from being 'mum' to 'dad' or vice versa? Contributor Tracey Lee suggested that

> sometimes this predicament can lead to a 'letting go' of the status of 'parent' which can have the effect of excluding the trans person from 'being' who they actually are to their child/children. For example, in dealing with their children in relation to their children's friends and their families, and of course in the context of the school where their child attends.

Young trans people may face a number of difficulties within the family. Rejection by the family and community, due to stigmatisation, may lead to the social and economic exclusion of trans children and young people (see Israel and Tarver 1997). Kessler (1998) describes difficulties and embarrassment for families of intersex children, whilst Kate N' Ha Ysabet described difficulties in the family concerning having a transsexual child:

> Having a child who is freaking us out has an effect on the rest of the family so that actually tends to initiate things like physical abuse, and problems in the rest of the family because having a trans person, having like this well, they don't know what's going on, they can't get on with life, they get angry because nothing they will do makes this kid any better. So they start beginning to hate the kid, because it's just a drain, a constant drain. Families are in this impossible situation, where they go to experts and say 'Well she keeps wanting to wear trousers all the time' and the expert says, 'Well treat her like a girl, really reinforce her being like a girl.'

A number of trans people identify as lesbian, gay, or bisexual, and are therefore affected by the social exclusion of these groups. This is particularly apparent in the areas of partnership and the family. Same-sex couples in the UK now have more rights than previously – for example gay and bisexual men now have the same age of consent as other young people. However, there are a range of ways in which LGB people continue to face exclusion concerning relationships and the family, including in particular a lack of partnership rights for same-sex couples, and limited adoption and fostering opportunities for LGB people. The absence of partnership rights for same-sex couples is important. It prevents the social legitimation of same-sex relationships (although this is being addressed to an extent by the civil partnerships that are being introduced in some UK cities). It also means that same-sex partners continue to lack the same rights as opposite-sex couples in the areas of pensions and inheritance tax, and, that in a same-sex relationship if one partner dies, the other may lose their home because there is no way of legally establishing them as next of kin <http://www.stonewall. org.uk/stonewall/>.

Education

Contributors discussed the way in which education can be problematic for trans people in a number of ways. As Pamela Summers said, school is a very gendered place. Young trans people are likely to be forced into gender stereotypes at school, with little chance of access to medical support, thus beginning a 'cycle of low self-esteem, leading to a mute acceptance of discrimination, which is the hallmark of systemic, self-sustaining oppression' <http://www.pfc.org.uk/>. Ann Goodley noted that, although things have improved, single-sex schools and lessons still persist in many places and teachers use expressions that reinforce gender categorisation, for example 'act like a man'. Playgrounds, toilets and so forth are demarcated along rigidly gendered lines. Kate N' Ha Ysabet described how transgressors of the gender code are violently sanctioned at school by bullying, and Ann Goodley discussed the way that tomboys are often idolised, whereas sissy boys are persecuted relentlessly. Sex education reinforces gender binaries, and in general taught material contains no description of the intersex body (Holmes 1998) nor any hint that transgender exists. The exclusion of trans people may continue into further and higher education. For example, many colleges and universities refuse to reissue degree certificates for graduates who have changed gender roles, meaning that when they apply for jobs they either have to disclose status – risking discrimination – or only apply for jobs that do not require proof of their degree <http://www.pfc.org.uk/>.

The Media

Media depiction of trans issues is varied. Some progressive and sympathetic coverage is apparent, and research with the trans communities (project (a)) shows that various groups and individuals are actively engaged with the media. Negative or salacious media coverage is damaging to the inclusion of trans people, sometimes in very direct ways, for example <http://www.pfc.org.uk/> documents a transsexual woman's experience of arson following her appearance on a television programme about transsexual issues, whilst Purnell (1998) discussed the way in which 'crass reporting' fuels the public marginalisation of trans people. The media also plays a role in promoting normative models of gender – for example a newspaper article framed intersex as an abnormality needing corrective treatment and social erasure at familial and social levels (Hohler 1996). In addition, contributor Stephen Whittle described the exploitation of trans people by the media as follows:

> And they constantly, you know whether it's the newspapers or magazines, journalists or whatever they talk, they talk us they write our supposed words, they talk about what we do in our lives, how we are and so just because they are so utterly greedy and so utterly selfish.

Authors such as Raymond (1980) and Billings and Urban (1982) frame the media as reinforcing the dominant order (see King 1986, 1993). However, this is not substantiated in the findings, which show that the media plays a role in normalising gender diversity, as well as stigmatising it. There is a paradox concerning media coverage: where it is objectifying or salacious it tends to reinforce exclusion, but where it is educational, sympathetic or in some cases entertaining it can help enable social inclusion of trans people. The media thus appears to be a contested domain.

The Penal System

The number of trans prisoners in the UK is small, but they face severe difficulties (Whittle and Stephens on <http://www.pfc.org.uk/>). They are usually placed in prisons according to their sex at birth, which means that they must either face exposure, in which case they are vulnerable to bullying or assault (contributor Pamela Summers noted that rape is almost automatic for MTF transsexuals in male prisons), or deny their gender identity. It is extremely difficult to continue with the 'real life test' whilst in prison, although this is seen as necessary by the medical professionals who support continuation of hormone therapy, and surgery may be delayed. Bloomfield (1996) also identifies a number of serious issues affecting this section of the prison population. These include denial of access to treatment that would contribute to their rehabilitation as citizens, and abnormally punitive sentences, with some lifers being told that they will never be released because of their condition and simultaneously denied treatment. The denial of treatment (including hormones) to prisoners is linked by Israel and Tarver (1997) to heightened clinical depression and risk of suicide. Other ways in which transsexual prisoners are oppressed include strip searches by members of the opposite sex, breaches of confidentiality including a prisoner's records being sold to a newspaper, denial of information concerning conditions including access to medical records and case conferences, psychological cruelty and verbal and sexual abuse including a case of rape by a prison officer (Bloomfield 1996). In the US, rape is endorsed in some jails as those in 'relationships' are perceived to be more manageable by prison authorities (Israel and Tarver 1997).

Overall, trans people (particularly intersex, gender ambiguous or third and other sexed/gendered) face entrenched and multifaceted forms of social exclusion. This extends beyond the economic exclusion that is clearly a major issue for many trans people. It encompasses linguistic and bureaucratic erasure, risks associated with social space, and marginalisation in the arenas of relationships, the family, education, and in some cases, medicine and the media. The difficulties they face are compounded by rigidity in social institutions such as the penal system. Whilst the factors associated with social inclusion and exclusion operate differently for each person, so that some individuals participate widely in society and are included in many ways, there are underlying structures that militate against trans and intersex people experiencing full inclusion.

THE DISCURSIVE UNDERPINNINGS OF TRANS EXCLUSION

Discourses and cultural elements form an important part of the processes of social exclusion discussed by authors such as Burchardt et al. (2002). There are a number of discursive structures underpinning the exclusion of gender and sexual minorities, and these are historically and culturally specific. For example the right-wing attack on LGB and transgender people in the US is strongly influenced by the religious (mostly Christian) right (Swan 1997),[6] which can be traced back to religious domination based on class interests and the suppression of decentralised matriarchal religions (Feinberg 1996). I shall outline and discuss the following forces in brief: ethnocentrism, patriarchy, homophobia, sexphobia, body fascism and, finally, other forms of exclusionary discourse. I shall not discuss transphobia (which can be defined as the fear of, or stigmatisation of, trans identities – see Monro 2000b), and gender binarism, here, as these are discussed earlier in this chapter, and elsewhere in the book. It is important to point out that the discourses I discuss operate in complex, interlinking, and contextualised ways.

Ethnocentrism

Transphobia exists within the context of the cultural and economic dominance of Western societies over others, and the related erasure of awareness concerning non-Western cultural constructions of gender and sexuality (see for example Herdt 1994, Ramet 1997). Western transphobia has, in some cases, directly impacted on communities that could be called trans (see for example Nataf 1996). The extent of gender diversity among other cultures is used by some Western trans people to argue for gender plurality in Western capitalist societies, while others resist this and continue to see a binary system as natural. It would be easy to adopt an argument that non-Western capitalist and precolonial societies are or were perfect, but this would lead dangerously into an essentialised view of the 'natural goodness' of non-European peoples (see Slater 1992). Thus, for example, while the Hijra third gender people of India are part of Indian culture, they are also denigrated (Jaffrey 1996). What is clear, however, is that a wide range of cultural variance concerning gender has been, and continues to be, subsumed by the cultural hegemony of the West.

Patriarchy

The social exclusion of trans people is closely related to the operation of patriarchy. Patriarchy can be defined as social systems of male domination: 'the systematic and/or systemic "organisation of male supremacy and female subordination" ' (Beasley 1999: 55). Some research contributors to projects (a), (c) and (d) saw patriarchy as a cause of transphobia, particularly the way in which gender categories have been constructed and fixed as a means of enabling men as a class to dominate and exploit women. For example:

> I think that, because of the patriarchal society that we've had for more than 3,000 years in which it was important for a father to hear 'it's a boy' this means that his land, his line, his name, his property, his genes are protected ... in the post-imperialist period there is still somewhere in the back of the mind the idea that we need the men. To do the fighting, to protect the women, to protect the land and all that sort of rubbish. (Ann Goodley)

Gender and sexuality were both created within a patriarchal system, and they underpin each other – the assumption of binary gender and sexual orientation is the backbone of patriarchal society. (Kerry)

Pamela Summers echoed Ann, linking ownership via inheritance expressed through birth relations with the gender binary system, and Alex Whinnom described the difficulties which trans poses for the British aristocracy, who base succession on the male heir. These arguments are echoed in the literature. Feinberg (1996) argues for example that medical and legal systems are imposed on the natural order because of systems of inheritance, legitimacy, paternity, and succession to title. Patriarchal systems also underpin the institution of heterosexuality, which depends on the normalisation of opposite-sex couples, and is reinforced by particular notions of the family, legitimacy and inheritance. The gender binary system is central to ubiquitous social institutions such as the sexual division of labour; people who transgress the gender divide or sexual orientation norms pose problems for patriarchy. Trans challenges a capitalist system that is based on a rigid sexual division of labour and entrenched gender inequalities (see Feinberg 1996).[7] Kate N' Ha Ysabet raised this issue when she discussed sexism in the labour market. She said that she identifies as a woman but is socially classed as a man. If she has surgery and then gets a job as a man is she pulling the system to pieces, as 'I am sitting here pretending to have a cock because you're paying me, you believe that me having a phantom penis means I am worth 30 per cent more pay?' Overall, the patriarchal system rests heavily on the notion that sex and gender divisions are natural, and intersex and the other forms of gender diversity are erased in order to perpetuate the normative notions of gender and sexuality that underpin gender inequality.

Homophobia

Homophobia contributes to the social exclusion of trans people because trans and LGB identities and social spaces overlap. The term 'homophobia' was originally coined to mean the irrational fear of homosexuality (Weinberg 1972), and has now spread to include the social implications of this fear (see for example Llamas and Vila 1999). Homophobia operates in many different ways and contexts. For example, in our study of lesbian and gay equality in local authorities, we found evidence of indirect as well as more direct homophobia. In at least two authorities involved in project (b), discomfort was marked. For instance:

Officer:	Politicians, they're a long way from being able to even talk about those issues.
Interviewer:	*There would be resistance to even using the words 'lesbian and gay'?*
Officer:	Yes, I think with the current leadership, yes. (Officer, Northern authority)

Findings from research project (b) showed that there were cases of blatant discrimination, perhaps isolated incidents. For example in one authority there was a case in which a lesbian worker at a leisure centre had been seriously harassed concerning her sexuality, but the perpetrator had not been dealt with adequately. There were other ways in which discrimination manifested. For example, in two authorities contributors saw the championing of sexual equalities as a definite block to promotion. Homophobia was evident amongst black and minority ethnic groupings as well as white ones, for example:

> An Asian youth worker who was working with quite a well-developed and well-attended lesbian Asian youth group, and somehow some people in the Asian community found out about it, and basically it just kicked off ... and she had to go into hiding and there were death threats made against her. The group had to disband, and importantly, the council did not back her up. (Community worker)

As noted above, homophobia and biphobia (discrimination against bisexuals) are intertwined with transphobia. Transphobia can be seen to originate in homophobia, or, alternatively, homophobia to originate in taboos about gender crossing. For example, research contributor John Marshall noted that he would get labelled as a 'pouf' if he walked down the street in a dress. He described how men feel sexually threatened by transvestism, as it challenges their heterosexual identities. This is supported by Holmes (1998), who sees the taboo about intersexuality as being due to fears about homosexuality. Homophobia can be identified as consolidating male heterosexual power (see Prosser 1998); homophobic constructions are produced by and producing of normative gender relations and identities. Prosser (1998) argues that homosexuality is enmeshed with transgender and that heterosexuality is constructed by the social sublimation of transgendered identification. Butler (1997) discusses the way in which the foreclosure of subject identity formation occurs: 'impossible' desires, such as homosexual ones, are denied and this denial is carried through to the social level, where it results in the exclusion of 'others' who are cast as abnormal or persecutors. As contributor Zach Nataf suggested, trans people, women and queers share opposition to heteropatriarchy (heterosexism/homophobia and patriarchy) (see Chapter 5).

Sexphobia

Homophobia, biphobia, and transphobia can be traced to sexphobia, or fear and social taboos concerning sexuality. Weeks (1985) explains the way in which fears about non-procreative sexuality, including those stemming from religion, have historically fuelled bigotry against same-sex desire. Social taboos about sexuality are a means by which sexuality is controlled. The public management of sexuality is well documented (see for example Durham 1995). The framing of same-sex sexuality and trans as 'sexual perversions', and as pathological (Socarides 1991), rests on negative attitudes towards sexuality and the notion that sex is at the root of social order/disorder (see Rubin 1984). Transvestites are particularly affected by sexphobia, as transvestism is culturally linked with sexuality, despite the fact that there is no sexual motivation for many transvestites. Contributors noted the ways in which, historically, organisations such as the Beaumont Society have denied the links between some types of transvestism and sexuality, due to worries about the stigmatisation of erotic fetishism, and taboos about masturbation. Sexphobia also affects transsexuals – in general, the social portrayal of transsexuality erases the erotic aspects (Ekins 1997). This impacts negatively on some transsexuals – for example Roz Kaveney noted that one reason she was not sure she was a transsexual was because she was told by society that she could not be a transsexual because she enjoyed sex. Bland (1994) argues that the definition of transsexual as someone who does not cross-dress for pleasure denies them the possibility to do so, and that this is oppressive as it blocks the self-therapeutic aspects of sexual fantasy, causing people considerable distress. Another issue that transsexuals have struggled with concerns the sensationalism about transsexuality, which is due to cultural taboos about genitalia (Feinberg 1996). A further difficulty concerns the divisive effect that sexphobia has on the trans communities. Steven Whittle (personal communication 1998) discussed the self-perceived need for transsexuals to distance themselves from transvestites because of the stigmatisation of transvestite sexuality (see Chapter 5).

Body Fascism

Body fascism can be defined as unequal treatment of people on the basis of appearance norms, and the stigmatisation of those deemed unattractive. Literature documents the effects of body fascism among the wider population. Journalist Lacey (1999), for instance, notes how people who are considered beautiful are socially privileged in the workplace, relationships and wider society. Body fascism is a major problem for some trans people, and can be seen as a direct cause of transphobia. As contributor Ann Goodley said:

> Unfortunately we judge each other on how we present, and how we present is judged not just aesthetically but in terms of what is fashionable, what is acceptable, within the society within which we live and so on. It's very very difficult.

Body fascism is linked to pressures on trans people to fit social norms and to attempt to pass, as well as to considerable suffering amongst those who do not fit social norms. Several contributors discussed body fascism as a problem which has to be dealt with during the course of daily living, and I heard reports about MTF transsexuals and a cross-dresser who were stigmatised by other trans people because they did not fit feminine norms. Contributor Stephen Whittle discussed ways in which attitudes in the trans communities are changing:

> People are really not told any longer what they should be like. Nobody says, 'Oh of course when are you hoping to have your surgery', nobody sort of does that at all. I mean you might get some comment like, 'are you still taking hormones?' and somebody might say, 'oh no I'm not', and they say, 'oh yes I wondered whether I should?', you know and then people have a conversation about medical risks and so on and so forth ... but nobody says 'you ought to because you'll look more like a man or a woman' ... there's a big difference, a huge difference.

The effects of body fascism impact on choices concerning surgery. For example, surgeons' emphasis on the appearance of genitals rather than sexual responsiveness (Kessler 1998) means that transsexuals and intersex people may end up with less than optimim levels of sexual functioning. Body fascism also fuels the extensive use of purely cosmetic secondary surgery that many MTF transsexuals undergo. Kessler (1998) discusses feminist analysis of cosmetic surgery, arguing that cosmetic surgery shifts the boundaries of the socially acceptable so that a smaller range of appearances is considered normal and bodies become objectified. This leads to arguments for the rejection of cosmetic surgery (Kessler 1998).[8] Issues concerning cosmetic surgery are difficult, and need to be understood in terms of the lived experience of transsexuals who feel that they need surgery in order to be socially accepted: choices concerning how far to adapt to social norms have to be made at the individual level. However, explicit acknowledgement of the inequity of socially constructed, naturalised norms concerning appearance is important in creating social space for physical diversity. As Kessler says, 'If we want people to respect particular bodies, they need to be taught to lose respect for ideal ones' (1998: 118).

There are other discursive structures that contribute to transphobia, including class prejudice, disablism and mentalism. Class prejudice cuts across the gender and sexual orientation spectra, affecting people in different ways depending on their background, the opportunities they have, and the choices they make. It may impact particularly harshly on working-class trans and intersex people, whose options are more restricted than those of their more privileged counterparts. Disablism is also an issue, given the pathologisation of some trans identities, and mentalism (the stigmatisation of people with mental health difficulties) is also relevant, given the medical framing of transsexuality as a psychiatric issue and the effects of this on public attitudes. Class prejudice, disablism, and mentalism interact with each other and with the other discourses described above in varied ways. Everyone is affected by these different discourses, which privilege some individuals and stigmatise, marginalise or exclude others. It is crucial to avoid painting certain groups as victims, partly because individuals interact with the forces of discrimination in very varied ways, and partly because discourses are changeable and the development of sites of resistance is ongoing (for example the reclamation of the terms 'dyke' and 'queer' by LGB people and the development of notions of trans pride). At the same time, it is possible to see these discourses – and the related social institutions – as systematically acting against the inclusion of certain groups, whilst supporting the interests of others. These discourses serve to legitimise the social exclusion of certain groups fuelled by the (often unconscious – see Sibley 1995) choices of the populace, policy-makers and politicians.

CONCLUSION

Trans and intersex people are a diverse population, with varied experiences of social inclusion and exclusion. There are some general trends in the social exclusion of gender minorities, concerning not only areas traditional to discourses of social exclusion – poverty and employment – but also a number of social institutions such as medicine, the family, and education. The model proposed by Burchardt et al. (2002), in which cultural as well as economic factors are addressed, is crucial for the social inclusion of trans and intersex people. This is because their exclusion is underpinned by a set of processes in which gender diverse people and sexual minorities are systematically stigmatised and discriminated against – with discrimination increasing the further people are from gender binaried and/or heterosexual norms. These include:

- ethnocentrism;
- patriarchy;
- homophobia;
- sexphobia;
- body fascism.

The exclusion of trans and intersex people occurs at much earlier stages than those identified by social exclusion theorists – in the case of intersex, third/multiple gender people, androgynes and people with ambiguous genders, prior to linguistic and bureaucratic categorisation. These groups are excluded so severely that many non-trans people do not even realise they exist. The processes of erasure take place at discursive and cultural levels. The marginalisation of transsexuals and cross-dressers is less marked, although there are a number of difficulties, as I have shown. Overall, the stigmatisation of gender diversity feeds into – and is reinforced by – the processes of exclusion and discrimination that take place at a social structural level, for example the difficulties that schools, prisons, and (in some ways) the healthcare system face in attempting to deal positively with transsexuality, cross-dressing, intersex, and gender ambiguity and plurality. It is tied into the social exclusion of other groups, including in particular sexual minorities and women, via structural inequalities linked with homophobia and patriarchy.

There are difficulties with the concept of social exclusion, some of which are highlighted with respect to gender diversity. The focus on economic exclusion could draw attention away from other forces of inequality, and there is a tendency for notions of social exclusion to individualise social problems. In addition, as Levitas (1998) suggests, the term represents a division between an excluded minority and an included majority – this is problematic, especially for people who straddle included/excluded divides.[9] A further problem concerns the way in which mainstream society relies on the normalisation of certain types of gender and sexuality, and the stigmatisation of others, in order to legitimate inequalities. Despite these difficulties, framing the social inequalities that trans and intersex people face via social inclusion/exclusion discourse is useful in a number of ways. Notions of social exclusion as a process can be utilised to unpick the ways in which different factors (such as people's physiology, choices, experiences of discrimination or violence, and economic constraints) all act together to form people's positions as socially excluded or included. Areas where stigmatisation affects them particularly strongly can be pinpointed and policy interventions made. For instance, the amendments to the Sex Discrimination Act (UK 1999) mean that transsexual people can now prosecute employers who discriminate against them. Whilst social exclusion discourses could be misused to gloss over entrenched structures of inequality, they do open a window of opportunity for inclusion. The dangers concern social inclusion work that discursively reinforces gender and sexual minorities as being 'the problem', rather than tackling gender binarism, transphobia, homophobia and biphobia at social structural and discursive levels.

4

Social Policy Implications

Traditionally, social policy has tended to overlook sexual orientation and gender, and to assume a heterosexual male subject.[1] A body of literature has developed that is critical of 'gender blind' approaches, providing an analysis of traditional models of social policy from the position of women (Lewis 1998, Woodward 1997, Lister 2000). Some authors have developed challenges to the heterosexist nature of social policy (Carabine 1996a, 1996b, Wilson 1997). These contributions have been important in moving debates forward and in providing analytical tools for deconstructing social policy, highlighting the ways in which women and sexual minorities are marginalised by policy processes. However, feminist policy analysis constructs 'male' and 'female' as separate, discrete categories, and overlooks trans, intersex, and other forms of gender diversity and fluidity, whilst existing work on sexuality and social policy pays little attention to sexual orientation fluidity or multiplicity. Gender diversity and bisexuality add extra dimensions to the analysis of social policy, partly because trans, intersex and bisexuality raise particular policy issues, but also because they destabilise the rigid structuring of social policy along gender and sexual orientation binaries. How do trans, intersex, and bisexuality trouble the systems of categorisation that writers in the field of social policy use? What omissions and tensions are revealed by examining social policy in relation to gender and sexual diversity?

The gender binaried nature of social policy systematically acts to erase and marginalise people with fluid sexualities, trans people, and intersex people. Sexual orientation equality[2] work in general is often marginalised by policy-makers, and, when sexual minorities are included, policy-makers rarely explore issues concerning bisexuality. Do bisexuals require different provision to lesbians and gay men, or do they simply move between heterosexual and lesbian or gay identities and interests (see also Chapter 7)? What implications does the erasure of bisexuality on a wider level, both within mainstream society and within the lesbian and gay communities, have for policy-making? Trans people are usually marginalised and, when they are included, this is usually limited to transsexuals and in some cases cross-dressers, whilst intersex people and other gender diverse people are overlooked. What policy issues would inclusion of these groups raise? There are different ways in which social policy-makers can address the inclusion of trans and intersex people, including liberal and radical strategies, and a number of different models of social policy-making. Some aspects of traditional approaches to policy-making are useful, for example the incorporation of policy initiatives that address the interests of trans people into the policy cycle. However, these are limited, because they fail to address the discursive exclusion of gender and sexual diversity. This can be addressed by post-structuralist analysis, which provides useful tools for understanding the policy silences concerning sexual and gender diversity.

This chapter aims to chart the ways in which sexual and gender diversity and fluidity are shaped, contained, and hidden by the policy process in the UK, and to provide some suggestions for the fuller social inclusion of people with fluid or diverse gender and sexual identities. Policy can be seen as a web of decisions, or as actions without decisions (Hill 1997), or can be defined as 'a set of shifting, diverse, and contradictory responses to a spectrum of political interests' (Bacchi 1999: 42). The current policy environment is set within a wider context of fundamental shifts in the social, economic, and political make-up of society; shifts which have destabilised the organisation of social welfare that was established in the post-Second World War era. The connections between the state, social welfare and the populace, and the distributions of rights and responsibilities between the state and citizens, have been called into question. This destabilisation was caused by a number of factors, particularly the interactions between two sets of opposing critiques of welfare provision – social authoritarian and neo-liberal critiques, on the one hand, and critiques stemming from radical Marxists and new social movements, on the other (Lewis 2000). As Lewis remarks, 'it was not just the form, content, and distributive criteria of social welfare that were subjected to challenge, but it was the categories and boundaries through which welfare was conceptualised, produced, and distributed' (2000: 3). The following discussion of social policy and gender and sexual diversity is set within the context of this destabilisation, and in particular, the way in which constituencies of new welfare subjects have impacted on social policy. Trans, intersex, and LGB people are less visible as welfare subjects than some other minorities, but trans and LGB people are organised and are seeking recognition of their rights and needs regarding social policy, and this is having some impact on policy work. For example, Holmes notes that: 'Under pressure from such people [men who want to be able to wear clothing traditionally associated with women] policy-makers are beginning to concede that it's discrimination to deny men this basic right to freedom of personal expression' (2003: 2).

This chapter has a number of different sections: a brief overview and critique of some of the traditional approaches to social policy in relation to gender and sexual diversity; an exploration of the application of post-structuralist analysis in this field, drawing on the work of Bacchi (1999), and including a brief illustrative case study of sexualities initiatives in local government; a discussion of the different models of equal opportunities in relation to gender and sexual diversity, and indications of some of the key areas for social policy development concerning gender and sexual diversity. Social policy is constituted by, and of, a set of interlocking unequal social relations (Lewis 2000), mirroring the processes of intersectionality that are described in Chapter 2. Here, I will focus on gender and sexuality (specifically bisexuality, trans and intersex), whilst recognising the importance of other areas. Discussions in this chapter are limited to the UK policy arena.

TRADITIONAL APPROACHES TO SOCIAL POLICY

There is a wide range of theories concerning the social policy process. This section discusses two of the mainstream approaches to social policy, rational comprehensive and incrementalist models, in relation to gender and sexual diversity. I will demonstrate the inadequacy of these approaches, but will also argue that they have a number of advantages.[3] Rational comprehensive models are positivist, assuming an objective reality and relying on the idea that people are able to make rational choices based on their perceptions of their social world. The implementation of strategies to tackle problems is seen as being relatively straightforward, relying on a goal-oriented process that is implemented in stages: agenda setting, problem definition, formulation, implementation and evaluation. Rational comprehensive approaches have advantages in that they are pragmatic, thus amenable to being used as a driver for social change concerning gender and sexuality. For example, the 2002 Equalities Standard set a statutory requirement on local authorities to implement a five-stage Equalities programme in the areas of gender, race and disability, and was followed in 2003 by a further set of regulations concerning equalities in the areas of sexual orientation, age and religion. The staged formulation of the Standard provides policy-makers with tools to structure implementation. However, the positivist project underlying the rational comprehensive approach is flawed in some ways, especially in relation to non-normative identities. People with fluid gender and sexual orientations (like others) do not necessarily experience decision-making as linear or rational. Similarly, policy-makers are subject to irrational processes, which can be related to unconscious fears concerning gender and sexuality.[4] In addition, as Bacchi (1999) says, rational comprehensive models are focused on solving problems, meaning that other issues are excluded and that the status quo is reinforced. This is particularly apparent in relation to gender and sexual diversities, because many policy-makers simply do not see these as being valid areas for consideration.

Incrementalist models are based on the notion of power as fragmented, and a concern to ensure that this is not concentrated in the hands of an elite. They draw on political pluralism (see Lindblom 1959, Hill 1997).[5] Lindblom argued that decision-making involves focusing on a limited number of alternatives and ignoring the consequences, in other words, 'muddling through'. Change occurs through a series of small adjustments, but these do not necessarily preserve the status quo: they can be radical or conservative depending on the situation. Incrementalism is based on presenting policy changes as if they are minor, or on utilising other strategies to minimise opposition, such as restricting interest group participation. Where the policy implications of inclusion are relatively minor, incrementalism can be a useful strategy for supporting sexuality and gender diversities. This is particularly apparent in the case of statutory sector consultation processes. The incrementalist approach has been evident, for example, in the field of Local Authority Equalities work concerning sexual orientation and gender throughout the 1990s and subsequently. Findings from research project (b) showed that those authorities that have been successful in implementing initiatives have tended to 'ease them through', a strategy typical of incrementalism. However, incrementalism is unlikely to serve as a means of implementing some of the more radical aspects of gender pluralism. It would be impossible to gain full social inclusion of intersex people, gender fluid people, and people with multiple genders without fundamental social change. In addition, like the rational comprehensive model, incrementalism focuses on finding solutions, and problem definition risks overlooking gender and sexual minorities, potentially reinforcing the status quo. To summarise, both rational comprehensive and incrementalist models of social policy are useful because they are pragmatic, but they fail to unpick the deeper issues behind the marginalisation of gender and sexual minorities.

POST-STRUCTURALIST APPROACHES TO SOCIAL POLICY

This section aims to address how the 'social' is constituted in relation to gender and sexual minorities. In order to do this, I draw on the post-structuralist approach of Bacchi (1999), who deconstructs the norms and discourses underpinning policy formulation and implementation, addressing the contested nature of the policy process. As Lewis says:

> What counts as 'social' as a focus of social policy in a specific society at a particular historical moment matters deeply for members of that society ... how gender and ethnic divisions are conceptualised, and how they are seen to link with the aims and practices of welfare agencies – such issues have significant social consequences. (2000: 2)

Bacchi, unlike mainstream theorists, treats policy studies as inherently political. She maintains that political initiatives constitute the shape of the issues to be addressed, so that 'problems' themselves are discursively constructed based on actors' interpretations of the situation. This process structures social policy because certain groups are constructed in certain ways, and the limitations of this produce specific social effects. For example, framing something as a 'social problem' may mean the portrayal of certain subjects as 'sick' or 'troublesome'. Overall, Bacchi rejects the pragmatism of other approaches and instead looks at the way that problems are constituted and at the erasure of challenging issues from the policy arena.

What analytical tools does Bacchi's approach provide? Instead of aiming for policy solutions, Bacchi addresses the way in which certain things are considered to be 'inappropriate' for consideration. She suggests that policy is discursively constructed in different ways in different contexts, and that discursive representations are 'nested'. In other words, certain assumptions and norms underpin large areas of social policy, and within this, other types of discourse operate in different ways. She interrogates social policy using the following questions:

- How is the problem constructed?
- What presuppositions or assumptions underlie this representation?
- What effects are produced by this representation?
- How are subjects constituted within this representation?
- What is left unproblematised?
- How would responses to the 'problem' change if the 'problem' is thought about differently?

Bacchi's approach, like other post-structuralist positions, can be criticised in a number of ways. First, there is the difficulty with a lack of pragmatism. Post-structuralist methods appear to be an idealistic luxury in the 'real' world of policy-making and practice, where political and financial constraints impact in many and varied ways. For example, Taylor-Gooby (1994) argues that postmodernist (and post-structuralist) theory is mostly blind to the increasing universality of economic liberalism, which impacts significantly on policy-making. Bacchi responds to this type of critique by identifying a contradiction in post-structuralist accounts, between deconstruction and a transformational, positive political project. When used in a transformative way, post-structuralist approaches are valuable. As Bacchi says, there are material limitations on the way that things are constructed but it is possible to change constructions (at least to an extent). Another difficulty concerns relativism (where everything is made up of competing representations, none of which are more 'valid' than the others), which Bacchi deals with by arguing for the use of deconstruction in order to make the construction of the 'real' visible, suggesting that theories should be evaluated in terms of their effects on the ideological construction of reality, in other words, how they intervene in real struggles.

Bacchi's approach to social policy can be used to explore the ways in which policy processes act to shape or erase gender and sexual diversity. Many social policy initiatives are constructed without much reference to gender, and when gender is addressed, it is often framed as a women's issue. For instance, Escott and Whitfield, writing for the Equal Opportunities Commission, produced a report titled *Promoting Gender Equality in the Public Sector* which appears to be targeted at the equality of women, excluding trans and intersex people who do not identify as male or female, noting for example that 'it is necessary to challenge those public bodies which do not share the commitment to reducing inequality between women and men' (2002: vi). Trans people and other gender diverse people are generally omitted from consideration. Where they are included, they are constructed as problematic, and the gender binaried nature of society is not questioned. The processes of exclusion via language, legislation, and bureaucracy that were documented in Chapter 3 are apparent in the social policy arena. For example, the benefit system assumes that people are either male or female, and gives maternity benefits only to those people who identify as female, rendering FTM trans people who have children invisible and excluded from provision. People whose gender identity is discretely male or female benefit from this, whilst others are heavily disadvantaged. Assumptions concerning the normalisation of the gender binary system underpin this dynamic.

Post-structuralist analysis reveals the ways in which social policy frequently perpetuates the social dominance of heterosexuals and relegates same-sex desire to the category of 'other'. For example a LGB community leader told me that 'lesbian and gay politics – for me, it's still about invisibility. It's improving, but it's lowest on the list of issues in local authorities, the voluntary sector, and the NHS.' Complete erasure of non-heterosexual realities and policy issues is still common amongst policy-makers in the UK, although this will change to an extent with the new legislation. Where sexual minorities are addressed, their issues tend to be seen as discrete, pertaining only to those groups, and this means that they are kept contained and do not affect the heterosexual majority. The underlying assumptions concern the supposed normality of heterosexuality. However, lesbians and gays have made some inroads into the policy arena at a national as well as local level, and European directives (specifically the Human Rights Act 1998) are reinforcing this. Within this framework, other areas of non-heterosexual expression are often foreclosed. Findings from research project (b) showed that where policies concerning sexual orientation are in place, bisexuals are often marginalised both at symbolic levels (for example not being included in group titles), and in everyday policy work. The lesbian and gay policy-making arena is beset by struggles concerning the inclusion of bisexuals (see Chapter 5); struggles which can be seen as a result of the omission of non-binaried subjectivities at a broad social as well as policy level.

Case Study: Sexual Orientation Equality Work in Local Government

How can Bacchi's work be applied to a specific area: local government work in the area of sexuality and gender diversity? This section will address, first, the erasure of sexual orientation equality work in general, and second, the erasure of non-binaried identities from sexualities work. Sexual orientation equality work in the UK has a history of marginalisation. Until the 1980s, sexual orientation was seen as being outside of the remit of local government. During the 1980s, some progressive local authorities developed lesbian and gay equalities policies (see Cooper 1994, Carabine 1995), but these sparked a backlash which was linked with the right-wing development of notions of 'loony', as well as the introduction of section 28 (legislation which was in place in the UK between 1988 and 2003, which prohibited local authorities from 'promoting' homosexuality) and the subsequent retrenchment of lesbian and gay equalities work in local government. Sexual orientation equality work has subsequently developed in a piecemeal fashion, dependent on factors such as the impact of local politics, key players, legislation such as the 1998 Community Safety Act, and local commitment to community representation.

The discursive construction of sexual orientation equality initiatives has changed since the 1980s. In the 1980s, some radical authorities adopted strategies aimed at challenging heterosexism amongst workers and the wider population. Now, sexual minorities are framed as service consumers, or, to a lesser extent, as victims, and problems regarding sexual orientation are seen as relating mostly to violence and discrimination. Certain areas are seen as legitimate, particularly statutory matters, employment rights, work about HIV/AIDS, and challenging overt homophobia. Other areas are seen as less legitimate, particularly those that publicly celebrate sexual and gender diversity (such as Mardi Gras events) and those involving sex in public places (such as cruising and cottaging). What are the effects produced by this representation? In some cases, a less homophobic environment within local authorities, and an inclusive approach towards many aspects of LGBT people's lives. For example, Aberdeen City Council (2003) details a number of areas for action concerning equalities work and the LGBT communities, including education/training, awareness raising, access to services and community safety. In other cases, the marginalisation of sexualities work has continued, although this is not only due to the way the problems are framed or not framed, but also to subtle and overt strategies of resistance. Policy-makers and practitioners benefit from the erasure of sexualities work – it is sometimes seen as complicating policy-making and practice and as being politically sensitive, and in addition, it has resource implications. However, some officers and councillors in authorities also recognise the importance of the well-being of LGBT people, as workers as well as community members.

Until the mid-1990s, sexualities work was represented as lesbian and gay work, with little questioning of the sexual orientation binary system. After this, mostly in response to changes within the sexual and gender minority communities, some local authorities began to include bisexuals and, to a lesser extent, trans people. However, research shows that bisexuals sometimes remain excluded (projects (b) and (d)). For example:

> Straight society, for example social policy-makers, erase us. For example [city council] were happy for us to have a stall at the women's day, so I think things are changing. But we've written to them [as a bisexual group] and they say their policies only include us when we are in same-sex relationships. And, for example, at some meetings about the organisation of queer events, although the event is marketed as GLBT only lesbian and gay groups are called for input at the initial planning stages. With Community Strategy planning, [bisexual group] never received a letter. We are not a lesbian or gay group so we are not mailed, because bisexuality is not recognised as a valid sexual identity. So we are excluded from the policy process. (Kerry)

One contributor noted that, 'a lot of organisations include bisexual and also transgender but without thinking about what that means' (LGB community leader). In local authority policy-making, where sexual and gender minorities are dealt with at all, problems are usually framed with respect to the needs and interests of lesbians and gays. Where bisexuals are included, this is on the basis of a perception of common issues and oppressions, or a broader policy commitment to inclusion that overrides inter-group squabbling. There may be little consideration of the separate issues that bisexuals face. In addition, certain gender groups, especially non-binaried gender diverse people, are overlooked due to assumptions that transgender means either transsexuality or cross-dressing. Overall, where bisexual and trans people are included, in many cases, inclusion is symbolic, with little policy development or implementation. Findings from project (b) also showed that there is opposition to bisexual and transgender inclusion, coming from within the communities in some cases (see Chapter 5), but also from some key lesbian and gay players (officers, councillors) in the local authorities.

The assumptions underlying the erasure of bisexual, trans and intersex subjectivities include the notion that people with these identities are so unusual as to be unworthy of consideration. The ideas underlying the marginalisation of trans, intersex, and bisexual people are constructed in the context of the history of local government work; lesbians and gays spearheaded sexualities work, so that bisexuals are now seen as less central. What is left unproblematised by the current situation are assumptions about the stability of lesbian, gay, and heterosexual identities, as well as the acceptability of the exclusion of bisexuals and gender diverse people.

The post-structuralist approach developed by Bacchi provides a number of useful tools for unpicking the marginalisation of trans and intersex people, as well as sexual minorities. It can also be used for beginning to understand the way that trans, intersex, and bisexual people are sometimes excluded by policy-makers who support equalities initiatives for women, as well as lesbians and gay men. Post-structuralism can be used to gain a more in-depth understanding than that provided by traditional approaches. It enables the foregrounding of the gaps and elisions that exist in social policy with respect to gender and sexual diversities. It opens crucial space for questioning the ways in which policy issues and initiatives are constructed. Post-structuralism can therefore be used to inform traditional notions of policy 'problems', and cycles of policy implementation, targets, and evaluation, which are important tools for driving progressive policy concerning gender and sexual diversity forwards.

EQUAL OPPORTUNITIES

Another way of conceptualising and implementing social policy in the field of equality is provided by equal opportunities (now often called equalities). Equal opportunities developed from liberal political philosophy, which emphasised the rights of the individual and the universally applicable standards of justice and citizenship (Webb 1997). Definitions of equal opportunities vary. Following Bagilhole (1997), a working definition concerns not treating anyone in a blatantly discriminatory manner; treating people fairly.[6] The meaning of the term depends on the way in which equality itself is defined. Equality of opportunity concerns equal access, with individuals being judged on the basis of merit. Equality of condition involves a focus on parity of circumstances, whilst equality of result is more radical, entailing policies aimed at transforming inequalities.

Various factors contributed to the development of equal opportunities initiatives and legislation in the UK. During the 1940s and 1950s ideas concerning equal opportunities were based on notions of fairness and morality (Bagilhole 1997). In the 1960s and 1970s, developments included more radical goals as a result of pressure from the women's and gay and lesbian liberation movements. In the 1980s equal opportunities became increasingly problematic, given the wider movement away from welfarism, but in the 1990s and later, equalities work was repackaged because the business case for equal opportunities became apparent. A 'managing diversity' approach was advocated as part of this, developed initially in the US and then adopted increasingly in Europe (Webb 1997) and elsewhere. 'Managing diversity' meant that equal opportunities were framed as adding value to organisations, as well as making them more representative. Equal opportunities have now become normalised so long as they are tied to a managerialist approach (which as Bagilhole (1997) argues could be seen as a sanitised, bureaucratised version of equalities work). However, there has also been a concurrent reaction against equal opportunities, connected with the backlash against feminism and 'political correctness' (see for example Faludi 1992). Recently, the progressive impact of European Union legislation has become increasingly important, although Britain has been cautious and reluctant to bring itself in line with other European Union states.

How can we analyse equal opportunities in relation to gender and sexual diversity? One way to do this is to explore the way in which different models of equal opportunities can be applied to gender and sexual diversity.[7] Jewson and Mason (1985) argue that there are two main elements of equal opportunities: liberal approaches and radical approaches. The two approaches are fundamentally different in terms of political basis, aims and methods. Liberal approaches focus on fair procedures, the bureaucratisation of processes, and making access more equal. They aim to ensure equity at an individualised level by removing unfair distortions in the way the labour market operates, via institutionalised practices in employment. They advocate minimum amounts of state intervention (Jewson and

Mason 1985: 315), and use a 'short agenda' (short-term policy goals), concerning issues such as minimising bias in recruitment (Cockburn 1989 in Bagilhole 1997). Early equalities policies were based on liberal perspectives, so, for example, early race equalities work supported perceptions of assimilation and multiculturalism, with emphasis on learning respect for different cultures and under-lying assumptions that being black meant being disadvantaged. Multiculturalism can be criticised for focusing attention on black people rather than white people and their power structures, as well as neglecting the connections between ethnic minority communities and other groups, such as poor white people and women (see Bagilhole 1997).

Radical approaches provide a critique of liberal meritocracy, which is seen as legitimating existing inequalities whilst concealing their real causes. So, for example, ideas concerning 'ability' are understood to contain a series of value judgements, which are socially constructed and transmitted. Radical approaches frame equalities at the level of the group, rather than the individual, using standards derived from feminist and other critical discourses, as opposed to free market ideology. They advocate state intervention as a means of tackling inequalities, and support for the struggles of specific subordinated groups. Their primary aim is equality of outcome, rather than equality of access, and the means by which this is to be achieved is the politicisation of decision-making, rather than the bureaucratisation of procedures (Jewson and Mason 1985: 318). Radical approaches support redistribution (Webb 1997) and a fundamental reordering of society. They have a 'long agenda', aim-ing to transform organisations and wider society over a long period of time. Since the 1980s, the more radical approaches to equal opportunities have become diluted, or shrouded in liberal rhetoric. Most current and recent equalities work appears to draw strongly on liberalism. As noted above, there has been a shift towards approaches that are diversities oriented, as opposed to equalities oriented initia-tives, although according to some contributors to research project (b) there has been a recent revision of this in some policy areas, towards an overall integration of equalities and diversities approaches.

There are disadvantages and advantages concerning liberal and radical approaches to social policy. The most obvious problems with liberal stances are the individualism and the associated lack of struc-tural critique. However, on a more practical front, there are difficul-ties with the bureaucratisation of procedures that is characteristic of liberal types of policy work. The formalisation of organisational and policy procedures may have negative impacts, such as damaging informal channels of communication (Jewson and Mason 1985). However, there are advantages to liberal strategies. Many of the contributors to research project (b) stressed the need for cautious reform in the area of equalities work; incrementalist, collaborative policy-making, rather than oppositional or radical work. Liberal forms of equalities are more likely to be socially acceptable, hence efficacious, whilst radical approaches are problematic because they aim for more fundamental change, and risk causing a backlash. Difficulties with liberal approaches are ongoing. For example the multicultural, individualistic stance on which diversities initiatives are based was criticised by some of the contributors to research project (b), who saw it as diluting equal opportunities work due to a failure to address the systematic social subordination of certain social groups. Other contributors argue that diversities initiatives are useful; they appeal to the wider population in a way that prevents gender, race, disability, sexuality and other equalities issues from seeming alien and easy to dismiss by heterosexuals and non-trans people. Diversities initiatives appear to be helpful because they provide a structure in which the complexity of identity categories, including the overlaps between different social groups, as well as those groups that are marginalised from the main equalities categories, can be addressed.

What approaches to equalities policies are appropriate for supporting the inclusion of bisexuals? Bisexuals are hard to group together because of the variety of personal and social expressions that they experience and because they have fluid sexual identities, meaning that group-based approaches are problematic. Diversities approaches include heterosexuals as well as lesbian and gay people, and extension to cover bisexuality is relatively unproblematic. However, the diversities approaches to bisexual inclusion are limited, because they are unlikely to tackle institutional and cultural heterosexism. In addition, they appear to fail to address certain aspects of some bisexual identities, especially polyamory. For example, findings from research project (b) concerning same-sex adoption in one diversities-positive local authority indicated that being in a stable one–one relationship (or single) is likely to be considered a prerequisite to adoption, meaning that those people in polyamorous relationships would be excluded. Full equality for lesbians and gays, and thus for bisexuals, remains perhaps unattainable without a more robust approach to equal opportunities, one which addresses the structural basis for heterosexuality and monogamy.[8] A 'long agenda' is arguably necessary with regards to bisexual equality. However, this is not necessarily in conflict with the 'short agenda' of the liberal position, which, in practice, seems to be the most efficacious means of achieving progressive social change for bisexuals.

What types of equalities approach are best suited to supporting gender diversity? The broadening of binaries, non-gendered, and gender plural stances that I outlined in Chapter 2 could all be implemented via radical approaches. Challenges to the gender binary system are inevitably political, as they have potentially far-reaching implications not just for a gender minority but also for the male and female majority (because they open up possibilities for choice concerning gender, and they destabilise normative binaried assumptions), and so an approach which deals with the contentious nature of social change concerning gender openly might seem to be the best approach. However, there are a number of difficulties associated with the radical stance with regards to transgender. Trans and intersex people are very diverse populations, and placing them together is not fully viable in social policy terms, as their interests and needs are different. The more individual approach favoured by liberals may fit trans and intersex social policy interests better. This is particularly true of the majority of trans and intersex people who wish to assimilate into male or female categories, rather than achieve fundamental change to the gender binary system. For the minority who wish to identify as other than male or female, liberal and diversities stances may be useful on a pragmatic level. Neo-liberal discourses concerning the business case for equalities, and equality of access to services, are powerful with respect to gender pluralism. For example, as discussed in Chapter 3, a proportion of trans people are currently unable to work due to disability or discrimination (Whittle 2002). Social policies that support gender diversity could significantly enhance the ability of gender diverse people to join the labour market. Likewise, the business case for consumer responsiveness provides support for equalities initiatives concerning gender diversity. Consumer responsiveness means that trans and intersex people would not be treated as distinct groups with specific political agendas, but as diverse populations who may have certain gender-related characteristics and interests, as well as other interests concerning for example being older, younger, or from minority ethnic groups. Diversities initiatives may also be more helpful to transgender people than other approaches to equalities because the latter tend to focus on race, gender, disability, and more recently, sexuality, age and faith. The danger of the liberal approach and diversities initiatives is that reforms may be insufficient. As noted above, it is hard to identify and tackle structural inequalities when taking an individualistic position to equalities work. Overall, findings from research projects (a) and (d) certainly support the idea of a 'long agenda', given the extent to which the gender binary system is entrenched, but also strongly support pragmatic, realistic aims that would not provoke the type of backlash associated with 1980s radicalism.

GENDER AND SEXUAL DIVERSITY: SOME POLICY IMPLICATIONS

Things must be broken down to the simplest level for managers. Bisexuality is too problematic, so it gets ignored ... simplistically, I think any policy should include options for as diverse a range of sexualities as possible. Sexuality policies should include all sexualities and be constantly reviewed as things change.

Kerry

This section aims to explore some of the policy implications of gender and sexual diversity, focusing on trans, intersex, and bisexuality.[9] As I have shown, there are a number of ways of looking at social policy in these areas. Mainstream and post-structuralist approaches have advantages and disadvantages, as do liberal and radical strategies. The themes that are central to analysis of these different approaches, including pragmatism versus idealism, diversity and individualism as compared with universalism and group-based approaches, and radicalism as an alternative to reformism, will run through my discussions of social policy and gender/sexual diversity. In addition, I will structure my explorations in relation to the three types of theory concerning gender diversity that I identified in Chapter 2; the broadening of male and female categories; degendering, and gender pluralism. Whilst these are ideal types, overlapping in practice, separating them out is a useful analytical strategy. Although their ultimate aims are the same – gender and sexual equality – to an extent they have different, and sometimes conflicting strategies and outcomes. Exploring these differences may be useful, as a way of informing the development of social policy strategies that balance the different interests and needs of gender and sexual minorities.

It is important to reiterate the temporary, limited nature of my discussions of policy implications in this field. I am not trans, or intersex to any significant degree, and whilst I am bisexual, I cannot speak for all bisexuals. Discussions about policy in this area should be multifaceted and ongoing.

Core policy issues that emerged from research project (d) include the importance of supporting visibility (for example including bisexuals together with lesbians and gay men), and the need for policy-makers and providers to address the emotional and relational issues that people with fluid or multiple sexual orientations experience (for example providing help lines, training social workers in anti-oppressive practice) – as well as, of course, supporting the rights of people with same-sex desires and/or relationships (see Chapters 6 and 7).

In general, the social inclusion of bisexual, trans and intersex people requires the support of existing consultation mechanisms, for example the central government interdepartmental transsexual working party, and the establishment of new structures, in particular a means of consulting effectively with intersex people, and others who may identify as different from male or female. Support for community groups, infrastructure organisations and networks is crucial for capacity building in this area, so that bisexuals, lesbians and gay men, trans people, and intersex people have the resources to enable them to contribute to the policy process.[10] Resourcing of community groups and infrastructure organisations should also include the establishment of structures to ensure that groups genuinely attempt to attain internal democracy, as there is a danger of more marginalised individuals and groups within the already marginalised sexual and gender minority groupings being further erased or overridden, especially when there are differences of interest (see Chapter 8).[11] Stringent accountability measures are also necessary, as findings from research project (d) showed that, in one case, monies were being diverted to fund key activists' activities at the possible expense of other group users' interests. In addition, involvement of gender and sexual minorities in wider party politics, and in policy networks, should be encouraged. Overall, establishing the framework and resources necessary for sexual and gender minority participation in politics and policy-making is a central policy recommendation to come out of research projects (a), (b) and (d), cutting across the different approaches to gender and sexual diversity. Finding ways of making the issues and identities found in the sexual and gender minority communities accessible to policy-makers and practitioners is also crucial. For example, contributor Giles said: 'Having categories enables them to think in small, easy, steps ... "genderqueer" lets people get a handle on it – if you say "I'm somewhere in between" they can't get a handle on it.'

Beyond the above guidelines, there are, as I have said, a number of social policy routes that could be pursued in relation to gender diversity, which I discuss in relation to the three theoretical approaches I outlined earlier: the expansion of male and female categories, moving beyond gender, and gender pluralism.

The Expansion of Male and Female Categories

This approach consists of widening definitions of 'male' and 'female', so that people who might be considered 'other' are able to assimilate into society as either female or male. As I pointed out in Chapter 2, this is currently the most prevalent approach, cutting across both mainstream policy-making and the political goals of much of the trans communities.[12] This is a pragmatic solution for many gender diverse people, but it does erase those few people who cannot, or choose not to, fit into the gender binary system. It is also a workable option for most members of the sexual minority communities, as well as the heterosexual majority. It operates inclusively except for where people identify as neither male nor female – those people who identify otherwise may be excluded, although in practice a fair amount of sexual diversity is found in some sexual fringe communities which still mostly adhere to gender binarism, including the bisexual and fetish communities.

The implications of broadening out gender binaries include:

1. The introduction of legislation to support pre- and post-operative transsexual people in their reassigned gender identity (this is currently being developed by central government in England) including in specific types of institution, such as prisons.
2. The depathologisation of gender diversity, including the removal of transsexuality and transvestism from psychiatric diagnostic manuals, and discussion of gender issues in terms of gender identity rather than 'problems' (see Zandvliet 2000).
3. The continued/increased provision of resources, including access to surgery and hormone treatment, for transsexuals.

4. The cessation of intersex genital mutilation – surgery that is unnecessary for physical functioning – on intersex infants and children until each individual is able to choose which gender they would like to live as.

5. The assignment of intersex infants to one gender at birth on a temporary basis, until they are old enough to choose whether to live as male or female (see ISNA guidelines).

6. The introduction of equalities legislation for same-sex couples, including full partnership and parenting rights.

7. The reworking of legislation and social regulations/norms concerning men who wish to wear dresses, skirts, make-up and high heels, so that they are not discriminated against (see Holmes 2003).

8. The introduction of broader gender equalities initiatives, for example stronger paternity leave legislation to enable men to care for their children.

9. The introduction of social and cultural initiatives that increase the acceptance of diverse ways of being male and female, for example anti-bullying initiatives that tackle the victimisation of effeminate boys in school, and initiatives to increase the number of women in traditionally 'male' jobs and higher ranking male-dominated positions.

10. The positive portrayal of diverse ways of being male and female and different forms of relationship in the statutory and other sectors.

Moving Beyond Gender

As I have described, moving beyond gender, or degendering, involves the removal of gender signifiers and codes from social life as far as is possible, and the concurrent minimisation of sexual orientation categorisation systems. This means that the differences between women and men would be limited as much as possible. One major implication of degendering is the removal of all questions concerning gender from official and commercial forms, unless these are specifically necessary, as for example in the case of treatment for reproductive health issues. Others include the changing of terms that are unnecessarily gendered, for example the use of 'chair' or 'chairperson' rather than 'chairman', and unnecessarily sexualised, for example the terms 'husband and wife' being replaced with the term 'partner'. Other implications include the less rigid gendering of babies and children, for example the introduction of educational initiatives to counter the rigid colour coding of infants and the use of gender specific toys. Implications for primary and secondary education include minimising the division of girls and boys into separate groups for teaching or class/playground management, developing educational materials that include people who are non-gender stereotypical, and, as with the 'broadening' approach, tackling the bullying of children who do not fit gender or sexual orientation norms. In addition, sex education would focus less heavily on physiological differences and more on aspects of sexual relations that cut across gender and sexual orientation (not necessarily uniformly), such as negotiating safer sex, intimacy issues, and considering parenthood. Wider social implications would include reform of the welfare system to minimise gender differences, for example flattening out policy and practice that assumes that people are heterosexual, and changing therapeutic practice guidelines to support people who are fluid in their gender or uncertain as to their gender identity (see Zandvliet 2000). Degendering would also entail government support for the minimisation of gender differences in the business world (for example in advertising), and increased media portrayal of androgynous or non-stereotypical women and men.

Gender Pluralism

Gender pluralism is generally compatible with the first two approaches, but moves beyond them in that it develops support for people with a range of gender and sexual identities. Instead of focusing on broadening out existing categories, or attempting to eliminate gender as far as possible, it celebrates gender diversity and the sexual diversity that is linked with this. The policy focus for gender pluralism is, therefore, on creating space for the addition of new categories and identities to those that are already established, so that a spectrum (or universe) of genders becomes possible; intersex, androgynous, gender plural, male, female, trans, a related universe of sexual orientations is developed; heterosexual, gay, lesbian, bisexual, polysexual, and fluid (as shown above, certain identities, especially genderqueer, involve a combination of non-binaried genders and sexualities). Social policy in this area is particularly reliant on mechanisms for community inclusion and responsiveness to pressure from new welfare constituencies, because the territory is new and change must be led by the people who will be most affected by it. However, possible areas for policy work include:

1. The creation of 'other' categories on forms and documents.
2. The recognition of socially viable categories for people who wish to identify as other than male or female – particularly intersex people, who are born 'other' and might chose to identify as intersex if it was socially possible. This would involve significant changes to a whole raft of legislative and statutory procedures.
3. Depathologisation of all forms of gender variance (including intersex, transsexuality, multiple genders, and transvestism) and the development of strategies to enable access to treatment with minimal pathologisation, where treatment is necessary for conditions relating to gender variance.
4. The naming of intersex, androgynes, gender fluid, gender plural, and polysexual on equalities documents and strategies.
5. Governmental pressure on community groups to be inclusive of people with non-male/non-female identities and non-binaried sexualities (for example funding to be tied to inclusive policies).
6. Statutory resources to support the equality of non-male/non-female people, for example funding for work in central government concerning these groups.
7. Legislation to support relationships between people of non-binaried genders, and those between a man or a woman and a person who identifies as androgynous, intersex, or gender diverse in other ways.
8. The cessation of operations on intersex people that are unnecessary for physical functioning, unless individuals wish for these (as above).
9. Continued provision of surgery and hormone therapy for transsexuals where wanted, but also the provision of alternative options such as non-operative reassignment – and the provision of full equal rights for trans people who do not wish to have surgery, or who identify as other than male or female after surgery.
10. Full social support for men who wish to wear attire traditionally associated with females (including legislation to prevent discrimination).
11. Educational and anti-discriminatory initiatives aimed at tackling ignorance and prejudice towards people of other genders.

As I argued in Chapter 2, gender pluralism is the only type of approach to social policy in this area that will fully include all people. The other approaches create space for diversity, and mostly combine productively together and with gender pluralism. However, ultimately they may act to continue excluding people who cannot or do not wish to live within the gender binary system, in terms of both their gender and their sexual identities.[13] Perhaps gender pluralism is impossible within current mainstream Western society, although the extent of change associated with women's and gay and lesbian rights, as well as, for example, disabled people's rights, over the last century would indicate that this is not necessarily the case. If gender pluralism is to be pursued, constructing it within a strong liberal framework, which draws on post-structuralism in analysing processes of exclusion, may be the most viable option. People who do not fit male or female norms suffer considerable amounts of discrimination and social exclusion (as shown in Chapter 3) and deserve to have equal rights, including the right to determine their gender and sexual identities. Rights and victimisation discourses have considerable purchase amongst the general public. The broadly liberal diversities initiatives appear to be amenable to supporting a range of different identities, including gender pluralism and bisexuality. Moreover, liberalism involves incrementalist, reformist strategies, which are less likely to provoke negative reactions from prejudiced or ignorant people; this, combined with robust participatory democracy (see Chapter 8), may be the most viable way forward. The risks associated with liberalism are insufficient change, and an individualistic approach that fails to tackle structural inequalities.

CONCLUSION

Traditional analysis of social policy has tended to overlook gender and sexuality issues, and the literature that addresses social policy from feminist or non-heterosexist positions erases trans, intersex, and bisexuality. Sexual and gender diversity are marginalised or hidden by mainstream policy processes, although the models of social policy that are associated with these, such as rational comprehensive and incrementalist approaches, may be useful in driving forward progressive change once erasure of these groups has been addressed. Post-structuralist analysis of social policy is useful in developing a critical understanding of social policy in relation to gender and sexual diversity, because it provides tools for uncovering the erasure of sexual and gender minority groups, and the assumptions that underpin this. Post-structural analysis can be demonstrated by looking at sexual orientation equality initiatives in local government. Local government policy processes often marginalise lesbian and gay people, and, where they are included, bisexuals or trans people are generally not. Whilst post-structural approaches are important in deconstructing the hegemony of heterosexism and gender binarism within policy-making, they are insufficient in reformulating and changing policy. Post-structuralist analysis lacks the pragmatism necessary for policy-making, so that a combination of mainstream and post-structural approaches is likely to be most useful.

Equal opportunities policies have been one of the key means of driving forward social change in the areas of gender and race, and, more recently, sexuality. Liberal forms of equal opportunities, which emphasise fair procedures, equal access, and a short-term agenda using bureaucratic procedures, are one means of operationalising equalities policies. This type of approach is similar to the managerialism that has become popular since the early 1990s, which emphasises the maximisation of worker's abilities and consumer satisfaction, thus providing a business case for equal opportunities. Liberal and managerialist forms of equalities have dominated the equalities and diversities arena since the 1980s, and they have enabled some positive developments, including nascent support for bisexual and trans inclusion. These approaches can, however, be criticised for being individualistic, hiding the group-based nature of structural inequalities and failing to achieve equality of outcome. Alternatives are provided by radical approaches, which focus on achieving fundamental social change via a long agenda. The difficulties with radical approaches arise from their tendency to homogenise groups (due to a reliance on class-based activism) and their exclusion of the smaller groups within minorities (such as bisexuals, trans and intersex people), as well as a history of provoking resistance from conservatives. Therefore, strong liberalism, that supports the equality of bisexuals, trans people, intersex people, as well as others, and that draws on the 'long agenda' aspect of radical approaches may be the best way forward.

The policy implications of gender and sexual diversity concern, primarily, the establishment and support of better resourced communities and infrastructures to enable trans, intersex, and bisexual people to engage with the policy process and formulate policy interventions – as community members, policy-makers, and practitioners. As with other sections of the voluntary and community sector, there is also a need for funders to aim to ensure that community groups are representative and democratically accountable, given the divisions within the communities. Support for a robust community sector and mechanisms for influencing the policy process will enable the communities, together with policy-makers, to tackle issues concerning diversity and gender and sexual pluralisation. There are specific policy issues concerning bisexuals, especially a need to support visibility and inclusion, as well as the development of policy and practice that support people experiencing sexuality fluidity, multiplicity, and in some cases, multiple relationships. There are a number of ways of conceptualising policy-making in relation to trans and intersex. The 'broadening gender binaries' approach involves many of the current types of reform, such as the resourcing of transsexual surgery, legislation to support gay and lesbian people and transsexuals, the cessation of unnecessary surgery on intersex infants, and a general commitment to gender equality. The 'degendering' approach involves the removal of unnecessary gender indicators and divisions, for example male/female categorisation on forms and the rigid colour coding of infants, and changes to the welfare system to minimise gender differences. The third approach, gender pluralism, goes beyond the broadening gender binaries and the degendering approaches because it supports people with identities that are other than male or female – people who would be excluded at least to a degree by the first two approaches. It would include, for example, the creation of additional gender categories in language and official documents, and legislation to support gender pluralism. The viability of gender pluralism as a political goal is open to discussion. Although there are some divergences, it is likely to be generally compatible with the other two approaches, given the emphasis on self-determination and equality that runs through all of them.

5
Activism: Tensions and Alliances

The communities that have evolved around lesbian, gay, bisexual, trans and other non-mainstream sexual and gender identities are, to an extent, insulated from the hegemonic norms concerning gender and sexuality that permeate mainstream society. These social spaces provide a rich arena for the formulation of identities that challenge heteronormativity, and in some cases, gender binarism. However, the way that these communities have been historically formulated, as well as the ongoing impact of intersecting inequalities both within and outside of the communities, mean that the spaces associated with these communities are sites of contestation. There are a number of conflicts concerning identity and politics within, and between, the sexual and gender minority communities, as well as alliances that cut across these divergences.

This chapter outlines and discusses some of the tensions between different sections of the LGBT communities,[1] and the formation of alliances across these communities, focusing on the inclusion of bisexuals and trans people. Bisexuals and trans people have shared affiliations with lesbians and gay men, historically and currently, but alliances are uneasy, given the rigidity of categorisation on which lesbian and gay identities are based, and the way that these identities are constructed (by both gay/lesbian and heterosexual actors) as being oppositional to heterosexuality. Bisexuality and trans have also been contentious issues within the feminist movement. There has been a history of condemnation of both of these groups by binary-based feminisms, especially cultural, separatist and radical feminisms. This has impacted significantly on the inclusion (or exclusion) of trans and bi women within the lesbian communities, as well as generic women's space. The deconstruction of rigid gender and sexual orientation categories raises important questions for activism concerning gender and sexuality. What is the basis for alliances when the boundaries between communities are destabilised? Is a political approach that focuses on difference between the communities a useful strategy? Is a universalist approach, in which underlying universal commonalities form a basis for collaboration, more helpful?

This chapter will begin by outlining the history of the conflicts within and between the LGBT communities, and describe some of the current tensions. I will then address feminisms in relation to trans and bisexuality, focusing on radical, cultural and separatist feminisms, which have perhaps had the greatest impact on the way that feminists perceive trans people and bisexuals.[2] Tensions between the different communities are illustrated via a case study of LGB work in local government. I will then discuss alliances, before exploring issues concerning universalist and diversity-based approaches to activism. I will not discuss intersex in any depth in this chapter, as there has been a limited amount of activism concerning intersex in the UK. In addition, whilst acknowledging that there are conflicts between the gay male communities and trans and bisexual people (see for example Califia 1997), I will focus here on feminisms and the lesbian communities. The chapter focuses on issues associated with the Western sexuality/gender rights movements, whilst acknowledging that other tensions exist, including those associated with broader inequalities such as nationality and ethnicity (see for example Roen 2001).

LESBIAN, GAY, BISEXUAL AND TRANS COMMUNITIES: THE TENSIONS

This section aims to set the scene for discussions concerning the conflicts and alliances between the different sexual and gender minorities. I begin by briefly demonstrating the historical overlap between gender and sexual diversity, and the involvement of trans people in the early gay and lesbian liberation movements. The section then provides an overview of the way in which tensions concerning gender and sexual diversity have been played out within the lesbian, gay, bisexual and trans communities.

History

The categorisation of gender and sexuality has historically been more fluid than it is at present (see Nataf 1996, and Chapter 6). Same-sex men's communities initially developed in social spaces organised around companionship and sexual expression, and involved not only same-sex sexualities but also behaviours that would now be defined as transgender, as illustrated by a description of the prosecution of a Molly House in 1726: 'Some [a policeman reported] sat on another man's lap, kissing them, and using "their hands indecently." Others would dance, curtsy, and mimic the voices of women' (Bullough 1976: 480–1). Same-sex desire between women tended to be located in informal networks, and there is considerable evidence for a crossover between same-sex desire and cross-dressing or cross-gender identification. For example, Cromwell (1999) documents cases in which women who loved women lived (and passed) as men in order to maintain their relationships. The overlaps between gender and sexual diversity were also evident in the work of some of the authors who contributed to the development of sexology in the late nineteenth century – for instance Karl Ulrichs modelled homosexuality as a third sex (Adam 1987). The overlaps between same-sex desire and transgender were obliterated by sexologists in the early part of the twentieth century, although these overlaps continued to an extent at the grass roots, where gay and lesbian subcultures provided space for, and were partly constituted by, gender diverse and bisexual people.

LGBT People and the Development of Activism

Trans and bisexual people played a pivotal role in the early gay liberation front, which had acceptance of sexual diversity as a goal <http://www.transhistory.org>. The gay liberation movement then drew boundaries that excluded trans (and bisexual) people. This was partly because one of the prerequisites during the early stages of treatment for transsexuality was that transsexuals would become heterosexual after surgery; gay people had well-founded worries that treatment for transsexuality was being used to 'cure' homosexuality. It was also due to the impact of lesbian feminism. Adam (1987) describes the early stages of the movement towards lesbian autonomy, which was spurred on by lesbians' experiences of being outnumbered by gay men, who took male privilege for granted. Lesbians began organising women only events in 1970, and 'lesbians around the world began withdrawing from gay liberation in 1972 and 1973' (Adam 1987: 92), with splits taking place in gay liberation movements in Western nations. The political positions of radical, cultural and lesbian feminists were diverse, but, overall, lesbian separatism defined lesbianism as a 'women-identified experience … sharing of a rich inner life, the bonding against male tyranny, the giving and receiving of practical and political support' (see Adam 1987). As Epstein (1999) notes, lesbian feminism forged a political community by drawing clear lines around a lesbian feminist identity, which was distinct from (and developed in opposition to) those of gay men, bisexuals and trans people. 'To lesbian separatists who endorsed strongly essentialist conceptions of femaleness and lesbianism, male-to-female transsexuals were not "real women", and bisexuals were "traitors" who continued to "enjoy heterosexual privilege" ' (Epstein 1999: 50).

Radical and lesbian feminisms contributed to a social milieu in which identity politics, and the boundaries between women and men – and lesbians and heterosexuals – became value-laden and policed. The emphasis on a homogeneous identity meant that differences had to be subsumed. However, 'over the course of the late 1970s and 1980s, the unifying model of lesbian feminism became less stable, as lesbian feminist communities were racked with disputes over racial and sexual diversity' (Epstein 1999: 49) (see Chapter 2). These included what are now known as 'the sex wars': conflicts about the political acceptability of butch/femme identities, sadomasochism and pornography (Vance 1984). The 'sex wars' were played out in the communities in a number of ways, for example disputes at the London Gay and Lesbian Centre during the 1980s about SM and transsexuality (Roz). There were alternative views amongst some lesbians, who maintained affiliations with the gay movement, which had continued with its willingness to 'embrace such politically incorrect people as drag queens and butch lesbians' (Adam 1987: 96), and fierce disputes broke out between what were seen as 'pro-sex' and 'anti-sex' women. These disputes also related to race and class differences, for example 'Rita Mae Brown and Martha Shelley were attacked as male-identified for promoting coalition between lesbians and people oppressed by class and race' (Adam 1987: 96).

Separatist feminism, and misogyny amongst some gay men, led to tensions between lesbians and gay men that continued through the 1970s and subsequently. In the 1970s gay men's responses to political lesbianism ranged from the purging of any signs of masculinity, through attempts to accommodate lesbians' demands, to stances in which 'gay men suspected that many lesbians simply found it convenient to identify with a large and respectable mass movement [feminism] than with a group of stigmatised "perverts" ' (Adam 1987: 96). The AIDS crisis provoked a sea change in relationships between lesbians and gay men, as 'Many lesbians became involved in the AIDS movement, thereby tightening, at least temporarily, the political and personal connections between lesbians and gay men'

(Epstein 1999: 53). This, and other changes, such as the impact of queer politics, has meant that the divisions between lesbians and gay men are now less strong (see the case study on local government below).

The Current LGBT Communities

As I have shown, bisexual and trans people have been historically marginalised by the lesbian and gay communities. Sexual identities and the relations between communities are, as elsewhere, developing in an ongoing way. For example, contributor Craig discussed the position of married men. He suggested that married men who have sex with men would historically have cottaged, but that, because many of the cottages are now closed or more heavily policed, a lot of these men now use the internet. Contact during cottaging and cruising was mostly non-verbal, but the internet requires men to verbalise their identities and desires – they are forced to categorise themselves, so they say they are bisexual. This has opened up new possibilities in the way that these men interact with others.

As well as ongoing developments in the bisexual communities, there are also wide variations in the way in which the communities interact, for example:

> I think they [bi women and lesbians] are different camps, but there's a lot of variety in how they interface, mainly because it depends on individuals. So any generalisation has to take into account the immense variation. My impression is that white lesbians have been the most separatist from bi women, and that black and Asian groups are more likely to be mixed lesbian and bi. (Jennifer Moore)

> There is contradictory stuff in the gay community about fetishising bisexual men, when bisexual men are seen as being more masculine than gay men. My sense is that men are saying they are 'bisexual', are adopting an identity as straight acting and straight looking, as non-camp, and that this is linked for them with bisexuality ... at the same time, married men feel stigmatised by gay men, it's complicated. (Craig)

Although there are variations, there is a tendency for bisexuality and bisexuals to be excluded by lesbians and gay men. Within the communities, some lesbians (and gay men) prefer to avoid bisexuals (see Rust 1995: 219), and bisexuals are sometimes shut out of lesbian and gay social space. For example, Kerry told me that 'lesbian and gay groups are reluctant to let us campaign with them. [The blocks] are the lesbian and gay groups themselves. The only way it can be achieved is if a bisexual individual endlessly goes to meetings.' Bisexuality is also subsumed to an extent by the lesbian and gay communities, as findings from research project (d) showed that some bisexuals deal with biphobia by pretending to be lesbian or gay – or by continuing to identify as such whilst having some level of sexual engagement with opposite-sex partners. Bisexuality is also marginalised by (some) lesbian, gay and queer theorists, or is framed as reinscribing oppositional categories, so that 'In effect, bisexuals become the theoretical and cultural carriers of heterosexual hegemony within lesbian or gay, or queer, community' (Hemmings 2002: 11).

Biphobia within the lesbian and gay communities has been well documented by authors such as Ochs (1996); it manifests as a denial of the existence of bisexual people and the invisibilisation of bisexual people (as well as overt hostility). Biphobia is linked in with subculture structuring mechanisms, for example Jennifer Moore suggested that:

> there's a hierarchy which both bi women and lesbians subscribe to, which says that being lesbian is better than being bi. I know that I catch myself at it and have to remind myself that 'it isn't better to be lesbian'. I think it partly comes from the 1980s theme that 'the lesbian is the ultimate feminist' and partly from generalised biphobia, in particular the suggestion that bisexuality is a halfway house.

Why are bisexuals stigmatised by lesbians and gay men? Dunphy (2000) and Ochs (1996) locate this exclusion primarily in the way that bisexuality challenges sexual orientation binaries – this is unsettling for people whose identities are invested in these binaries. Ochs usefully describes the origins of this exclusion, tracing it to, for example, the privileging of heterosexual identities which some bisexuals access – some bisexuals do have a greater ability to pass as heterosexual than lesbians and gay men, especially when they are in relationships with opposite-sex partners. This is particularly relevant given the levels of stigmatisation that 'out' gays and lesbians face (although 'out' bisexuals also face stigmatisation). Exclusion has taken place for a number of other, less savoury, reasons:

- notions of purity concerning sexual orientation – these conformist ideals have led to divisive politics (Hutchins and Kaahamanu 1991: 221);

- various types of stereotyping – for example bisexuals are seen as promiscuous, as apolitical, as parasitical to the lesbian and gay communities, or as likely to leave same-sex partners for opposite-sex ones (see also Dunphy 2000);
- stigmatisation via the labelling of bisexuals as HIV carriers.

Trans people are also marginalised by the lesbian and gay communities, although inclusion of trans people within the LGB communities has also increased (see Monro 2000b), and intersex people are now a named included group in some bisexual circles (research project (d)). In general, as one contributor observed, 'People like things to be clear, for example Kenric [a lesbian dating agency] will accept post-operative trans women but not pre-operative trans women. But it is much better in 2003 than in 1970.' My research showed that people often see trans people's concerns as being different to those of LGB people – for instance, a Stonewall representative told me that 'transgender issues are gender issues' (project (d)). In some cases this difference seems to be used as an excuse for institutional transphobia, in others, there is a concern to support trans equality but avoid homogenising differences. Transphobia in the lesbian and gay communities (I have not come across prejudice against trans people in the bisexual communities) is linked with underlying identity conflicts – for example Bergling (2001) relates the way in which effeminate or camp men are ostracised by (some of) the gay communities. Trans people also face a considerable amount of exclusion by gay, lesbian and queer theorists (see for example Califia 1997, Hemmings 2002). Trans was heralded by queer theorist Butler (1990) as transgressive and challenging to heterosexism, but trans people have resisted the appropriation of transgender by queer theorists; queer approaches can be seen to appropriate transgender experience and to trivialise or dismiss transsexuals' experience (Hemmings 2002: 122).

There are a number of ways of challenging the exclusion of bisexuals from the lesbian and gay communities. Authors such as Dunphy (2000) discuss challenges to the stereotypes that perpetuate the exclusion of bisexuals. For instance, the notion that bisexuality is 'just a stage' on the way to a lesbian or gay identity could be supplanted by the idea that a lesbian or gay identity might be 'just a stage' in transition to a bisexual identity. Others (for example Young 1995) question the definition of lesbian identity. For instance, if lesbianism is defined as sexual involvement only with other women, this excludes celibate women, whilst if it is defined as never having sexual thoughts about men this excludes many lesbians. Seen in this way, 'lesbian' and 'gay' identities are complex and overlap with 'bisexual' identities. Similarly, notions of lesbian and gay identities as political are problematic – the lesbian and gay communities include people who are apolitical about their sexuality, and some heterosexuals support lesbian, gay and bisexual rights politically. Some of these arguments also apply to trans people, especially when gender diversity as a marker of lesbian and gay identities is taken into account, and alliances concerning tackling shared types of discrimination and abuse are formed. Once the boundaries between lesbians, gay men, bisexuals and trans people are seen as less distinct, the exclusion of bisexuals and trans people becomes less tenable.

Conflicts within the Trans Communities

I have flagged up some of the divergences within the lesbian and feminist communities. There are also conflicts within the bisexual and trans communities. Tensions within the bisexual communities centre around hierarchies of inclusion concerning whether some-one is 'bisexual enough' (sleeps with enough people of different genders) and polyamorous (sexually involved with more than one person in an open and caring way), which in certain circles is seen as being better than monogamous or celibate. In addition, as I note in Chapter 8, there are hierarchies concerning 'coolness' and some groups, for example people of colour, are less well represented.

Tensions within the trans communities revolve primarily around debates concerning terminology, status, political strategies and inclusion. For example:

> Transgender is now almost synonymous with MTF transsexuality – they've hijacked the term. And, our gay movement has recognised transgender, but everything they say is about MTF transsexuals. (Graham Holmes)

> In the transgender community, there's sometimes a huge divide especially between trans men and trans women. For example until comparatively recently trans women have tended to have much more experience of mutual support ... the whole row about passing, questions about passing, the judgements about this, for example 'she's an embarrassment to be seen with'. Trans men tend to pass more. (Roz Kaveney)

Until the 1990s, the goal for most transsexual people was to pass and assimilate into mainstream society as the gender to which they have been assigned, and the emphasis on conventional gender identities continues to be important for many transsexual people. This emphasis on assimilation has contributed to the development of a hierarchy within the transgender communities, with post-operative transsexuals placed at the top, followed by pre-operative transsexuals[3] and then cross-dressers (see Bornstein 1994). Clear presentation as the sex the person identifies as seems to be valorised within large sections of the trans communities – for example hyperfemininity tends to be seen as desirable within transvestite culture. The hierarchy is linked with broader structures of inequality concerning patriarchy, privileging people who are gender normative and penalising others. It also ties into heteronormativity and homophobia. Rejection of LGB people and subjectivities is apparent in some sections of the trans communities – for instance contributor Craig noted that 'lots of married men do cross-dressing. Some go on to do sex with men, but this is taboo in traditional cross-dressing communities.' The hierarchical system also acts to marginalise people who cannot – or choose not to – fit into clear categories, for instance non-passing transsexuals and some cross-dressers. For example:

> I've been verbally abused, I've been threatened, and I've been warned that if I persist in going out in public without my wig I'll get beaten up. Ironically, this behaviour has not come from the public, but from members of the [transvestite organisation] ... some have even said that presenting as a mixture of male and female is unacceptable ... freedom of choice is anathema to some in the cross-dressing community. (Holmes 2003)

Since the early 1990s, when the radical transgender movement began, trans people who wish to disrupt, or live outside of, the gender binaried system have challenged gender hierarchies. For these people, passing as male or female may not be a goal (although it may be a survival strategy), and the older hierarchy is not subscribed to. Whilst trans people may often adopt both radical and assimilationist stances in practice, the tensions between these positions remain a source of difficulty. For example, from the assimilationist perspective, the gender pluralist disruption of mainstream gender binaries that the non-male/non-female identities can catalyse is problematic, as it means that mainstream society no longer looks at gender through binaried spectacles – this makes passing harder. From a gender pluralist perspective, the conservative trans insistence on being closeted and assimilating erodes a potential basis for organising, and perpetuates the social erasure of gender diversity. It impacts on some gender diverse people's lives in negative ways – for example I heard reports of some trans organisations marginalising intersex and androgynous people who had little recourse to alternative organisations. Tensions concerning inclusion are mirrored in debates within the movement, debates, for example, concerning whether people with non male/female identities should be included in a movement primarily run by transsexuals.

FEMINISM: THE EXCLUSION OF BISEXUALITY AND TRANS

Feminist analysis of trans has been dominated by the heavily binaried radical and separatist feminisms, which have served as a basis for the exclusion and stigmatisation of trans women. Bisexual women have faced criticism from these groups of feminists. In this section, I outline the feminist critiques of trans and bisexuality, and explore counterarguments. Needless to say, these overlap and are combined with lesbian critiques, but I have attempted to separate them out here.

Feminism and Trans

Transgender has been a divisive and volatile issue for the feminist movement (see Whittle 1998a), with disputes concerning the presence of transsexual women in women-only space taking place since the 1970s. Feminist debates about transgender have centred around the work of (mostly radical) feminists, especially Janice Raymond (1980, 1994), Mary Daly (1984), Sheila Jeffreys (1996) and also, more recently, Germaine Greer (1999). Jeffreys, Daly and Greer broadly follow the work of Raymond, who argued that transsexuals who identify as women are really men, and that transsexuality is a patriarchal means of reinforcing gender stereotypes (1980). Raymond saw MTF transsexuals as deceptively invading women's space, minds and emotions. She stated that 'All transsexuals rape women's bodies by reducing the real female form to an artefact, and appropriating this body for themselves' (1980: 104), and that 'The transsexually constructed lesbian-feminist feeds off woman's true energy source, i.e. her woman-identified self. It is he [sic] who recognises that if female spirit, mind, creativity and sexuality exist anywhere in a powerful way it is here, among lesbian-feminists' (1980: 108). She argued that lesbian feminists who accept transsexual women are 'guilty of mutilating their own reality' (1980: 119). Overall, her position can best be summarised by this quote: 'I contend that the problem with transsexualism would best be served by morally mandating it out of existence' (1980: 178) (via legal limitations of changing sex). Raymond has continued to argue that transgender people reinforce, rather than challenge, gender norms, although she does provide some suggestion of recognition that trans may not simply be an evil patriarchal tool, in her statement that 'A real sexual politics says yes to a view and a reality of transgender that instead of conforming to gender, really transforms it' (1994: 632).

The radical feminist stance on trans has had a profound and damaging impact on relations between trans people and the feminist movement. Since the feminist debates of the 1970s, typified by Raymond's position on transsexuality, transsexual women have experienced a very considerable amount of exclusion from the lesbian and feminist communities. This has included, for instance, female transsexual employees in women's organisations being forced to resign, transsexual women who have been raped being refused support by Rape Crisis Centres, and Women's Centres refusing them access (Monro 2000b). The trans people who took part in the study on transgender politics were unanimous in their rejection of the radical feminist position, which was seen as victim-blaming, abusive, erasing of trans people's agency, and limited, given the many gender positions that trans people occupy. The only caveat was provided by one transsexual commentator, who suggested that Raymond's (1980) critique of the gender stereotyping that took place in the medical establishment was an important catalyst for change.

Raymond's work (1980, 1994) is seriously flawed in a number of ways. Methodologically, her research can be seen as unethical because she deceived her subjects when gaining access by failing to let them know she had an anti-transsexual agenda (Califia 1997) and misrepresented them, for example by denying their experience of being female by referring to them as male. This goes against feminist methodological guidelines such as honesty and empowerment of participants (Reinharz 1992). Raymond's notions of transsexuals invading and taking over women's space are largely unfounded: as one contributor said, the thinking is irrational – transsexuals have not been known to rape women, and the use of rape as a metaphor is insulting to rape victims and denies the extent to which transsexuals are at risk of sexual abuse. Raymond's account is problematic in other ways; theoretically and in terms of political strategy. She shifts between biologist and constructionist accounts of gender. She argues that transsexual women are unequal to genetic women because they are born male, and, together with other feminists such as Greer (1999), uses biological factors in her pronouncements on transgender people. A biological stance is, in itself, untenable because there are wide chromosomal and hormonal variations in sex in the general population (Rothblatt 1995). Raymond's constructionist account is also problematic: she sees transsexual women avoiding experience of patriarchy because they are brought up as male. Whilst this rings true to a degree, many transsexual women experienced themselves to be female early in their lives, and have acted accordingly, only to be sanctioned by the gender normative system. In addition, transsexual women experience sexism in the same ways as other women. The idea that transsexual women cannot construct themselves as female is dangerous; it locks us into a gender determinist position where people are seen as being unable to change.

It appears that the issue at the root of the radical feminist attack on trans is the perceived threat that transgender poses to radical feminism. As I argued in Chapter 2, trans poses difficulties for this branch of feminism, because radical feminism rests on the notion of discrete male and female categories and an equation of men and masculinity with oppression. Trans scrambles gender binaries, because trans people cross genders, or exist between or outside of female/male categories. The difficulties that this raises for feminism have led to gender inconsistency being suppressed (More 1996). Several of the trans contributors suggested that the reason for Raymond and other feminists' attacks on transsexuality was their own self-interest. For example:

I think for me it was about the power of a small group of, you know, privileged white feminists who wanted to make the definitions about who was in and who was out and who was right and who was wrong, and, you know, build a power base of their own and the book [*The Transsexual Empire*] was part of that. (Zach Nataf)

It's about other people creating their own empires especially the Janice Raymonds of this world ... over and over again, whether it's the level of very local politics. Like who should be allowed into Women's night at Paradise [club], who should sit on the Police, you know the gay and lesbian police committee. (Stephen Whittle)

Trans identities and politics highlight the way in which feminist aims concerning the dismantling of the gender system remain unmet by radical and separatist feminisms. Ironically, the focus on distinctions between women and men, and the erasure of gender diversity, may act to reinforce the gender binary system, if these are adhered to long term rather than being used as a temporary, limited, strategy. The normative political agenda associated with these types of feminism was also criticised by some of the contributors to research project (a), who argued that challenging gender stereotypes should be a choice for trans people, in the same way that it is for others.

Why has the radical, separatist stance on transgender had such purchase on the feminist, lesbian and trans communities? It is partly because of the historical context in which it was developed: a women's community that was formed in reaction to women's experiences of male domination and oppression and that perceived itself to be embattled. Non-trans women's fears, grounded in the realities of women's inequality, became manifest via the scapegoating of gender minorities. This was possible because the fundamental aspects of radical and separatist feminisms meant that people who transgressed gender binaries were ontologically incomprehensible: they did not fit within a gender binaried worldview. Perhaps the impact that these types of stance had is also linked to the way in which they diametrically opposed the dominant medical construction of transsexuality. There was a lack of a middle ground, where the progressive part of Raymond's work – the critique of a homophobic, sexist, gender-binaried medical establishment – could be utilised, but the transphobic part rejected. This has been compounded by the lack of feminist discourse that is supportive of trans people (including transsexuals), with the exception of the work of trans authors such as Feinberg (1996) and others such as Califia (1997).[4] The post-structuralist, postmodernist, and diversity oriented accounts of gender that have affected other areas of feminist thought have not yet fully impacted on feminist accounts of trans – or on feminist grassroots politics concerning gender diversity.

Feminism and Bisexuality

Feminist interpretations of bisexuality vary widely depending on the type of theoretical 'lens' through which it is viewed. For example, liberal feminists would tend to be inclusive of bisexual people, whilst post-structuralist feminists might deconstruct the category of 'bisexuality', problematising the way in which it seemingly incorporates assumptions about there being two genders, but would perhaps support the complexification and increased diversity associated with bisexuality. Radical and separatist feminists, however, have a very different 'take' on bisexuality. In this section I analyse the separatist feminist critique of bisexuality. Anti-bisexual feminist sentiment amongst the feminist and lesbian communities has contributed a great deal to the marginalisation of bisexual women within these communities. However, a number of bisexual feminists have responded to separatist critiques, arguing that bisexuals can contribute to gender equality and that feminism is important for the bisexual communities.

Early second-wave feminism was dominated by heterosexual concerns and the viewpoints of heterosexual women, although some authors supported the idea that women should have choice concerning the gender of their sexual partners (George 1993). The development of the lesbian movement in the early 1970s challenged this, and attitudes about bisexuality amongst lesbians varied: some were inclusive, whilst others saw bisexuality as a cop-out. George describes the way in which bisexuality became increasingly unacceptable within the feminist movement during the 1970s, so that

> within the context of a strong political lesbianism, bisexuality became seen as the apotheosis of cowardice, decadence and fence-sitting ... for some years in the 1970s and 1980s it became very difficult for an active feminist to be open about her bisexuality. (1993: 46)[5]

This continued with, for example, the publication of anti-bisexual materials by authors such as Jeffreys (1999).[6]

Why have radical and separatist feminists condemned bisexuals? The core reason is that bisexuality poses a fundamental challenge to those forms of feminism which frame lesbians and heterosexuals as separate, discrete, groups; construct men as a class of oppressors; link heterosexual sex directly with women's inequality, and frame lesbianism as *the* political way forward. Bisexual women, like heterosexual women, experience opposite-sex desire and may have relationships with men. However, they cannot be written off (as unable to have same-sex relationships) in the way that heterosexual women can. Instead, they problematise the boundaries between separatist lesbian feminism and heterosexuality. Bisexual women break down notions of men as oppressors, especially as bisexual women frequently have relationships with non-hegemonic, or bisexual, men. They also highlight the way in which separatist feminists are invested in gender: separatist communities are constructed against 'others', in this case men and heterosexuals. Bisexual women may identify as feminists, and may have gone through lesbian feminism; their choices to identify and act otherwise serve as an uncomfortable reminder of the limitations of lesbian feminism. It may seem strange to refer back to the debates of the 1970s and 1980s when thinking about bisexuality and feminism, but these debates are still alive and kicking today, visible, in particular, in the discussions that are taking place about bisexual inclusion in the sexual minority communities. Lesbian feminists such as Jeffreys (1999) continue to vilify and misrepresent bisexuals, whilst at the same time usefully highlighting some of the difficulties associated with the bisexual movement, including the sex stereotyping and female exploitation that occur in some sections of the swinger and sexual fringe communities.

Lesbian feminism has had a profound impact on the development of sexual politics, despite the fragmentation of the feminist movement during the 1980s, the backlash against feminism, and the rise of queer politics. Bisexual feminism, by comparison, is far less developed and influential (see Chapter 6). There are various reasons for this, for example:

- the bisexual movement had origins in the apolitical swinger's movement, as well as the feminist movement;
- the movement as a whole is newer and smaller;
- separatist and radical feminists have rejected alliances;
- bisexual political interests straddle those of heterosexuals and lesbians/gay men;
- there are debates about whether a separate bisexual politics is necessary;
- the anti-sexist men's movement is underdeveloped;
- there has been a backlash against feminism (see Faludi 1992) (fuelled perhaps to an extent within the bisexual communities by the prejudice that many bisexuals experience at the hands of lesbian feminists).

In addition, bisexuals are an extremely diverse population, making development of a coherent, unified political position difficult. The bisexual communities include people of all genders, and a wide range of sexual preferences. There are sizeable swinger, polyamorous and fetish contingents for whom the type of sexual practice or relationship arrangement may be equally or more important than gender. There are also people who are bisexual in practice (for example men who sleep with men) who do not identify with the bisexual communities at all – as well as people who think they might be bisexual, but are not connected to any bisexual community. This diversity renders a politics based on gender categorisation – in particular feminism,[7] that signifies in its wording a focus on women – is less obviously relevant to the bisexual communities as a whole. In other words, people whose sexuality is not based on attraction to one sex are likely to be less interested in gender categorisation, and on forms of politics that rely on it.

Despite the difficult relationship between feminisms and the bisexual communities, there are a range of bisexual feminist voices represented in the literature, from Weise's (1992) edited collection, through Mattesson's (1991) account of being a male bisexual feminist, to Hemming's 2002 work, which interrogates definitions of bisexuality from a post-structuralist perspective and explores the fraught relationship between bisexuality and the lesbian communities. Some authors, for example Elliott (1991), argue that bisexuality provides an important challenge to the restrictive norms imposed on women by lesbian feminism, suggesting that:

> Bisexuality could be the best thing that ever happened to lesbian feminism. It delivers the benefits of loving women – and the freedom to do so – to more women. Moreover, it ensures the proliferation of lesbian feminist values into the mainstream, rather than allowing them to be cordoned off within a subculture which does the mainstream the favour of removing its members and values therefrom. (1991: 327)

Bisexual feminists point out that many bisexual women have a history of activism in the lesbian communities, bringing a progressively critical approach to heterosexual relationships. Unlike heterosexual women, they are not obliged to rely on men as sexual partners. Bisexual women can act as 'bridge builders' between lesbian and heterosexual feminists, facilitating necessary alliances (Bower 1995: 107). Bisexual feminists tend to discuss alliances between feminists. For example George says:

> Feminists have spent too much time attacking each other. But both lesbians and bisexual women are oppressed by a heterosexist society: oppression is

imposed on a less powerful group by a more powerful group, and neither lesbians nor bisexual women have power. Although our immediate struggles may not always seem identical, ultimately our enemies are the same. (1993: 60)

Overall, radical and separatist critiques of trans and bisexuality can be seen as reactionary attempts to reinforce gender binaries – although this was not the initial aim of these feminisms. The trans and bisexual movements can be seen to provide a framework for challenging the gender and sexual orientation dualisms that lie at the root of radical and separatist feminisms. They reject the fatalistic notion that men's oppressiveness is inevitable, providing a contribution to a politics supporting the inclusion of people of different genders and sexualities in the project of gender equality. This does not mean that separatist feminisms are untenable per se, just that they are temporary, limited strategies. For example, as Sturgis points out, bisexual feminism does not deny the contributions or identities of those who identify as lesbian or heterosexual, or the necessity of separatism in some cases (1996: 44). However, other types of gender and sexual politics are equally important and valid.

CASE STUDY: LGB WORK IN LOCAL GOVERNMENT

How do the tensions between the different sexual and gender minority, and feminist, communities play out in practice? This section provides a brief case study of the ways in which these communities currently intersect within a specific arena – local government equalities work. Findings from research project (b) revealed a wide range of approaches – and conflicts – concerning sexual orientation and gender. The relationships between lesbians and gay men have altered to a degree since the 1980s; there are more links between lesbians and gay men and less antagonism. However, tensions between these groups still exist, especially concerning the way in which gay men's interests tend to dominate – for example most of the community fora and community centres concerning LGBT (or LG/LGB) issues, focus on concerns such as HIV prevention rather than lesbians' and bisexual women's health issues. In addition, whilst there appears overall to be awareness in the lesbian and gay communities concerning ethnicity, ability and other characteristics connected with social inequalities, the communities continue to be heavily structured in various ways; there is a dominance of white models of same-sex sexuality, a valorisation of youth (especially on the gay men's scene) and a tendency for lesbian and gay people with disabilities to be hidden.

About half of the authorities that were surveyed included bisexuals and in some cases trans people in their equalities initiatives. The frameworks that support inclusion are based on:

• notions of shared oppression;
• a mutual struggle against discrimination and strength in numbers;
• a questioning of why bisexuals and trans people would not be included;
• the view that separatism is a dated political strategy. For example, one lesbian community member said, of her locality, 'we have been the dinosaurs that talk about "Lesbian and Gay" traditionally'.

Views amongst contributors concerning bisexual and trans inclusion varied widely. Some contributors saw the issues trans people face as fundamentally different to those of LGB people, because their concern is with gender and matters such as birth certificate change. There were a number of reasons given for excluding bisexuals, for example the idea that bisexuals can take refuge in heterosexual privilege, that they bring heterosexuals into gay space, and in one case, a questioning of whether bisexuals actually exist. In a few instances the concerns were framed in terms of resource constraints, and a minority of contributors cited the cumbersome nature of the term 'LGBT' as a reason for not using it. The most extreme view came from a lesbian local authority officer, who told me that 'coming into lesbian and gay space and sticking their tongues down each other's throats. I think they [bisexuals] should fuck off.' A lesbian community activist provided a more representative exclusionary stance:

> Bisexuals are different as they have a different political agenda – my personal view is that they have an easier time ... they can be part of the straight community or not – they are fundamentally different. The transgender issue is different as their focus is not lesbian and gay particularly – it's a different mindset – being trapped in the wrong body – a different remit. (Community member, Wales)

A number of lesbian and gay contributors criticised the exclusion of bisexuals and trans people. For example, a gay community member discussed homophobia within the gay communities – he saw the exclusion of bisexual and trans people as being underpinned by psychological processes (unconsciously fuelled prejudice). Another said 'I was astonished to find out how homophobic my colleagues were towards bisexuals.' A few lesbian and gay contributors saw trans people as being more socially excluded than lesbians and gay men. In addition, a few contributors discussed increasing fluidity concerning sexual orientation amongst younger people, describing the way in which lesbian, gay, heterosexual and trans forms of categorisation can be restrictive or irrelevant. For example a youth worker discussed the way in which some young non-heterosexual people have gender issues, and the fact that some young people want to bring straight friends along to LGB youth groups. Notions of a commonality of oppression and inclusion were perhaps most apparent overall, for example:

> we know what the differences are but the person who thumps you does not. Let's not get hung up on stupid wee issues – because that is what they are. Lots of gay men get queer bashed because they look feminine. The definition of homophobia is about people being perceived to be gay. We have heterosexuals being beaten up because of this. (Community member, Scotland)

TOWARDS RAINBOW ALLIANCES

The inclusion of bisexuals and trans people in some sections of the lesbian and gay communities is linked with changes in the dominant discourses within the communities. As noted above, the lesbian separatist frameworks that were present in the 1980s are now far less apparent. Notions of social inclusion, equalities and diversity are common, whilst queer theory has emerged as one of the major radical discourses within the communities (see for example Bell and Binnie 2000). Notions of inclusivity across a range of areas have become more prominent – for instance a community member suggested that

> the [other] big issue that needs to be done with LGBT is enabling people to recognise that we are a totally inclusive community, so there are black people, there are people with disabilities, we are all ages, we're mothers, fathers, we're colleagues.

These changes impact on the way that the communities are constructed. A representative of a national LGB organisation said:

Contributor: I'd say that LGBT is now the majority grouping used in discourse, and I think this will be future guidance. It came from the communities themselves, and a more assertive transgender community, some queer thinking.

Interviewer: *Can you explain?*

Contributor: A rethinking of traditional models. People are less grounded in a rigid politics of autonomy based on particular forms of oppression and so there are broader alliances, but also LGBT has been slow to link up with other alliances, such as race.

The changes in the discourses found in the sexual and gender minority communities are highly compatible with the formation of rainbow alliances. The term 'rainbow alliance' was developed as part of the queer movement towards embracing diversity and sexual and gender fluidity, and the recognition that the deconstruction of rigid gender and sexual categories necessitated forms of political organisation which were different from those associated with discrete or separatist identities. Instead of a politics bound up with being female, or lesbian, or gay, there is a movement towards a politics associated with the right to self-determination, with pluralisation, and with a celebration of diversity. All parts of the gender and sexual spectrum are included in rainbow alliances, although in practice alliances are located around non-heterosexual and gender transgressive subjectivities. The rainbow symbolically covers both universalist, all-embracing politics (the whole rainbow) and an acknowledgement of diversity (the separate colours); as such, it provides a powerful means of unifying sexual and gender minorities and staking a claim for equality with heterosexual men and women, whilst also acknowledging differences between the various groupings.

Political alliances can be seen as necessary for gender and sexual minorities, given the importance of size and visibility to the effectiveness of social movements. Many bisexuals and some trans people stress the importance of alliances with lesbians and gay men. For bisexuals, these alliances can be seen as inherent to identity and lifestyle, as same-sex desires and activities place bisexual people within lesbian or gay social space, and render them subject to the same kinds of discrimination that lesbians and gay men face even if they do not identify with gay or lesbian culture. The importance of alliances was stressed by some of the contributors in research projects (a), (b) and (d). Several of the bisexuals I interviewed emphasised the importance of alliances between bisexuals and lesbians and gay men. A Stonewall representative noted that

> bisexuality is about sexual orientation in the same way as lesbian and gay are. It is helpful to work on them all at once – obviously there are differences, just as with lesbians and gay men, but it makes us stronger.

There are also alliances between sections of the bisexual and trans communities:

> At a typical BiCon conference I'd say that I've talked to people who represent four to five different genders, people who might identify as androgynous, or plural, or both. There are many genders, and people feel more free to choose genders within the [bisexual] community. (Kerry)

> it depends partly on which strand of bisexuality you're talking about. Some bi people are coming simply from the 'I like men, and I like women.' On the other hand, some people who consider themselves part of the bi community have gone a lot further to rejecting the significance of gender. Some bi people don't think the gender of the person they're with is important at all, and are therefore equally happy with people of other genders than men and women. But even the 'I like men and I like women' branch of bisexuality has gone a little way towards questioning gender rules, so clearly it's no coincidence that a lot of trans people feel at home in the bi community. (Jennifer Moore)

Many trans people also either identify as LGB, or go through stages of experiencing same-sex desire, so that they can be automatically allied with non-trans LGB people. The trans people in my research (projects (a) and (d)) gave a number of reasons for alliances with LGB people including:

- historical overlaps between what are now termed trans and LGB identities, and, for some people, current overlaps: trans can be read as 'not straight', and many lesbian and gay people can be seen as having gender issues;
- a history of social and political overlaps – for example contributor Yvonne Sinclair described how she and other transvestites

launched their TV/TS group in collaboration with a gay group in the 1970s;

- the contributions of trans people to what is framed as lesbian and gay politics – for example drag queens were on the front line at the Stonewall riots;
- shared, if sometimes different, experiences of oppression;
- the small numbers of trans and intersex people (especially people who do not identify as male or female), and the related difficulties of achieving social change because of this;
- for some trans people, the centrality of LGB liberation to trans liberation – acceptance of LGB people is seen as opening the way to trans liberation;
- alliances around related issues, such as HIV/AIDS activism.

Despite these important reasons for the development of rainbow alliances, there are some difficulties with such alliances. Many of these have already been discussed; the most important include historical divergences, conflicts over identity and cultural ownership, and disputes over political aims and methods (separatism is quite clearly incompatible with rainbow alliances if it is seen as an ultimate political goal). Another problem concerns the extent of differences between the communities. As contributor Jennifer Moore argued, 'it's important to distinguish between creating alliances to address political issues, and expecting to share social groups'. Lesbians and gay men may not wish to share social space with bisexuals (or trans or intersex people) but the rejection of political alliances indicates prejudice that needs to be tackled. However, even political alliances may be difficult when there has been considerable hostility or ignorance, or where people cannot relate to those with whom they might build alliances. For instance intersex contributor Salmacis said:

> Well, the problem I've got with Pride is, I'm not male, I am not homosexual, I am not lesbian. I identify myself as female because I'm physically predominantly female, and I'm comfortable with that, but I'm not a lesbian. I'm not heterosexual because I'm celibate. Apart from the fact that in most respects sex would be an impossibility anyway because it's been botched up.

Another difficulty with alliances concerns the impact of prejudice within the communities – for example, homophobia amongst transvestites and transsexuals, and transphobia amongst lesbians and gay men. These groups, in some cases, seek to distance themselves from what they perceive to be the stigmatised identities of other minorities – they hope to appeal to mainstream notions of normality and in so doing jettison alliances with other minority groups. This trend was apparent in findings from research project (b), when contributors discussed other areas of equalities initiatives. For example, people working in the field of race equalities sometimes distanced themselves from LGBT equalities work, which was seen as more politically sensitive (as well as in some cases problematic on the grounds of faith). Clearly, experience of being a member of one minority does not automatically mean that people become sensitised to the needs and rights claims of other minority groups. In fact, the research on trans (project (a)) indicated that stigmatisation of other groups may be even more marked where identities are fragile or threatened, where identities are being consolidated in opposition to others (for example butch lesbian identification of butch as a female rather than masculine identity), and/or where wider social stigmatisation is intense. The resources needed for the development of awareness of difference are also more limited where groups are embattled. For instance, there has been little attention to the whiteness of the trans communities and the probable need for attention to the interests of ethnic minority trans people in the UK, but the trans communities are reliant on individuals contributing resources on a voluntary basis, so arguably have limited capacity to address diversities issues.

Overall, the lack of coherence and the introspectiveness of the LGBT sector can be seen as signs of political immaturity, as a more mature sector would support diversity and tackle prejudice in a more concerted way. They can also be seen as markers of the continued successful operation of hegemonic norms. As Ochs (1996) says,

> All of us, bisexual, lesbian, gay and transgendered, must resist getting lost in the 'divide and conquer' strategy that we are invited to participate in by the dominant culture. There is no long-term benefit in creating a hierarchy of oppressions … If biphobia and homophobia are not allowed to blind us, then we can move beyond our fears and learn to value our differences as well as our similarities. (1996: 236)

UNIVERSALISM AND DIVERSITY

The proliferation and increasing complexity of sexed and gendered identities raises some important issues for activism concerning gender and sexual minorities. Is a broad-based, inclusive movement likely to be the best means of securing equality for people of all genders and sexualities? Or would such a movement override difference,[8] subsuming the interests of smaller groups and perhaps opening space for mainstream, hegemonic norms to be reinstated? The universalist, or broad-based, inclusive approach has a number of advantages:

- it acts as a 'level' – everyone is seen as equal and worthy of social inclusion;
- it is not strongly identity based, so that those occupying ambivalent, changing, or unconceptualised positions are included;
- it supports activists who choose not to use their identity for political purposes, campaigning more generally – for example contributor Mike said that his preferred form of political activism is generic, concerning supporting diversity, rather than saying 'this is me … which for some reason devalues it';
- because it emphasises the equality of everyone, it acts to challenge the prejudice that can become entrenched in subculture groupings, as well as the mainstream. For instance, it can be used to challenge racism in gay communities, or prejudice against trans people in the women's movement;
- it includes anyone who wishes to support equality, rather than shutting out those who do not have a particular identity (for example bisexuals being excluded from lesbian and gay events). As Hutchins and Kaahamanu (1991: 217) say, 'when the entire continuum of sexual behaviour is validated, it liberates everyone from the tyranny of being forced to choose sides';
- because it is inclusive, it is resistant to being labelled as unfairly supportive of minorities – this type of argument is often used by right-wing critics of specialist provision for groups facing discrimination.

The universalist approach would seem to be appealing to those concerned with creating a more socially just society, as well as those who are exploring new forms of gender and sexual identification. In fact, the current UK policy emphasis on social inclusion takes a liberal, universalist approach, and it is in the context of this – and community activism concerning inclusion – that bisexuals and trans people are gaining some level of visibility and social legitimacy. On a conceptual level, universalist approaches provide a means of moving beyond a politics in which certain groups are potentially shut out or alienated. However, there are some problems with the universalist approach:

- because it fails to address social inequalities in a focused way, it can easily end up glossing over these inequalities and replicating the dominant social order. As Sturgis says, 'Embracing a "we're-all-really-the-same" humanism obscures the very real power structure of male domination' (1996: 43);
- it tends to be individualist, so failing to make connections between classes of people – for example women – and inequalities, and failing to tackle the structural embeddedness of inequality – for example, institutional disablism;
- because it is not necessarily connected to lived experience in the same way that particularist identity politics are, it can end up failing to address marginalised groups' needs and interests;
- it is difficult to create social change without people being personally motivated – abstract ideals of a more just society are often not enough to galvanise people into action.

What of the alternatives to universalism, namely, difference-based approaches? Current difference-based approaches focus on established categories of people, such as women, addressing the particular needs and rights that these groups might have. These approaches enable the experiences of particular groups to be addressed in more detail than is possible with universalistic approaches. Difference-based approaches enable groups to be treated as a class, whilst at the same time recognising that particular groupings are cross-cut by (or formed in relation to) other socially ordering variables, such as class and ethnicity. There are certainly advantages to particularist stances to gender and sexual diversity. For example:

> We tend to favour a diversity approach, as everyone is different – their skills and needs. If you treat everyone equally it's not necessarily an appropriate way to treat people and they will suffer. For example if an employee who has childcare needs is treated the same way as other employees it's detrimental. Similarly with lesbians and gay men and transgender people – you need to take on board everyone as an individual and treat their needs. (Stonewall representative)

> For me, it's a case of respecting people's differences. People aren't equal, in whatever area. You make space for what people are – more equal opportunities, that's equality. No, we are not the same. (Jane)

At the same time, difference-based approaches demand that difference be conceptualised – people with fluid sexual orientations become known as 'bisexual'; people of diverse genders become classed as 'trans', and others, who may have these tendencies but choose not to (or are not socially able to) express them, remain male or female, and gay, lesbian or heterosexual. They risk 'freezing' both established categories and established roles (for example the social norm that dictates that women are primarily responsible for childrearing). The crucial irony, and an irony that has received considerable coverage in the literature, is that identity politics demands categorisation, but that that categorisation can then, in itself, become restrictive or hegemonic (see Dunphy 2000: 75). Further subdivisions are one way of dealing with this problem. Relational forms of categorisation, such as 'lesbian-bisexual' may be useful in avoiding the privileging of specific (bisexual) identities (see Hemmings 2002), and other alternative forms of identification, such as 'all genders', or 'polysexual', may solve the problem of categorisation becoming restrictive in some ways. These terms include those people who resist the current forms of identification usually used as a basis for particularist politics, potentially serving as a basis for the development of diverse rights claims. The difficulty with narrow forms of identification (such as lesbian-bisexual) is that they are too narrow to form an effective basis for activism; the difficulty with broad categories is that they may lead back towards a universalising approach, risking obscuration of the specificity of experience and the effects of structural inequalities. Gender and sexuality activism requires a fine balance between universalist and particularist approaches. Where a particularist stance is taken as a basis for activism, the acknowledgement of differences, and the creation of separate spaces or organisations, may be appropriate, but underlying support for other gender and sexual orientation groups is crucial. For instance, as contributor Kerry argues, many people have different issues from those of bisexuals, but people do not have to be the same to work for equality – the issue is one of being understood, and understanding other people who are different. Similarly:

> In some cases, they say 'this is a group for lesbians and gay men' – this I respect, as it is about realising they aren't the same, you can't necessarily provide for both. (John)

> We don't represent transgender people though we support for example Press for Change and the Gender Trust when they think it is helpful. We

don't have the expertise within the organisation to work effectively for transgender people. It'd detract from LGB work, and it wouldn't be helpful for us to work on transgender issues. Though there is an exception in Scotland where someone does work on transgender issues as well as LGB issues. (Stonewall representative)

CONCLUSION

This chapter provided an overview and analysis of some of the tensions between, and within, the LGBT communities. I began by demonstrating the close historical identity overlaps between these different groups, and then described the ways in which the early gay liberation movement became fragmented along gender lines, focusing on the development and impact of lesbian feminism. I then outlined the ways in which trans and bisexual people are ostracised and excluded by the lesbian and gay communities, tracing the reasons for this exclusion, which include the trans and bisexual disruption of the gender binaries on which lesbian and gay identity categories rely, the impact of radical and separatist feminisms, and prejudice and stereotyping concerning bisexuality and trans. The chapter addressed conflicts between and within the LGBT communities, including tensions within the trans communities. It then moved on to more in-depth analysis of feminism and, firstly, trans, and secondly, bisexuality. I argued that although the recognition of difference is necessary, feminist prejudice against trans people and bisexuals – and the resulting exclusion of these groups from women's organisations and feminist politics – is unjustifiable for a range of reasons. Trans and bisexuality challenge the gender binarism that lies at the heart of radical and separatist feminisms, and feminists of this ilk reject these identities because they do not fit into a binaried analysis, even where people of these groups support gender and sexual equality – as many do.

The chapter then moved on to explore the possibility of 'rainbow alliances' – alliances that recognise and support diversity across the range of gender identities and sexual orientations. Alliances across the LGBT communities have developed considerably over the last few years, and are seen by many contributors as being crucial to the development of a progressive and effective movement, for a number of reasons, including:

• the existence of people who bridge different sections of the communities, for example lesbian trans women;

- the importance of mutual support, given the limited numbers of people involved;
- shared experiences of oppression, especially around issues such as community safety;
- the capacity of alliances to support identity fluidity and multiplicity.

There are, however, difficulties with rainbow alliances, which can be conceptualised using notions of universalism and diversity. Universalism, which is a broad-based inclusive approach, is valuable because it includes everyone, does not alienate people with mainstream identities, and allows for a greater amount of identity fluidity and complexity than particularist approaches. It provides a means of moving beyond a politics in which certain groups are excluded or alienated. However, it tends to be individualist, failing to address social structural inequalities and thus potentially reinforcing the dominant order. Those with marginal identities are easily overridden and their interests subsumed by groups with louder voices. Particularist or diversity approaches, address these problems by focussing on the interests and needs of different groups. They foreground the differences between people and groups, avoiding models of equality that frame everyone as being the same. Particularist approaches are important in dealing with differences, but can be problematic if they encourage factionalism or 'freeze' systems of categorisation. In addition, some groups are too small to be easily formulated in political terms, so that it is hard to organise them in activist terms, and a broader-based, more universalist strategy could perhaps be more effective if non-members of those groups took on their issues. Overall, gender and sexuality activism entails balancing universalist and particularist approaches. There is a need for broad-based activist alliances, recognition of shared agendas and acknowledgement of identity complexity and overlap. This may include, in some cases, support for separate space, but only within the broader remit of political support for diversity and self-determination.

6
Gender, Sexuality and the New Social Movements

> I think of intersex as a civil rights movement still in the stage of breaking the silence. I compare intersex awareness to other movements that have earned their place in the world. You cannot remove our existence by removing our anatomy.
>
> Morris 2004

New social movement (NSM) theory has developed in relation to earlier ways of conceptualising social protest and change, especially those concerned with the Labour movement. The understandings developed by NSM theorists are useful for analysing the social movements that are emerging around the gender/sexual diversity nexus, because they address fluidity, complexity, grass-roots social action, and issues concerning identity politics. Whilst there is a certain amount of NSM literature addressing the feminist and the gay and lesbian movements, there is little in the fields of trans, intersex, and bisexuality. In what ways can the gender and sexuality related movements be conceptualised in terms of the insights provided by NSM theorists?

This chapter analyses feminisms, the masculinities movements, the lesbian, gay and bisexual movements, and the trans movements via the prism of NSM theory. I will begin by defining NSMs and the way in which they have developed. I will then outline the key characteristics of NSMs, before proceeding through an overview of some aspects of NSM theories. As Engel (2001) says, these theories are complex; I review them briefly here, due to space constraints. The chapter then provides a snapshot of the development and characteristics of the social movements in the sexuality and gender fields, with the exception of paedophilic and right-wing organisations (NSMs can be seen as any group of citizens that are activists (Zirakzadeh 1997)). Of course, some social movements overlap; as contributor Roz Kaveney pointed out, networks of interest groups are an important source of activism, and a network can be developed in relation to one issue and then mobilised to tackle another. I will not address one of the key debates in the NSM literature, the issue of whether the NSMs are really new, as this is covered elsewhere (Tucker 1991), or the relationship between sexuality and gender movements and other NSMs (see the section on inter-sectionality, in Chapter 2).

NEW SOCIAL MOVEMENTS

There is a large body of literature concerning NSMs,[1] and a wide range of approaches to their analysis. NSMs are difficult to define, as they do not have clear boundaries, and the term 'social' is very broad (Byrne 1997). I draw here on the work of a range of authors, who define NSMs as follows: as those movements which may challenge established cultural, economic, or political orders (Kirby 1995); as a political phenomenon that involves a group of non-elite people trying to build a new social order (using confrontational as well as civil tactics) (Zirakzadeh 1997); or as involving collective action following individual perceptions of shared concerns (Obershall 1997). In addition, as Woodward says:

> Identity politics developed and defined these social movements through a deeper concern for identity: What it means, how it is produced and contested. Identity politics involve claiming one's identity as a member of an oppressed or marginalised group, and this identity becomes a major factor in political mobilisation. (2002: 202)

NSMs can be seen to have originated in Western democracies in the anti-Vietnam and CND protests of the 1960s (Dalton and Kuechler 1990). They represented a challenge to both Western liberal politics and 'revisionist' and 'Stalinist' Soviet policies (Woodward 2002), and are characterised by pluralist, non-class-based ideologies (Larana et al. 1994). There were various key factors behind the growth of NSMs, including the shift from industrial to post-industrial society, the related decline in the working class and growth of the 'new middle class' which formed a basis for the NSMs, and disillusionment amongst many people concerning state reform as a means of change (Kirby 1995). NSMs are set in the context of the weakening of traditional leftist forms of political action and a decline in interest in mainstream political parties, as well as problems with the drive for economic growth (see Byrne 1997). Larana et al. (1994) emphasise the roles of material affluence, information overload, and confusion about the range of cultural alternatives in creating a climate where NSMs have been able to develop. According to some authors, NSMs have a number of key characteristics:

- They are complex – as Byrne (1997) says, NSMs are complex coalitions which employ a range of political stances and strategies.
- They use participatory, democratic, pluralist, decentralised, and non-bureaucratic forms of organisation (see Dalton and Kuechler 1990).
- They have a much looser organisational structure than formal organisations.
- Their membership may be uncertain, with unclear, contested leadership (Obershall 1997). NSMs are likely to have a small core of key activists, a larger group of part-time activists, and sympathisers located on the edges of the movement (Obershall 1997).
- They employ radical as well as other forms of protest. NSMs may involve oppositional political tactics (Larana et al. 1994).
- They are likely to draw support from a socially diffuse group of individuals, rather than people coming from a distinct socio-economic background (see Dalton and Kuechler 1990).
- They exhibit a tendency to blur individual and collective identity, so that movements may be 'acted out' through individual behaviour, and disclosure of experiences and feeling for the purpose of gaining political recognition may be seen as a form of collective action (Larana et al. 1994, Taylor and Whittier 1992); the view 'the personal is political' may be seen as an important strategy for social transformation (see Taylor and Whittier 1992).
- They involve an awareness of shared identities, and of the way in which group interest conflicts with mainstream cognitive frameworks and goals (Morris and McClurg 1992) – although it is important to point out that people can have strong identities but reject activism concerning these.

How do individual NSMs develop? In a nutshell, NSMs involve a number of people becoming unhappy about something, feeling that the mainsteam ways of addressing it are insufficient, beginning to believe that they can act to change things, and having opportunities that allow them to do so as a collective. According to Young (1993), although most social movements begin with the belief that injustice is occurring and that there is a need for change, social movements can also concern the prevention of change, or can be organised as counter movements to other NSMs. Social movements grow in response to changes in the conditions of life that produce discontent, and ineffectiveness in the usual ways of addressing this discontent. Following Taylor, it is possible to identify three sets of factors underlying NSMs: 'the political and cultural context that supports and constrains protest, the mobilizing structures and strategies through which power is expressed, and the frames of meaning challengers use to identify their grievances and collective commonalities' (1999: 1). One aspect of the political and cultural context concerns the possibility of the dramatisation of a (hegemonic) system's vulnerability (see Larana et al. 1994), which is linked with the availability of opportunities for successful actions (for example a weakness in the opposition, or powerful allies) (Obershall 1997). Other factors affecting the success of NSMs include the availability of 'master frames' (definitions) from other NSMs, which the new movement can follow, and activist subcultures which act as repositories for cultural resources for activism (Larana et al. 1994). Obstacles to mobilisation are outlined by Obershall (1997), who discusses the way in which movements benefit everyone with an interest in their success, regardless of whether they personally contribute, so that getting people to take part in activism is a major challenge for NSMs. Another problem is the impact of oppositional movements, especially if the challenger is protected by the status quo. Overall, the development of a new social movement is dependent on a number of key factors, including member dissatisfaction with the status quo, the availability of opportunities to change things, and people contributing.

New Social Movement Theory

In brief, NSM theory has evolved through a series of stages (see Kirkby 1995 and Engel 2001 for a fuller description). These can be typified as (1) Classical social movement theory; (2) Resource mobilisation theory; (3) Political opportunity theory, and (4) the political process model (PPM). In this section I will provide an overview of some aspects of these approaches, before discussing their applicability to gender and sexual minorities in subsequent sections.

(1) Classical social movement theory was pluralist. People were seen as being bonded by shared values, and as represented by the state in an unproblematic way. Because democracy was assumed to exist, collective action was seen as an aberration (Engel 2001) – the result of people having psychological difficulties and grievances due to the changes associated with modernisation (Zirakzadeh 1997).

(2) A number of theoretical approaches emerged in the 1960s, including resource mobilisation theory (Zirakzadeh 1997), which like classical social movement theory emphasised agency and the micro level, as opposed to structuralist explanations (Engel 2001). Resource mobilisation theory, which was dominant in the 1980s, emphasises the utilitarian aspects of social movements, looking at collective action in terms of cost-benefit analysis and (supposedly) objective variables such as organisation and resources. Resource mobilisation theory fails to explain the way that structural inequality gets changed into subjectively experienced discontent (Mueller and Morris 1992).[2]

(3) The political context for NSMs has been analysed by political opportunity theorists, such as Tilly (1978) and Tarrow (1998), who examine the link between changes in institutional politics and NSMs, and the extent to which opportunities exist for outside organisations to influence these. Political opportunity structure theories filled the gap that was left unaddressed by the American school of social movement theory (classical and resource mobilisation theories), as it provided a macro-level analysis. As Engel says: 'political opportunity structure is a macro analysis that evaluates how different governing structures affect mobilization by providing possible institutional opportunities such as electoral realignments' (2001: 14). One difficulty with political opportunity structure approaches is that, whilst political opportunities within established organisations are one determinant of a movement's success, there are also factors within the organisation itself, in particular the pre-existence of mobilisation structures and connections between individuals (Freeman 1975, McAdam 1986), and the organisation of the movement or collective action once it is underway (Gamson 1990, McAdam 1986, Taylor 1999).

(4) The factors addressed by the first three models have been homogenised using the political process model. The PPM cuts across micro-, meso- and macro-level aspects of social movements, addressing the reasons for people's participation in social movements, the ways in which they are able to participate, and the external or

institutional environment (Engel 2001). It highlights three central factors in the development of movements:

- pre-existing organisational strength;
- collective identity formation and liberation;
- changing opportunities.

The PPM models two sets of interrelated dynamics. First, movement formation, which involves the interaction of opportunity structures and the ways that organisations take advantage of opportunity with psychological changes within groups, with group identities changing from isolated, victimised positions to collective empowerment. Second, movement maintenance, which involves the range of organisations that make up the movement, spanning a continuum from those that are based on contagious spontaneity (rioting) through to established, structured, interest groups. The PPM analyses the stages in which movements develop, from initial collective insurgency through to an emphasis on sustainability and some level of centralisation. Engel (2001) notes that for a movement to continue, collective identity must be sustained, and organisational change must take place in response to external events such as counter movements or governmental control. There appears to be a movement towards a greater inclusion of cultural factors in recent NSM thinking. As Engel suggests, 'Recent scholarship is moving towards re-evaluating culture as a variable in social movement development and maintainance' (2001: 125). The cultural aspects of NSMs include both collective action frames and collective identities (Taylor 1999). Collective action frames are discussed by Benford and Hunt (1992), who describe the way in which actors communicate power via scripting, in which collective frames (definitions) of the situation are built on, so that people come to understand that there are key players, certain ways of doing things, and certain responses and actions associated with a movement, and these perceptions support the movement.

This chapter will primarily use the PPM, as it provides an integrated analysis of the key factors affecting the development of NSMs – the pre-existing strength of organisations, collective identities, and changing opportunities. It will also include analyses of political opportunity structures and cultural factors, such as collective action frames.

MOVEMENTS ASSOCIATED WITH GENDER AND SEXUALITY

This section aims to provide an overview of the social movements associated with gender and sexuality, applying some of the concepts drawn from the NSM literature, and focusing primarily on those movements that have not yet been addressed by NSM theorists. The women's liberation movement and the gay and lesbian movement are generally recognised in the literature on NSMs, with the women's movement being discussed as early as 1955, although, there is an absence of any systematic theory of gender and social movements (Taylor 1999). There are a number of other loose gender and sexuality related groupings that could be seen as NSMs, including the men's movements, the bisexual movement, and the trans movement. I will look at these different movements in turn, whilst acknowledging that many people have alliances with more than one of them and that they overlap organisationally, as well as in individual terms. I will begin discussion of each movement with a brief overview of the movement's development, before applying some of the concepts from NSM theory.

The Feminist Movement

The roots of the Western feminist movement can be traced back to the work of early feminists such as Mary Wollstonecraft, whose book *A Vindication of the Rights of Woman* (1792) was produced in response to texts concerning the rights of men.[3] Early feminisms, both in Europe and the US, were framed mostly in terms of moral improvement (Connell 2002), and were connected with both liberal and socialist political movements. Nineteenth-century feminist movements asserted women's rights as individuals, as equal members of society, and as contributors to society via their roles as mothers and workers (Rowbotham 1992).

> By the turn of the twentieth century there was a world-wide labour and socialist movement which had its own intelligentsia, and which provided – most notably in Germany, but to some extent around the capitalist world – an organisational base for radical women. (Connell 2002: 118)

The early twentieth century saw the birth of first-wave feminism and the suffrage movement in the West, including subgroups such as the birth control movement (see Connell 2002). Women's rights oriented movements were also emerging in some other countries, for instance in Russia and India (Rowbotham 1992).

Second-wave feminism, which developed after the Second World War, involved the rapid mobilisation of women in the late 1960s and early 1970s. Initially, their radicalism concerned fighting against gender, race and class oppression simultaneously, but by the mid 1960s it had become gender specific (Connell 2002). A number of strands developed, along ideological divisions concerning the primacy of gender and class as determinants of women's inequality, and then, in the 1980s, there was a growth in multiple identity politics within feminism which was provoked by a re-examination of theories of gender by black feminists and others (see Chapter 2). The ideological basis for these different feminisms will not be examined here (see also Chapter 5); rather, we will address the way in which they can be seen as NSMs.

The feminist movements can be seen as classic examples of NSMs as they tend to have flat hierarchies, to be decentralised, to have complex organisational forms and coalitions, and to blur collective and individual identities by emphasising the way in which the personal is political. Their complexity is discussed by Rowbotham:

> human wants and needs are never simple, and women are as capable as men of having contradictory and different desires. Consequently, there are many types of women's movement, some aiming to conserve, rather than change women's position. Moreover, within the movements for change there are many conflicting emphases and perspectives. (Rowbotham 1992: 5)

How does the PPM apply to the feminist movement? As I showed above, the PPM outlines three factors affecting the development of movements: the pre-existence of relevant organisations, changing opportunities, and the formation of collective identities – and identity liberation. As I have shown, feminisms existed prior to the development of second-wave feminism, meaning that some organisational and cultural resources were available to nascent activists. In addition, many strands of the women's movement have sought to make use of the opportunities for change that exist. The feminist movement developed in the West in the 1960s, an era of economic prosperity, liberal politics and the pill. Opportunity utilisation is apparent in many instances – for example a Ugandan university held a conference titled 'Women's Worlds' in 2001 in the context of support for women's equality from international aid organisations, creating an opportunity for African women's organisations to influence political institutions. However, much women's organisation and activism has not been constructed primarily in relation to the opportunities provided by mainstream institutions, making the use of political opportunity theory problematic. The more radical, separatist aspects of the women's movement sought to create alternatives to what was perceived as a masculinist system, by, for example, creating women-only spaces and engaging in activism that challenged masculinist establishments, such as military bases. This oppositional dynamic is addressed to an extent by the PPM, which, as I have shown, models movement maintenance as taking place in response to external events.

Identity liberation, and the formation of shared identities, are crucial to feminisms – although, as I have shown in Chapters 2 and 5, the path to collective identity formation is not always a smooth one. Some of the theories that primarily address the identity and cultural basis for social movements (which is included to a degree in the PPM) are perhaps particularly helpful in theorising the women's movements. Consciousness raising served as a crucial aspect of early feminism, and the construction of non-mainstream identities remains an aspect of feminisms, although these are varied (Taylor 1999). The analysis and disruption of mainstream ways of framing gender is central to feminisms and feminist identities. This includes not only the more recent post-structuralist approaches, but also earlier radical, Marxist, and other feminisms, for example: 'From its inception, the postpartum support group movement connected women's emotional distress with the gender division of labour in American society that designates women primarily responsible for the care and nurture of children' (Taylor 1999: 22). Overall, therefore, the women's liberation movement is a classic example of a NSM, and it can be theorised using the PPM, political opportunity theory and frame theories.

The Men's Movements

a progressive men's movement is very recent and is very small. In academia it appears as men's studies, in society it takes the form of men's consciousness groups, and there are also some men's groups within political parties and trade unions which address issues of masculinity and power.

Dunphy 2000: 141

The men's movements can be traced to the work of men such as John Stuart Mill, whose essay 'The Subjugation of Women' (1889) argued for women's equality, and Friedrich Engels, whose *The Origin of the Family, Private Property and the State* (1884) provided a Marxist account of women's inequality (see Connell 2002). However, the modern men's movements are often seen as developing in response to the feminist movement. Gay activists were the first to address hegemonic masculinity in the political context, and to align themselves with feminists (Carrigan et al. 1987). In the 1980s, new links were made between gay theory and feminist analysis of gender, and one of the men's movement, the anti-sexist men's movement, developed (Connell 2002). Men have had contrasting responses to feminism (see Chapter 2). For instance, Byrd and Guy-Sheftall (2001) analyse the way in which African American men have engaged with feminisms and womanism, providing a critique of heterosexist black fundamentalism.

The small progressive men's movement in the UK became seriously divided in both areas for action and organisational form, and by the mid 1990s was limited to a few campaigns against violence against women, some consciousness raising groups and programmes of counselling, and academic research. In addition, the right-wing 'men's rights' lobby, especially in the US, provided considerable competition to the progressive men's movement. This traditionalist, patriarchal network constructs men as the victims of feminism, aims to reverse what is seen as the gains of feminism, and utilises tactics such as bombarding the Equal Opportunities Commission with complaints about 'discrimination against men'. By 1997, the UK men's movement had developed an organised form, seeking to repeal all equal rights legislation and criminalise abortion (Dunphy 2000). Dunphy describes the way in which this men's movement is an uneasy alliance of misogynists and men with genuine worries about issues such as the lack of paternal rights. He discusses the way in which 'it expresses the anger and resentment of numbers of heterosexual men at having to account for their masculinity in an era of unprecedented social and economic change' (2000: 145); their sexist and homophobic attitudes would previously have gone unchallenged. The mythopoetic men's movement, again stronger in the US than elsewhere, shares some ground with the right-wing men's movement in that it may reassert a hegemonic essentialist masculinity. The mythopoetic men's movement sees the identity crisis that men are facing as due to issues such as men's lack of relationships with their fathers, and seeks to put men in touch with their true selves through initiation ceremonies, stories and myths (Ferber 2000). True masculinity is modelled as 'earthy, nur-turing and playful', as opposed to 'toxic masculinity', which is neglectful and violent.[4]

The men's movements have a number of the characteristics that are typical of NSMs, including a mixed membership and an empha-sis on collective identity. The PPM is relevant to understanding the factors leading to the men's movements, including the pre-existence of relevant organisations, changing opportunities, and the forma-tion of collective identities – as well as identity liberation. Although there was not much of an organisational history that was specific to the men's movements, these movements utilised existing main-stream organisational opportunities and, in some cases, existing patriarchal discourses. The gendering of mainstream institutions, and the greater socio-economic power that men as a class have, mean that men overall have enhanced access to political opportuni-ties, both as actors within organisations and as activists outside of them. The way that the right-wing men's movement has utilised opportunities to influence these institutions, for example attacking feminism in newspapers (Dunphy 2000), illustrates their use of mainstream organisations. The continuation of male dominance within these institutions underlines the way in which political opportunities are unequally structured. Similarly, the right-wing men's movement had no qualms about developing and using mobil-ising structures, whereas the anti-sexist men's movement stumbled over the hierarchical element of these in a way that was detrimental to the movement (Dunphy 2000). Perhaps this illustrates the way in which these approaches to NSMs are predominantly theorised by hegemonic men, for hegemonic men. The emphasis on formal organisation, as well as on the capacity which is necessary for an organisation to take advantage of political opportunities, is unequally gendered; some feminists are wary of the inequalities that are built into formal organisational forms, and women are still less prominent in the public sphere, where these theories are located.

Identity issues are also important to the formation of the men's movements. The culturally based frame theories are useful for understanding male activists' subjectivities. For example, gay male gender identities can be seen to provide spaces in which scripts of normative heterosexuality are rewritten, and as areas of slippage between cultural conceptions of masculinity and non-normative sexuality – such as the way in which 'macho' styles eroticise signs of masculinity in homosexuality (Gutterman 2001). Another area where cultural scripts can be rewritten is male pro-feminism, including the use of privileged status by men as a platform from which to disrupt gender and sexuality categorisation (Gutterman 2001). Male sexism is also supported by framing strategies – for instance, according to Sampath (2001), Trinidadian discourses concerning 'respectability' are linked with femininity and discourses concerning 'reputation' are developed in reaction to this, centring on male working-class enjoyment, including sexual banter, from which women are excluded because it would damage their 'respectability'. This example also illustrates the structural approach to social movements (see Kirby 1995), as Sampath (2001) links the rise of these discourses to socio-economic changes, such as the decline of heavy labour on the island and the growth of service industries in which women are the main earners. The impact of socio-economic changes on thinking concerning masculinities is more widely evident in the work of authors such as MacInnes (1998), who describes a current crisis in masculinity, with men going through changes and uncertainty concerning their gender identities, as being linked with revolutions in modernity, including capitalism, liberalism and demographic transition.

The men's movements can, like feminisms, be analysed using the PPM and political opportunity theories. The men's movements demonstrate the way in which political opportunities are unequally gendered, and the gendered bias of political opportunity theorists, who overlook the way in which men often have more access to the public sphere than people of other genders do. Cultural theories, especially frame theory, are useful in understanding the way in which non-hegemonic parts of the masculinities movements involve the reworking of identity scripts.

The Lesbian and Gay Movement

Adam (1987) documents the development of the gay and lesbian social worlds that preceded the gay, lesbian and bisexual movement as early as the twelfth century in Europe (see Chapter 5). A gay male subculture was established in some places by the nineteenth century, and the first gay rights organisations sprang up in Germany in the later part of that century (Adam 1987). Authors such as Magnus Hirshfeld and Oscar Wilde, as well as cultured individuals such as Natalie Barney, who was the centre of a lesbian friendship network in Paris, all impacted on the development of the lesbian and gay subculture. The early gay movement ended abruptly in Russia,

Germany and the occupied territories with the rise of Nazism and Stalinism, and the influence of McCarthyism and its assault on homosexuality in the US after the Second World War also impacted on the movement. Gay and lesbian rights organisations began to appear in the 1960s in the US, and in 1969:

> New York Police raided a Greenwich Village gay bar called Stonewall. Bar raids were an American institution ... what made Stonewall a symbol of a new era of gay politics was the reaction of the drag queens, dykes, street people, and bar boys who confronted the police first with jeers and high camp and then with a hail of coins, paving stones, and parking meters. (Adam 1987: 75)

Gay liberation was born, and the older homosexual organisations were deposed by a more radical set of activists, with organisations emerging all over the Western world, ranging from anarchic direct action oriented groups to more formally organised groups (Adam 1987). Lesbian feminism emerged in the early 1970s, with a separatist lesbian movement splitting off from the gay liberation movement, so that 'in the 1970s, the popularity of separatism led to the creation of a radical women's culture through organizations such as land collectives, print collectives, alternative businesses, and lesbian resource centres' (Cruikshank 1992: 160). However, feminisms diversified in the 1980s, and a number of factors contributed to the diffusion of separatism and the development of a more pluralist and commercialised lesbian and gay scene in the West. It is important to note that the movement varies widely internationally, with developments taking place in a wide range of other countries (see Baird 2001 for an international review of human rights abuses). Issues for the gay and lesbian movement in the UK include:

> Partnership rights for same-sex couples – other cultures allow the regulation of relationships and so on. We're hoping for legislation to allow recognition for legal rights, for example for inheritance tax, and rights of next of kin. At present, there are cases where people have bought property and have to pay unfair levels of tax and sometimes have to sell properties. Also, homophobia is more widespread, homophobic bullying in schools, for example the use of 'gay' as a standard insult. (Stonewall representative)

How do the theories of NSMs apply to lesbian and gay organisations? The lesbian and gay movement typifies NSMs in that it consists of a set of complex coalitions, radical as well as mainstream forms of protest, in some cases a flat organisational structure, and a mixing of private and public realms. The lesbian and gay movement went through the insurgent stage identified in the PPM model, although this coexisted with earlier, more formally organised groups. Although tensions between structured and unstructured organisations have continued, there has been a gradual formalisation taking place, with lesbian and gay equality now being somewhat institutionalised in many health and political settings in the UK. The most powerful community organisation, Stonewall, is professionalised and mainstream. Movement maintenance has, to an extent, been spurred on by state or other forms of homophobia, although it has also been stimulated by the business sector.

The factors contributing to movement development that are outlined by the PPM – organisational history, opportunity, and identity – apply to the gay and lesbian movement in a number of ways. As indicated above, the movement has had a rich cultural and political history, which formed a basis for developments. The arguably less full development of lesbian subcultures is perhaps one reason why the lesbian movement differs from gay politics; as Adam said: 'having a much less extensive public-bar sector than gay men have, many women came out for the first time in the midst of the women's movement' (1987: 89).

Political opportunities have more recently been provided – for example, research project (b) indicated that a policy emphasis on urban regeneration in the UK has fostered support for gay areas in cities. A recent UK example of a political opportunity which has allowed the development of pro-equality initiatives has been provided by the police response to the racist murder of Stephen Lawrence and the homophobic Admiral Duncan bombing. These terrible events catalysed authorship of the Stephen Lawrence report and the introduction of the Community Safety Act 1998 where homophobic hate crime is discussed.

Cultural and identity aspects are crucial for understanding the lesbian and gay social movements, especially the shift from pathologised identities to positive, politicised collective identities that has formed the basis for the modern lesbian and gay movement. The PPM is insufficiently developed in terms of the way it models the cultural aspects of the lesbian and gay movement. First, it is overly centred on the more formally organised, assimilationist aspects of the movement (Engel 2001) and, second, it underemphasises the development of lesbian and gay social spaces and cultures, which are particularly crucial to the movement. For instance, Cruikshank (1992) describes the importance of lesbians being able to live in the lesbian world developed in the 1970s by lesbian feminists; this reinforced their sense of pride and lesbian identification. Framing theory is important to understanding the movements – for example there was a shift in framing when the early, closeted, pathologising models of homosexuality gave way to affirmative models. Framing models can be expanded in relation to the lesbian and gay movement by addressing the way in which frames are developed by actors within the movement, as a means of supporting the movement and challenging dominant social arrangements, as with for example 'utopian' gay communes in the 1970s (see Engel 2001). They can also be used to explain the forces that oppose the movement, for example moral conservatism and the Christian Right. Overall, the lesbian and gay movement can be analysed using concepts drawn from the PPM and frame theory in a number of ways.

The Trans Movements

In Chapter 5, I describe the way in which early gender diverse subcultures were similar to those concerning same-sex desire; the two overlapped and merged in terms of culture and identity. Gender diversity became separated from same-sex desire in the early twentieth century, although, as noted earlier, there were subsequent overlaps in social space and political activity. The transvestite and transsexual communities first emerged in the US in the late 1950s in the context of widespread social hostility towards homosexuals and trans people (King 1986, 1993). The roots of the contemporary trans movement can be traced to the early stages of the Gay Liberation Movement: the Stonewall riot and the activism this provoked in the US and the Gay Liberation Front (GLF) and radical drag in the UK (see Kirk and Heath 1984). The first US radical organisations that would now be termed 'transgender' or 'trans' were groups such as the Street Transvestite Action Revolutionaries, which were formed in the 1970s after gay activists rejected trans people (Wilchins 1997). MTF transgenderist Virginia Prince founded the Foundation for Personality Expression around 1960 (King 1986, 1993) and the magazine Transvestia in 1963; this marked an important watershed in trans politics and led to the establishment of national and international networks. Initially intended for heterosexual transvestites and MTF transsexuals, these networks broadened in the 1980s to include all trans people and others (MacKenzie 1994). This occurred in tandem with changes in discourses concerning gender: Rubin (1999) and Prosser (1998) discuss the importance of the work by Stone (1991); Butler (1990, 1993); Bornstein (1994) and others in opening the way for unconventional gender possibilities. In 1992 Annie Ogborn founded Transgender Nation, a broad-based, inclusive movement that located trans people's problems at the level of wider society, and focused on activism rather than support (Wilchins 1997). This was linked with the development of Transgender Menace and Gender Public Advocacy Coalition (GenderPAC): activist organisations based in the US. The Intersex Society of North America (ISNA) was founded in 1993 and by 1996 there were groups in Canada, Australia, New Zealand, South Africa, The Netherlands and Germany as well as other similar groups in countries such as Japan (Chase 1998). There are now over 3,000 intersex-related support and patient advocacy groups on the internet (Morris 2004).

The influence of American trans politics on the UK situation is strong. The trans movement in the UK developed through a mixture of grass-roots activism and community networks and alliances. The first organisation in the UK was the Beaumont Society, founded in 1967 by British transvestites who had met Virginia Prince (King 1986, 1993). Other organisations included the GLF-backed London Transvestite/Transsexual group, the Leeds TV/TS group, and the TS Liberation group at the ISIS commune (King 1986, 1993). The Self Help Association for Transsexuals (SHAFT), was founded in 1981 (Kate N' Ha Ysabet) and later split into the Gender Dysphoria Trust and the Gender Trust, with an affiliated group called GEMS (King 1993) (and, later, another group, Gendys). These developments were followed by the formation of Press for Change (PFC), which is currently the main organisation campaigning for transsexual people's rights, although there is a range of others. Transvestite groups have now sprung up in most British cities and there are various special events and clubs devoted to transvestism and to fetishism. Groups initiated by intersexuals are not very established in the UK, although there are support groups for parents, and a UK intersex network on <http://www.ukia.co.uk>. There are also transgender working groups or sections of many gay, lesbian and bisexual organisations.

Overall, the trans and intersex movements focus on issues such as equality, social inclusion, and the right to self-determination (see Monro 2000b, 2003). However, the US and UK trans movements vary considerably in their political methods, with some parts of the US movement being more radical and oppositional than any aspects of the UK movement, which does not involve the type of activism seen as characteristic of NSMs.[5] Trans politics in the UK includes a wide range of types of political action, including the production of art, literature and academic analysis, the organisation of conferences and events, lobbying and participation in consultation with local and central government, liaison with health and other professionals, action such as writing letters to firms concerning mandatory male/female categorisation on forms, educational work and consultancy, networking and the use of the internet. As I have previously shown, there is a wide range of political aims amongst trans and intersex people. For example, '[Mens' clothing rights movements seek] the same freedom of choice in what they wear as is already enjoyed by women – this may not always include women's clothes, but may incorporate makeup, jewellery, and other feminine styles or accoutrements' (Holmes 2003). Overall, some of the crucial issues currently include:

- cessation of surgery and other treatment to force intersex people to fit into the gender binary system;
- the provision of information to intersex people regarding their conditions, and public education campaigns to promote understanding and tolerance;
- provision of equalities legislation for transsexuals (including people who are non-operative);
- psychiatric depathologisation of transsexuals, cross-dressers, and intersex people;
- access to appropriate healthcare for those trans and intersex people who require it;
- establishment of community safety measures to stop violence against gender diverse people;
- the opening of space to discuss gender diversity – including non-male and non-female identities.

How can the trans and intersex movements be analysed in relation to NSM thinking? The trans and intersex movements typify NSMs in that they are amorphous, overlapping groupings, populated by people with a wide range of identities and backgrounds. Organisational structure is flat and diffuse, and there is an emphasis on collective identities. Different groups of gender diverse people have different organisations, with some overlap between them – for example Press for Change is inclusive of intersex and androgynous people but in practice focuses on transsexuality (Monro 2000b). These groups have a small number of key activists, and many others with some level of involvement.

The development of the trans and intersex movements can be analysed in relation to the PPM, to a degree. The trans movement began with the collective insurgency, but this was both preceded by, and paralleled by, community-based self-help groups. The cycles outlined in the PPM are thus not clear-cut with respect to trans – the various strands coexist and are mutually sustaining. For example at a support group I went to discussions shifted onto issues concerning rights, which then generated enthusiasm for taking part in activism. This mixing of 'stages' is partially due to the differences within the communities, which encompass both conservative transsexuals who wish to assimilate into the mainstream, and who might take part in support groups or lobbying, but would not identify with a distinct trans politics, and trans people who are actively challenging gender binaries, who might take part in more radical cultural or political events. It is also due to the small size of the trans population, the lack of identity cohesiveness and the continued marginalisation of these groups. In addition, the medicalisation of transsexuality, which is to an extent necessary for treatment, places an unusual pressure on trans and intersex organisations to maintain ties with the medical establishment, something that is not found in other NSMs. In a sense, this highlights difficulties with the PPM model, which perhaps overlooks the way that sections of mainstream institutions and subcultures sustain each other. For instance, there is now a well-organised international support network of intersex condition-specific support groups, which have close working relationships with professionals <http://dmoz.org/society/Transgendered/Intersexed/Activism/>. This complex set of relationships has paradoxically both created an organisational base, and held the movement back, as much of the energy that could have gone into affirming self-determination and challenging rigid gender binaries has been taken up with concerns to do with treatment. There is a further difficulty with the PPM with regards to trans and intersex. The political climate in the UK has changed since the 1960s, when NSMs emerged. Direct action was seen by some contributors to research project (b) as less sophisticated and productive than engagement with the political opportunities that do exist; this stance seems to be mirrored in the current trans political formations. The trans and intersex movements have bypassed the insurgency stage to an extent, moving directly into the more formalised, professionalised stage.

The different aspects of the PPM – pre-existing organisation, changing opportunities, and collective identities – have some applicability to trans and intersex movements. First, as I have shown above, there were pre-existing organisational structures that supported the development of the trans movement, although it is important to emphasise the way in which the radical trans movement developed in opposition to the more conservative trans organisations. Organisational strength has come from a number of disparate sources: the various trans groups, the medical establishment, the fetish scene and other networks, and, increasingly, connections with the LGB movement.

Second, trans radicalism developed in the context of certain opportunities within mainstream society – for instance an increase in consumerism made access to private treatment for transsexuals and access to cross-dresser's accessories easier. The expansion of transgender networks in cyberspace provided important opportunities for activism and community-building – for example Feinberg (1996) discusses the way in which the third gender pronouns 'ze' and 'hir' came from cyberspace discussions. There is a great deal of transgender and intersex material on the net (see for example <http://www.tgforum.com>). Whittle (1998b) emphasises the importance of cyberspace for trans activism, allowing mobilisation and a shift away from concerns with passing, although it is important to point out that not everyone has access to the net. Another area in which possibilities for activism developed concern engagement with the increasingly tolerant lesbian and gay communities – for example, transgender was included under the 'Pride' banner in 1996 in the UK. In addition, the openings provided for lesbian, gay, and bisexual politics in the UK, which have been supported by the government drive to increase social inclusion, have meant that trans people have recently had more opportunities to influence the mainstream. Opportunities for direct influence have also developed in recent years, with the establishment of the Intergovernmental Working Group on Transsexuality, and sustained dialogue between politicians and the transgender communities – although these opportunities are only there for certain sections of the communities; cross-dressers, to an extent, and non-male/female people, remain shut out. The trans movement illustrates the strategic use of political opportunities, for example:

> it's a lot of single issues. I mean you take single issues. I mean I think it's very important that we do work around transsexual prisoners and transgendered prisoners. I think it's, you know, even though they're an incredibly tiny minority of the community but they are, you know, there is a matter of solidarity. One of the things one has to do about politics is find areas in which solidarity can be created and in which alliances can be created, not in the sense of the Labour Party's attempt to construct a sort of delegate culture of, you know, they're ... 'Well basically every minority will elect representatives and they all come and tell us what that community wants.' (Roz)

Third, the cultural aspects of NSMs – identity liberation and collective identity formation – are important for trans and intersex politics, although it is important to note that whilst a shift towards identity liberation has taken place in the UK, this is not evident everywhere. One contributor to research project (a) said that she thought that transsexual people were unable to activate on their own behalf and needed the advocacy of outsiders. Identity liberation is now taking place amongst trans and intersex people internationally, with the Intersexual Society of North America existing since 1993 and the UK Intersex Association aiming to 'campaign against the use of surgery and other medical treatment for coercing intersex people to physically conform to the cultural definitions of "normal" ' <http://dmoz.org/society/Transgendered/Intersexed/Acvitism>. As intersex person Esther Morris says, 'we need to move intersex away from the medical context and into our social consciousness' (2004: 27). Frames are important for transgender politics, in particular the reframing that has taken place in connection with the development of the terms 'transgender' and 'trans', that emphasise inclusivity (Nataf 1996), self-determination and activism. However, some contributors discussed the personal cost of being involved in transgender politics; whilst they adopted liberated identities, they still had to face social discrimination if they were out. Overall, the trans movement in general illustrates and provides support for the PPM, although the limited development of the movement points perhaps to a need for the re-emphasis on structural inequalities.

The Bisexual Movement

There were early communities of bisexuals, such as the Bloomsbury Group in the UK in the early twentieth century. However, the contemporary bisexual movement began in the early 1970s in the US, in the context of the sexual revolution, and there were bisexual groups in some places of Europe by the end of the 1970s (Hutchins and Kaahamanu 1991, <http://whatexit.org/tal/mywritings/bipolitics.html>). Early bisexual groups focused broadly on sexual liberation, and were often more connected with the heterosexual 'swinger' communities than the lesbian and gay communities, although many bisexuals were associated with the early gay and liberation movement, which advocated sexual freedom (see Chapter 5). The erasure of bisexuality by the mainstream and lesbian and gay communities resulted in the development of a separate bisexual community (or communities) – based on lifestyle politics, and a political agenda concerning visibility (Lawrence Brewer, BiCon 2003). The first specifically activist bisexual groups emerged in the 1980s, for example San Francisco's BiPol. HIV impacted on the bisexual movement from the 1980s onwards, as the bisexual communities lost members, took part in HIV activism, and addressed the stigmatising attitudes that framed bisexuals as carriers. The queer movement of the 1990s also affected the movement:

> with its emphasis on diversity, radical politics, and direct action, this movement brought out people who had become disillusioned by the assumption of apoliticism of existing gay and bisexual organisations. Part of the new movement emphasises the inclusion of bisexuals, transgenderists and others. <http://bitheway.org/Bi/History/htm>

There was an explosion of publications concerning bisexuality in the early 1990s and subsequently (see for example Firestein 1996, Storr 1999), as well as an increase in the number of groups and media coverage of bisexuality (Hutchins 1996), all of which have fuelled the movement. The increased inclusion of bisexual under the 'lesbian and gay' banner has taken place since the mid 1990s, with, for example, a cursory search on the net revealing a huge range of LGB organisations.

The bisexual movement in the UK currently consists of small groups and loose national and local networks, and internet networks. It is fragmented, complex, and primarily concerned with identity issues, recreation, and support, rather than lobbying. A range of bisexual people are involved in other communities, for example the Sci Fi community. Bisexual politics tend to concern personal identity. Mattesson (1991) discussed the strategic use of identity to tackle bias: presenting as 'gay' when facing the straight community, in order to foreground his gay side, and 'bisexual' in the gay community, in order to fight prejudice against bisexuals. There are a number of ongoing debates within the bisexual movement concerning whether bisexuals should:

- engage in independent organising as bisexuals – including the strategic use of the term 'bisexual' despite its limitations, the engagement in the production of newsletters and the organisation of events, and support for the development of a specifically bisexual culture;
- work with gay and lesbian groups – and campaign for inclusion in these. As one bisexual contributor said 'I think we need quite a large social movement to get us to the stage of acceptance of same-sex relationships' (John);
- work for wider sexual liberation, including the liberation of trans people, queers and intersex people. As contributors said: 'one of the main strands of activism is to say to people: "yes you are welcome here, even if you don't fit the stereotypes. We don't fit them either" ' (Jennifer Moore), and 'the thing is for the bi community to educate people that there are as many forms of sexuality as there are individuals' (Mike);
- aim to get rid of labels completely (see Chapter 2) (Lawrence Brewer, BiCon 2003).

There are ongoing debates within the bisexual communities, as well as within the lesbian, gay, and trans communities, concerning the extent to which bisexual and LGT people shares issues (Lawrence Brewer, BiCon 2003). There are certainly overlaps, for example:

A lot of the prejudice that bisexual people face is similar to lesbians and gay men, especially if they are in same-sex relationships – the legal situation is the same. Bisexual people are quite invisible, there are not many out bisexual people as role models, and there are lots of stereotypical myths that are hard to break down. (Stonewall representative)

Arguably, there are activist issues that are specific to bisexuals (see also Chapter 7). On a conceptual level, challenging the monosexual model that is taken for granted in both gay and straight society, and, for some bisexuals, the binary gender system on which it is based is central to bisexual politics (see Nangle 1995). In other words, our desires do not have to be divided into gay/lesbian or straight on the basis of a fallacious gender binary system. On a more practical level, the issues that bisexuals deal with include bisexual-specific prejudice (Hutchins (1996), the issue of people having their sexuality defined independently of any current partner, and polyamory (although, as I have noted elsewhere, some contributors argued that, for example, 'we are unlikely to get beyond the stage of two people relationships – we need to deal with this before we get onto poly' (John)). Contributors discussed a number of political aims, for example:

> Recognition would be nice to begin with. It's real and it's not a phase – all those clichés. (Interviewer: why is it important?) It's validation. It doesn't need to be a big issue but it would be nice if it was more than a limited group of people who accept it. And about partnership rights – it is wrong that same-sex couples don't have rights. (Jane)

> The poly community don't know each other that well. What I want is to have more people for social support – talking about the problems, the good things. (Grant Denkinson)

The aims of the bisexual communities go beyond issues concerning sexual orientation. There appears to be a concern with inclusion and supporting diversity, for example there were discussions about tackling racism at BiCon 2003, as well as an awareness in which different marginalised groups share opposition to hegemonic norms concerning sexuality. For example, Grant Denkinson described the way in which

> when I think of disability ... when parts of the body don't react in the same way ... there has been an understanding of different ways of having sex – getting away from the idea of the missionary position, for example someone on the net saying that they are worried about impotence and a lesbian woman saying 'we do fine'.

Overall, the political goals of the bisexual movement include 'to achieve legal equality for same-sex relationships and to let people see bisexuality as an equally valid identity to lesbian/gay or straight' (Stonewall representative).

How does NSM thinking apply to the bisexual movement? The bisexual movement is perhaps even more exemplary of NSMs than some of the other movements, because it has a particularly flat organisational structure, is decentred, and consists of loosely knit groups and organisations. The personal tends to be seen as political, with an emphasis on visibility as a force for social change, and community members come from diverse backgrounds. However, as with the trans movement, there is little emphasis on direct action, and the extent of purely bisexual activism, at least in the UK, is limited to the organisation of events (including an annual conference), support organisations, and lobbying for the inclusion of bisexuality in equalities and other initiatives. Many people who behave in bisexual ways do not identify as bisexual, and of those who do, only a minority are political about this. Bisexual politics does, in practice, tend to get subsumed under lesbian and gay activism, and the issues that are substantively (as opposed to symbolically) mostly specific to bisexuals, especially polyamory, remain in the private sphere. The way that bisexuals can move in and out of lesbian and gay organisations paradoxically both weakens and sustains the bisexual movement, as some activists channel their energies into lesbian and gay focused politics – illustrating the way in which too much diffusion and complexity inhibits the development of social movements.

Following the stages set out in the PPM, the bisexual movement appears to have taken an insurgent form at times (especially when bisexual activists have been involved in the lesbian and gay movements), as well as the later stages of the PPM concerning identity affirmation. However, internalised biphobia does have a tendency to re-emerge, leading to questions about the neat movement from isolated victimisation to collective empowerment that is modelled in the PPM. The bisexual movement does not yet appear to be fully mature, given the levels of social erasure of bisexuality, the way that bisexuality is absorbed by the lesbian and gay movement, and the small numbers of people involved. The heterosexual privilege that bisexuals (who are not in same-sex relationships) have a certain level of access to may be another factor affecting the underdevelopment of the movement; as Engel's (2001) account of the PPM shows, a certain amount of resistance or repression is necessary for a movement to be sustained.

The core aspects of the PPM – pre-existing organisations, opportunities, and identity liberation – are relevant to the bisexual movement, particularly in explaining some of the reasons for the underdevelopment of this movement. Pre-existing organisations, notably feminist and lesbian and gay organisations, but also for example the co-counselling and alternative spirituality movements, have been important for the development of the bisexual movement, but historically there has been far less of an organised movement than has been the case with some other NSMs. The political opportunity structure for bisexuals overlaps in many ways with the political opportunity structures that lesbian and gay activists face, although there are differences. Mainstream political institutions have, on the whole, provided few political opportunities for the bisexual movement to engage with, at least until recently (see Chapter 5). On a broader social level, bisexuals are still fairly socially erased, whilst lesbians and gays are increasingly visible, and to an extent, tolerated. The lack of development of the bisexual movement can partly be accounted for by the lack of opportunity; changes in social structures and in discourse to support bisexual equality could disrupt both gay/lesbian and straight normativities, as these are monosexual and rely on a gender binary system for their existence.

Cultural elements of NSM theory are important for understanding the bisexual movement, especially because the communities are focused on lifestyle issues. Identity formation is a crucial aspect of the bisexual movement, but being bisexual and proud has a more patchy history than being gay and proud, given the stigmatisation that bisexuals face from monosexual culture. In addition, the fluidity that bisexuals experience may make it harder to sustain a strong counterculture identity; when in opposite-sex relationships, it is quite easy to identify with heterosexual culture. One collective action frame that could be developed is the notion of monosexuality, which places both lesbian/gay and straight people in the same category, highlighting the way in which homosexual/heterosexual categorisation erases fluidity and gender diversity. Other collective action frames are apolitical ones – for example youth and underground subcultures, specifically those found in some club scenes, according to some of the research contributors (projects (a) and (d)), include some bisexual activity and a tolerance of polysexuality in a way which affects cultural norms, but which is not very linked with the organised bisexual movement. The influence of non-political subcultures is an aspect of NSMs, which is perhaps poorly dealt with by the PPM; as Engel (2001) points out, it has a tendency to focus on formal organisations, something that completely bypasses the influence of subcultures. Overall, the PPM and frame theories are useful in conceptualising the bisexual movement, although the centrality of non-political fringe networks to the bisexual communities points to a need for the further development of theory in the area of subcultures.

CONCLUSION

In this chapter I provided an overview of the development of a number of key movements concerning gender and sexuality; the women's liberation movement, the men's movements, the gay and lesbian movement, the bisexual movement, and the trans and inter-sex movements. I outlined a number of approaches to theorising NSMs and looked at some of the ways in which these could be applied to social movements concerning gender and sexuality. NSMs share certain characteristics, including complex, diffuse organisational structures, broad (sometimes uncertain) member-ship, and a blurring of the public and private realms. There are a number of ways of conceptualising NSMs, and I have focused on the political process model (PPM), and have also drawn on political opportunity theories and cultural (especially frame) theories – both of these are compatible with the PPM. The PPM integrates previous models, highlighting the key factors associated with the develop-ment of movements – pre-existing organisational strength, collec-tive identity formation and liberation, and changing opportunities. It suggests that movements develop from initial insurgency stages through to an emphasis on sustainability and a certain amount of centralisation.

NSMs concerning gender and sexuality share many characteris-tics. They tend overall to move from a period of collective insur-gency through to more stable, institutionalised forms – although some have not attained the latter stage. It is important to note that insurgent and more formally organised, assimilationist elements of the movements often coexist, and that there is some evidence that insurgent, oppositional forms of politics are no longer seen as polit-ically efficacious. In addition, some movements in the UK, in par-ticular the trans and intersex movements, appear to have moved straight into the centralised, more formally organised stage and bypassed the insurgent stage – although these movements draw on master frames provided by the more radical US-based movements. All of the movements can be analysed using the PPM and other theories to some degree, although some of them highlighted points for further exploration. These include:

- the importance of cyberspace in providing political opportunities;
- the influence and role of non-political subcultures in the formation of NSMs – particularly in the bisexual movement;
- the complex nature of the relationships between NSMs and, mainstream organisations. This is particularly important for the trans movement, which has developed in close (if sometimes oppositional) relationship to the medical establishment;
- the fragmented and diverse relationships between different sex and gender minority communities, and the ways in which these groups access political opportunities *within* other movements. For example, the bisexual movement accesses (and contributes to) the opportunities created by a more developed lesbian and gay movement, whilst also being denied opportunities for inclusion in some cases – the extent to which inclusion takes place is further moderated by mainstream interventions such as directives concerning inclusiveness;
- the importance of loose coalitions in the development of NSMs – but difficulties with notions of discrete NSMs when gender and sexual identities are fluid and/or plural.

The trans, intersex and bisexual movements are, like the men's movements, far less developed than the feminist, and lesbian and gay movements. The men's movements are arguably less evolved because there is less motivation for men to initiate or maintain a movement in a society in which they are generally privileged, so that impetus either comes from a reactionary desire to reinstate male dominance, or a political empathy with women (and gender minorities). The situation is generally different for trans, intersex, and bisexual people, where a number of factors have contributed to underdeveloped movements. There are only small numbers of trans and intersex people, the communities are very diverse, and there is considerable tension concerning aims (see Chapter 5). There have, until recently, been very limited opportunities for influence, and there has been little history on which to draw. The bisexual communities are similarly diverse, with different aims. The identity fluidity associated with bisexuality means that bisexuals easily become politically assimilated into either heterosexual or lesbian/gay cultures. There have been few opportunities to challenge entrenched monosexuality, and much bisexual history has been appropriated by lesbians and gay men. These movements could be strengthened by a reclamation of history, an emphasis on identity affirmation, and greater use of the frames provided by the other movements, as well as more strategic use of the opportunities provided by mainstream and other organisations.

7
Citizenship

The notion of 'citizenship' has become important in politics and academic thought (Bussemaker and Voet 1998), forming a means of integrating collectivist leftist traditions and ideas of individual rights and responsibilities, which are more often associated with conservatism (Lister 1997). The concept of citizenship is strategically crucial for gender politics because it forms a central plank of political strategies across the political spectrum (see Roche 1992). However, studies of citizenship have traditionally paid little attention to women, trans and intersex people, and non-heterosexuals. 'The citizen' is generally assumed to be a white, male, heterosexual, able-bodied person. There have been important challenges to this in recent years, with the development of models of feminist citizenship and sexual citizenship. However, these models have tended to overlook people who transgress gender binaries. Where gender diverse people have been included, it has been in the literature about sexuality, rather than gender (see for example Evans 1993, Plummer 1995). Similarly, coverage of types of sexuality that transgress binary categorisation, including bisexuality and fetishism, has been limited.

This chapter aims to provide an overview of some of the key aspects of citizenship in relation to sexual and gender diversity, utilising existing mainstream literatures on citizenship, as well as those concerning feminist and sexual citizenships, as a basis for exploring bisexual, SM/fetish, trans and intersex citizenships. I will therefore begin the chapter by outlining three mainstream models of citizenship – civic republicanism, liberalism, and communitarianism. I then discuss the emergence of feminist citizenship and analyse the mainstream models of citizenship from a feminist perspective. The chapter then proceeds to address notions of sexual citizenship, before discussing these – and mainstream models of citizenship – in relation to the areas of bisexuality and fetishism. Lastly, the chapter develops models of trans and intersex citizenship (see Monro 2003,

Monro and Warren 2004 and Chapters 3, 4 and 8 for discussions of rights issues). There are a number of themes running through this chapter, including the tension between forms of citizenship that rely on the rights claims of distinct groups versus approaches that aim to broaden models of citizenship to include minorities. This key theme, concerning particularist versus universalist approaches, appears again in Chapters 5 and 8.

It is important to note that, despite the usefulness of the concept of citizenship, a slight caveat is in order. 'Citizenship' is a slippery concept, involving the inclusion of some groups and the exclusion of others, often along ethnic and national lines. It is historically and culturally situated, and has different meanings in different languages. Also, as Bell and Binnie (2000) point out, whilst citizenship is a potent concept in the area of sexual politics, it may involve compromise, such as the exclusion of aspects of sexuality that are seen as unacceptable. Critics of the concept of citizenship can be found across the political spectrum – radical critics argue that it is a means of suppressing protest and opposition (Turner and Hamilton 1994).

MAINSTREAM MODELS OF CITIZENSHIP

Citizenship can be defined as a collection of rights and duties determining socio-political membership, and providing access to resources and benefits (Turner and Hamilton 1994). Modern notions of citizenship stem from the French and American revolutions and the changes brought about by the Industrial Revolution. Bussemaker and Voet (1998) discuss three main ways of thinking about citizenship: (1) civic republicanism, (2) liberalism and (3) communitarianism.[1]

(1) Civic republicanism, which developed in Greece in the fourth or fifth century AD, was based on notions of individuals as having equal worth, the importance of individual involvement in politics, and the duties of citizenship (Bussemaker and Voet 1998, Daly and Cowen 2000). However, under this system, some people were more equal than others.
(2) Liberalism is perhaps the most influential form of citizenship in the West, being forged in relation to capitalism. Emphasis is on individual equal rights, with minimal state intervention and maximum market freedom.[2]

(3) Communitarianism was again developed initially in Greece. It has many variations, but is distinctive in its opposition to the individualistic liberal model. Communitarians construct citizens as being dependent on each other, emphasise social obligations, and discuss the existence of differences that need to be taken into account – although only some differences are recognised, and gender and sexuality tend to be excluded. The development of the welfare state in the West and elsewhere has meant a revisiting of communitarianism, and the influence of communitarian notions has persisted in line with a neo-conservative emphasis on duties, as opposed to rights.

There are different traditions of citizenship. In the UK, for instance, the focus is on the relationship between welfare, citizenship and social class; in the US it concerns the relationship between ethnicity and citizenship and in Europe emphasis is on the relationship between public and private realms (Turner and Hamilton 1994). There are also different levels of citizenship, for example the European Union, nation states and local government. Citizenship is layered through local institutions and other factors. For example the UK and the Netherlands have a colonial history, which contributes to racialised notions of the citizen and policies concerning issues such as immigration (Bussemaker and Voet 1998).

Feminists and sexual citizenship theorists have provided impor-tant critiques of traditional notions of citizenship. These have taken place in the context of other challenges, especially those of, first, neo-conservatives, who have criticised the liberal-social model developed by Marshall (1950), arguing for greater emphasis on duties rather than rights. Neo-conservative thought has had a huge impact on social policy and politics, a greater influence perhaps than any of the radical models. Second, there have been various challenges from other non-mainstream sources, including work by authors in the field of ethnicity (Kymlicka 1995, Lewis 1998), disability (Campbell and Oliver 1996, Swain et al. 1993) and age (Barnes and Shaw 2000). The radical non-mainstream models share a critique of the assumption that 'the citizen' is white, male, able-bodied and heterosexual, and in many cases highlight values such as compassion and care. Key issues in the area of ethnicity, for exam-ple, concern the desirability of supporting diversity whilst ensuring compatibility with values such as equality and justice (see Back and Solomos 2000). Overall, these alternative approaches to citizenship indicate a need to broaden notions of citizenship, and question the power inequalities inherent in liberal, civic republican and communitarian approaches.

FEMINIST MODELS OF CITIZENSHIP

Feminist models of citizenship start by critiquing the way in which women have been marginalised in debates concerning citizenship for millennia. From the fifth century BC to the mid twentieth century, citizenship rights were almost exclusively given to men, and where women were included, it was often only in their role as mothers. Inequalities persist despite support for formal equality in many countries, partly because mainstream notions of citizenship continue to be based on implicit assumptions that citizenship means the same thing for women and men, masking differences in their interests. Current notions of citizenship still hide gender inequality. For example in the UK the idea of the 'active citizen' erases gendered assumptions, such as an emphasis on parental responsibilities without recognition of the way in which these are unequally gendered (Bussemaker and Voet 1998). Challenges to masculinist notions of citizenship include the work of Pateman (1989), Lister (1997) and Walby (1994). These authors build on the shared ground between feminisms and citizenship discourses, referring to notions of justice, equality, participation and recognition of pluralism (Bussemaker and Voet 1998). However, feminisms have had an ambivalent relationship to notions of citizenship. Citizenship has had an appeal to feminists because it promised universal rights, but at the same time, it has excluded women. As Lister (1997) says, 'The reappropriation of strategic concepts such as citizenship is central to the development of feminist political and social theory. A feminist project to (re)appropriate citizenship does not, however, imply an uncritical acceptance of its value as a concept' (1997: 3).

This section aims to discuss mainstream notions of citizenship in relation to feminism, explore whether it is possible to broaden notions of citizenship to include women, and point out some of the issues that post-structuralism and gender pluralism raise concerning feminist models of citizenship. How useful are traditional forms of citizenship for feminist thinkers? I will look here at (1) civic republicanism, (2) liberalism and (3) communitarianism.

(1) Civic republicanism was based on the notion of freedom in the public sphere, and women were excluded from public life

in ancient Greece. The notions of participation which are an important aspect of civic republicanism were subsequently linked to
notions of gender inequality, in the work of Rousseau, Macchiavelli
and others. Bussemaker and Voet (1998) suggest that civic republicanism is useful for feminists because of the emphasis on participation and public debate, but that it is masculinist due to its history
and the extent of women's past and present political exclusion. In
addition, the emphasis on the public sphere leads to the denigration
of the private sphere, a point to which we shall return later.

(2) Classical liberalism has a number of advantages for women:
the discourse of equality via the philosophy of natural rights, and
the language of freedom and autonomy. Liberal arguments for the
equality of women have been widely used by the women's liberation
movement, despite the exclusion of women by authors such as
Marshall. However, the emphasis on individualism is frequently
masculinist, because it is assumed that women are taking care of the
private sphere (freeing up male individuals to engage in public life),
and liberalism may also mean a reluctance to address citizenship
obligations. Neo-liberalism is problematic for women because of the
focus on the market and avoiding state intervention, which does
not support women's equality and is a threat to the welfare state on
which many women rely.

(3) Communitarianism has advantages for women in that it
includes values such as compassion, care, shared responsibilities and
interrelatedness. However, it hides some differences under the 'veil'
of universalism. In addition, some types of communitarianism are
traditionalist in the areas of morality and gender roles. In practice,
communitarian notions of community are often locality-based, failing to address the communities of interest that may concern women
and sexual minorities (Bussemaker and Voet 1998). Overall, therefore, all of these approaches have advantages and disadvantages for
feminist citizenship – but all of them risk the erasure of women's
interests in different ways.

Is it possible to reformulate the ideal of citizenship, which originally excluded women, to fully include them? The extension of
mainstream notions of citizenship to include women focuses on
informal, rather than public, forms of political engagement, and on
reformulating notions of the public–private divide. Feminists such
as Lister (1997) explore the role of women in the public sphere,
pointing out that women are under-represented amongst the political elites. Instead, they tend to be involved in informal politics, so

there is a need for citizenship discourse to pay greater attention to this arena. In addition, according to Lister (1997) there is a need to re-privilege unpaid caring, as opposed to paid work. The central issue here is the public–private divide. On a discursive level, citizenship, and the liberalism from which much citizenship discourse derives, depends on the idea of the separation between the private (domestic, personal life) sphere and the public (paid work, politics) sphere. On a structural level, public–private inequalities profoundly affect women's citizenship. For example, a lack of available childcare blocks women's ability to participate in work and politics (Daly and Cowen 2000). The alternative is to expand models of citizenship to include the private realm, although this could also pose problems in relation to privacy and autonomy (see Chapter 8), as well as difficulties with implementation.

Feminist models of citizenship are important in foregrounding women's interests and interrogating issues such as the public–private divide. However, as demonstrated in Chapter 2, there have been debates within feminism and post-structuralist thinking concerning the category of 'women' (see Richardson 2000c) and the extent to which we can talk of universal female experience. If the notion of 'woman' is deconstructed, ideas of feminist citizenship – especially universal feminist citizenship that pertains only to women – become problematic. Drawing briefly on Chapter 2, if the 'broadening categories' approach to gender is taken, 'woman' and 'man' are seen as umbrella categories, covering a multitude of experiences and identities, and other categories concerning trans are included and seen as partially overlapping with the categories of male and female, so that the picture becomes more complex and finely grained, making rigid boundaries between mainstream and feminist citizenships untenable. If the 'degendering' approach is taken, the basis for asserting a feminist citizenship is undermined, because this would involve asserting gender difference. The 'gender pluralist' approach would entail support for feminist notions of citizenship, but only alongside other types of citizenship, such as trans and intersex – and the boundaries between different forms of gender citizenship would not be discrete, as some people would move between them or belong to several categories. The picture also becomes more complex when other differences are addressed. For example, Boris (1995) argues that race and ethnicity are central aspects of the definitions of citizenship. She argues that much contemporary feminist theorising invites us to ignore race, due to its focus on gender, and criticises the development of feminist thought concerning citizenship in reaction to existing models of democracy and the welfare state, where race has been inadequately problematised.

As I have argued elsewhere, there is a place for strategic identity-based politics, including feminist politics. This means eroding models of feminist citizenship because of debates concerning post-structuralism and difference would be counterproductive. The diversity of women's concerns and experiences does, however, mean that some of the issues discussed by feminist citizenship theorists may be irrelevant to some women, and that other factors, such as nationality and ability, must be taken into consideration. Certain groups of women, for example women with mental health problems, may have certain types of citizenship issues that are not shared by other women, and that are not necessarily dealt with by feminist theorists. In addition, the category of 'women' is clearly not discrete, or placed in opposition only to the category of 'man': the binary can be disrupted, and other identities introduced. Feminist models of citizenship do not take trans or intersex into account (see below), nor do they fully address the many instances of male non gender stereotypical behaviour, such as male caring. There is a danger that feminist notions of citizenship 'freeze' certain concerns that are relevant to certain women, whilst erasing the experiences of other women and non gender normative people.

SEXUAL CITIZENSHIPS

As I pointed out earlier, sexuality is often overlooked or ignored in discussions about citizenship. To quote Richardson (2000a), mainstream models embody an implicitly heterosexual notion of citizenship. This means that where same-sex relationships and desire are acknowledged at all, they are framed as marginal, and heterosexualities remain unexamined and unproblematised. Notions of sexual citizenship have developed in relation to this absence of discussion concerning sexuality. This section reviews the existing work on sexual citizenship, and then expands models of sexual citizenship with reference to bisexuality, fetishism and sadomasochism, before providing an analysis of sexual citizenship in relation to the three traditional models of citizenship.

According to Richardson (2000b), the term 'sexual citizenship' can be used to describe the sexual rights of groups, as well as access to general rights, and the impact of these rights on sexuality. It can include the recognition of the sexual rights of groups that are constructed as problematic, where, for example, there are competing claims for rights. There are difficulties with the notion of sexual citizenship – for example it can be seen as an attempt to assimilate alternative sexualities into the mainstream, or as a commodification of sexuality. Ironically, citizenship can be used to support homophobic arguments for providing rights so long as people keep their sexual identities private (Bell and Binnie 2000). However, as Richardson (2000a) says, it is possible to argue that recognition of the rights of sexual minorities broadens the scope of rights discourses.

A range of authors have contributed to the field of sexual citizenship. They include:

- Evans (1993), who was possibly the first author to theorise sexual citizenship. He focused on the interplay between the state and the market and the impact of this on sexuality, especially sexualities that are seen as 'immoral'. Whilst capitalism allows a certain amount of non-normative sexual expression, this is ghettoised away from the mainstream. Evans provides examples of non-normative forms of sexuality, such as bisexuality, and also discusses cross-dressing.
- Cooper (1995), who uses Foucauldian feminism in analysing state power in relation to sexuality and resistance to this. She argues for politically strategic sexual pluralism, rather than outright opposition to the mainstream.
- Plummer (1995), who takes another approach altogether, developing the notion of 'intimate citizenship' and arguing that this should be seen as a fourth aspect of citizenship, in addition to the traditional Marshallian model of political, social and civic rights. He defines intimate citizenship as a bundle of rights concerning people's choices about what they do with their bodies, emotions, relationships, gender identities and desires.
- Weeks (1998), who addresses the broader social preconditions for sexual citizenship, suggesting that there has been a new emphasis on sexual subjectivity and reflexivity due to a democratisation of relationships and the development of new subjectivities. Weeks envisages the end of the heterosexual–homosexual divide as being a likely future issue. He suggests a differentiated universalism, in other words, the balancing of different communities' claims, respect for diversity, and a sense of common humanity.

- Richardson (2000c), who exposes the heterosexism and male dominance embedded within notions of citizenship, and argues that where lesbian and gay rights are granted there is a high price to pay in terms of the extent to which sexuality then becomes prescribed and limited. Richardson also analyses lesbian citizenship (2000c), which is associated with radical perspectives and critiques of heteropatriarchy, as opposed to rights-based approaches.
- Bell and Binnie (2000), who discuss the queering of citizenship, which they define as bringing the erotic, and people's experiences of embodiment, into discussions about citizenship, and making space for dissident citizenship – including reshaping the terrain of citizenship by remaining outside of it. They critique the way that romantic love is constructed and discuss alternative sexual arrangements (especially adultery) as challenges to the institution of heterosexuality. They argue for the recognition of myriad dissident sexualities, and also emphasise the importance of transnational changes, such as the 'Europeanisation' of human rights law.

There are a number of issues that have not been adequately dealt with by existing authors on sexual citizenship. These include disabled people's sexual citizenship, single people's sexual citizenship, sexual citizenship and abuse, parenthood and sexual citizenship, and the sexual citizenship issues of people in non-Western countries, including issues concerning female genital mutilation, female infanticide, child prostitution, and dowry deaths. Addressing these concerns falls outside of the scope of this book, which focuses on the deconstruction and complexity of gender and sexuality binaries. Bisexuality and trans are important to the destabilisation of binaries, and it is to these that I now turn.

Bisexuality

There has been little discussion of bisexual identities by authors working in the field of sexual citizenship. This section begins by discussing bisexual citizenship, including issues concerning bisexual identities, difference within the communities, and polyamory. I then explore bisexual citizenship in relation to Richardson's (2000c) concepts of, first, citizenship as based on equal rights and second, citizenship as an expansion of the mainstream.

Bisexual citizenship can be seen as unique because bisexual identities are different from lesbian, gay, and heterosexual identities in a number of ways. Bisexuality typically involves the experience of fluid or multiple desires. Some bisexual people are attracted to people on the basis of characteristics other than sex, others desire men, women and others simultaneously, others shift in cycles between desire for women and men. Bisexuality is subjectively different from monosexuality, partly because the experience of same-sex desire, politics and expression 'queers' bisexual people even when they are in straight relationships. The complexification of desire which bisexuality involves ties in with the understanding that there are different heterosexualities: hegemonic heterosexuality and then a plethora of non-normative forms of heterosexuality, which include opposite-sex relationships involving bisexuals. Bisexuality paradoxically links with the queer transgression of sexual binaries, and with transgressive politics, but also entails opposite-sex desire and expression.

Like lesbian and gay identities, bisexuality is constructed differently depending on social and historical context. For example, Farajaje-Jones (1995) discusses the interrelationship between African American experience and bisexual experience. The dominant construction of bisexuality in African American culture is as pathological and promiscuous. However, there are also a wide variety of definitions of bisexuality and sexual fluidity, and bisexual expression may take place without identification with labels. The experience of being a 'wanderer', able to be part of, but never fully integrated in, different cultures (gay/lesbian and heterosexual) is perhaps one of the hallmarks of bisexual experience. This mirrors the experience of some other marginalised groups. For example, Prabhudas (1999) points out that being bisexual is to be both gay and straight, and that this is similar to being mixed race, where one is both black and white. Both groups are often rejected by people in established categories, and may be dismissed as 'in betweens'; both groups may have a role to play in bringing disparate communities together (see Chapter 5).

Polyamory, defined as being sexually involved with more than one person in an honest and loving way, is one aspect of some bisexuals' experience that is also found in other social scenes, for example some sections of the gay community, and the heterosexual 'swingers' scene. It can include various relationship models, from being single and having various sexual partners to having primary partner/s and others, to group sex (Rust 1996). Having relationships with more than one person may be challenging to the institution of heterosexuality, which is reliant on male–female dyads, as well as the assumptions about sexuality held by the lesbian and gay mainstream. Polyamorous people are excluded from full citizenship because marriage and partnership agreements with more than one person are illegal in most countries, and where they are legal it is only in certain contexts (e.g. some African countries allow a man to take more than one wife) and tends to disadvantage women. Nonmonogamy is stigmatised in Western countries, where ideals of long-term one-to-one relationships are extremely powerful (see Lano and Parry 1995). Overall, bisexual citizenship can be seen as sharing ground with both lesbian and gay – and mainstream – citizenships, but as also being specifically about the issues bisexuals face, such as visibility, inclusion, identity fluidity and polyamory.

How can bisexual citizenship be conceptualised? The main citizenship issues for bisexuals are:

• recognition of a bisexual identity, as opposed to being gay/ lesbian or straight at different times. This means the naming of bisexuality alongside other sexual minorities;[3]
• support for full equality for people in same-sex relationships;
• acceptance of the fluidity of desire, which means supporting changes to eradicate discrimination against lesbians and gays, but at the same time not framing lesbian and gay categories as discrete or fixed;
• recognition of the identity challenges that bisexuals face and the provision of support for such identities on a cultural and institutional level;
• statutory and other change to enable social recognition of polyamorous arrangements.

Richardson (2000c) outlines different approaches to conceptualising the lesbian citizen, which I will draw on in developing understandings of bisexual citizenship. First, there are equal rights approaches to lesbian citizenship which look at the way lesbians are penalised in the heterosexual system. As Richardson says, there are difficulties with these approaches – focus is on reform and assimilation, and the aim is to achieve equality with heterosexuals. However, the reforms necessary to support bisexual citizenship would arguably involve a queering of the mainstream, as sexual fluidity and multiplicity would become normalised, and the rigidity of heterosexual identification would be questioned. How does the equal rights approach apply to bisexuality? Clearly, bisexuals in same-sex relationships are socially penalised in the same ways as lesbians and gays, unless they closet themselves by pretending to be heterosexual (which is arguably easier in some cases than it is for lesbians and gays). Bisexuals in opposite-sex relationships access the same social and material privileges as heterosexuals, but are likely to experience the erasure of aspects of their identities. Bisexuals who are out as bisexual are likely to face similar or more serious prejudice to lesbians and gays, or worse stigmatisation given the levels of prejudice against bisexuals (see Ochs 1996). Bisexuals who are celibate may chose to ally themselves with either or both sides of the heterosexual–homosexual divide and experience privilege or stigmatisation accordingly, or continue to be out as bisexual and face biphobia. Polyamorous bisexuals experience double stigmatisation, as bi-sexuals and as non-monogamous people, although polyamorous bisexuals in primary heterosexual relationships may easily pass as heterosexual and avoid discrimination.

The second aspect of lesbian citizenship outlined by Richardson (2000c) concerns the notion of changing the models of mainstream citizenship, which are located within the current heterosexual system. This model appears reasonably conducive to bisexual citizenship: challenging the public–private divide that renders most bisexuality invisible would be likely to support the social inclusion of bisexuals. In addition, some of the critiques of this approach do not stand up in relation to bisexuality. For example, criticisms stemming from lesbian feminist theory, especially arguments for the separate development of lesbian politics and identity, are problematic for bisexuals (see also Chapter 2), who straddle the heterosexual–homosexual divide and cannot be completely separate from het-erosexuality unless they deny one side of their identity. If the discussion shifts to a separate transgressive politics, as outlined by Bell and Binnie (2000), notions of a separate bisexual politics become more feasible. However, there are also difficulties with this (see the critiques of separatist and queer politics in the chapters on theory and activism). Richardson discusses problems with assuming lesbian commonality as a basis for politics. Perhaps ideas of common-ality are even more limited for bisexuals, who are of different gen-ders and have a wide range of sexual desire and expression.[4] Another problem is that bisexuals in opposite-sex relationships, although more queer than heterosexuals, still bridge into the mainstream, meaning that transgressive politics may breed identity conflicts unless an alternative locus for transgression (for example the Goth scene) is taken. For example, contributor Kerry noted that

> we can find conflicts in our identity through trying to fit into the sex and gender polarised system, we can face discrimination from both lesbian and gay, and straight categories. Trying to fit into boxes and none of them really fit.

A further difficulty is that if heterosexuality is seen as multiple, and only certain sorts of heterosexuality as hegemonic, then opposition to heterosexuality per se becomes a problematic strategy. Therefore, for bisexual citizenship, a 'broadening the mainstream' approach is more useful than a separatist one. Perhaps one solution is to claim a bisexual 'space of citizenship' which people can move in and out of (see Richardson's 2000c discussion of lesbian citizenship).

Fetishism and Sadomasochism

Fetishism and sadomasochism (SM) are also areas that have not been fully explored in relation to models of sexual citizenships.[5] SM and fetishism cut across sexual orientation categories, and for some people, SM/fetish affiliation supplants heterosexual, lesbian, gay or bisexual identification. Fetishism can be defined as an erotic interest in objects (for example clothing). Sadomasochism is used in practice as an umbrella term covering eroticised power play, eroticised painful practices (such as whipping), bondage, role play, fisting, watersports and other practices (see Plummer 1995). SM 'play' is constructed as different to 'ordinary' intimate activity, and may or may not involve genital contact. The fetish scenes in the UK and the US are segmented into heterosexual, lesbian and gay scenes, with considerable crossover between these subcultures, and positive inclusion of trans people in most social spaces. Some SM practitioners 'play' (do SM activities) only in private, within monogamous couples. Others 'play' in fetish clubs or with a range of people who may or may not also be sexual partners in the conventional sense. Subculture norms include emphasis on mutual consent and negotiation, as well as physical and emotional safety, although in practice these rules may be contravened.

What place do fetishists and SM practitioners have within discourses of citizenship? SM and fetishism have been hugely contentious within the feminist and lesbian communities (see for example Jeffreys 1996, Ardill and O'Sullivan 1993, and Chapter 5).

The gay male SM scene is far more developed than the lesbian scene,[6] and SM practitioners are generally welcome within the bisexual communities and the more alternative parts of the trans communities. There has therefore been a fragmented approach towards SM and fetishism from within the sexual minority and feminist communities, and it is not possible to argue for a panacea approach. In addition, opposition to SM/fetish citizenship from the moral right is strong, given the wider range of intimate activities involved – these activities are non-procreative, and often transgress monogamy norms.

SM and fetish citizenship can be framed in terms of the equal rights approach developed by Richardson (2000c) in relation to lesbian citizenship. Many SM activities are currently illegal, and the Spanner case, where a group of consenting adult men were prosecuted for taking part in SM activities, reinforced illegality in the UK (Thompson 1994). SM/fetish citizenship would involve rights for consensual adult SM practitioners, the psychiatric depathologisation of SM and fetishism, and the decriminalisation of SM venues. The alternative approach, in which mainstream models of citizenship are broadened, would perhaps focus on issues such as broadening notions of what constitutes sexual activity, and challenging the public–private divide. The destabilisation of the private–public divide is an important theme for SM/fetish citizenship – as discussed in the chapter on democracy (Chapter 8), the SM and fetish scenes disrupt public–private binaries, as these communities have a set of semi-public social spaces in which sexual activity takes place. Overall, the provision of equal rights for SM practitioners would involve a significant disruption to heterosexual norms concerning monogamy and penis–vagina sex, as well as mainstream lesbian and gay norms. Whilst this would be a progressive step, there would be a need to emphasise the values of consent and open negotiation between equal adults. This is crucial, because deconstruction of sexual norms can be dangerous as well as liberating, particularly when combined with counterculture affiliations. My research showed that some people become psychologically damaged on the SM scenes, and that because activities are illegal and stigmatised there is usually no support available from services to enable them to deal with difficulties (project (a)).

How do models of sexual citizenship relate to the three strands of citizenship discourse that I described earlier – (1) civic republicanism, (2) liberalism and (3) communitarianism?

(1) Civic republicanism is relevant to people who wish to be open about their sexuality and play a public role via activism or reform. This includes people involved in the sexual fringes (for example SM practitioners, fetishists, sex workers and polyamorous people). The notion of individual worth that is part of civic republicanism is important for models of sexual citizenship, especially because sexual minorities face stigmatisation and exclusion.

(2) Individual worth and autonomy are also central to liberal approaches to citizenship, providing a crucial basis for rights-based claims to citizenship. Rights-based citizenship claims have become increasingly prominent since the 1980s (Richardson 2000c). However, debates about the advisability of seeking equality with the heterosexual system (for example marriage rights) continue (Bell and Binnie 2000), with some people seeking to remain outside of the system. The separation between the public and private spheres that is so central to liberalism is, as discussed elsewhere, also problematic for sexual citizenship. In addition, the commodification of sexuality that is associated with neo-liberalism, and that is evident in the LGB, fetish and SM scenes, can be interpreted as both progressive and regressive. Lesbian, gay, and bisexual people, and SM practitioners, have all become more visible as citizens because of the way in which commodities specific to those people have been developed and marketed. However, other forces, such as gender, age, ability, and class, structure access to commodities so that the free arm of the market fails to operate equitably. State intervention to provide commodities concerning sexual expression, such as sex toys, is hardly likely to become possible (or necessarily desirable), but greater state intervention could be used to facilitate the equality of, for example, same-sex couples in areas such as housing.

(3) The third branch of mainstream citizenship discourse, communitarianism, is useful for sexual citizenship in the sense that it fosters a sense of community and interdependence – something that has long been a hallmark of the sexual minority communities, who have had to maintain a certain level of solidarity in order to survive. However, the values at the core of these communities – choice about sexual expression, pride in diversity, and opposition to mainstream sexual and family norms (in some cases) – clash with the moral conservatism of many communitarians, whose vision of community is based on heterosexual nuclear families and localised communities. Similarly, there is a long tradition of community activism and voluntary work within the sexual minority communities (who obviously

also contribute to the mainstream), but this may remain unrecognised by proponents of mainstream communitarianism. This is especially the case when the voluntary or care work is linked with illegal or particularly stigmatised activities, for example condom distribution for sex workers and men who cruise and cottage (find sexual partners in public spaces), drugs-related support work, or mutual social support within the fetish scenes. Bell and Binnie (2000) argue that the notions of obligation found in discourses of citizenship are problematic, because they involve the imposition of mainstream notions of morality on sexual dissidents. However, arguably, it is only the narrow notions of obligation and responsibility espoused by the mainstream that are the problem. Rights do entail responsibilities, it is just that we need a broader model of obligation, one based on support for diversity, self-definition, and freedom of expression without harm to others. As Weeks says: 'In the fluid politics of the post modern world, values are important for gluing together disparate political aims and objectives, and for providing a focus for the clarification of principles and policies' (1995: 43). A broader definition of obligations and responsibilities, which includes supporting sexual diversity, would impact on mainstream notions of citizenship and broaden them out, as well as supporting the sexual fringes.

CITIZENSHIP AND GENDER DIVERSITY

Mainstream approaches to citizenship, and the challenges to these made by feminists, have involved assumptions that there is a clear distinction between male and female categories. Authors in the fields of feminist and sexual citizenship either overlook gender diversity completely, or mention it only quite briefly (for example Bell and Binnie 2000). This section of the chapter will address trans (and to a lesser extent intersex) citizenship, beginning with a brief overview of the concerns central to trans citizenship, before addressing these using some of the concepts drawn from, first, mainstream models of citizenship, and, second, sexual citizenship. I explore trans citizenship more fully elsewhere (Monro 2003, Monro and Warren 2004).

As noted above, trans and intersex people are extremely diverse groups, making generalisation difficult. However, certain key themes emerge concerning claims to self-determination and equality (see Chapter 6), which can be discussed in relation to feminist citizenship. As shown in Chapter 2, trans and intersex involve the problematisation of gender binaries, either because people are somewhere in between male and female categories (intersex, androgynes, third sex/gender people), or because they at some time in their lives move between female and male identities (transsexuals, cross-dressers, drag kings and queens). Trans therefore entails the scrambling of the boundaries between mainstream and feminist citizenships – at times some trans people identify or present as male, thus presumably entering the space of mainstream citizenship, whereas at other times they take female roles, and enter the space of concern to feminist citizenship theorists. In addition, many transsexuals and cross-dressers do not always 'pass' as the desired gender, and therefore may inhabit multiple citizenship spaces. Intersex and androgynous people, third sex/gender people, and those who refuse to identify as any gender, remain outside the current remit of feminist citizenship theorists as well as mainstream theorists, despite the fact that, like women, they face discrimination because of their gender. Feminist approaches to citizenship are important for gender pluralist citizenship in that they foreground concerns that many trans women share with other women, and because of the debates which authors such as Lister (1997) have developed concerning public/private and diversity/universalism, which are relevant to trans people as well as non-trans women. However, as I have shown, binary-based feminisms are poorly equipped to address trans and intersex – post-structuralist feminist approaches are more useful for understanding trans citizenship, as the deconstruction/reconstruction of gender is a central part of trans experience, and because the notion of multiple categories of woman can be extended to include multiple gender categories or positions.

Trans and Mainstream Models of Citizenship

How does trans citizenship relate to the three strands of citizenship discourse outlined above: (1) civic republicanism, (2) liberalism and (3) communitarianism?

(1) The civic republican (and liberal) idea that individuals have equal worth is a potent one for trans and intersex people. However, for those people whose existence is completely invalidated in the West (including intersexes, androgynes, and third sex/gender people), the concept of equal individual worth is at present

unachievable. For these people, the participation in politics that is emphasised by civic republicans is very difficult to attain, not just because they do not inhabit a socially recognised category, but because they are often caught up in basic survival issues which entail taking a strategic female or male identity (see Chapter 3). Cross-dressers are also likely to have only limited participation, because their public identity is usually the male one, and the trans aspect is kept private. Participation is becoming easier for transsexuals in Western countries, and some other countries such as India, where the Hijra communities take part in politics (see Chapter 2). Another aspect of civic republicanism is the concept of duty, which is also problematic for some trans and intersex people, who may lack the means to meet civic obligations, although intersex and trans people do contribute to the wider communities in active and varied ways.

(2) The rights-based model of citizenship underpinned by liberalism is used as a framework by many trans activists (see Chapter 8). Clearly liberalism provides a useful set of discourses for trans people, but the emphasis on market liberalism can (as with sexuality) prove to be a double-edged sword. For example, the development of access to private surgery and hormone treatment for transsexuals in the UK has meant that the state provision has been forced to become more supportive of diversity. However, access to private treatment is limited to those with a substantial income. State provision is still necessary, meaning that liberalism must be tempered with an interventionist strategy.

(3) Communitarianism provides a useful set of discourses for trans and intersex people. Informal and formal social networks are important for many people, for support and activism as well as social reasons. I experienced a genuine sense of community during my research with trans and intersex people (projects (a) and (d)). There is also an acceptance of differences, although, in parallel with mainstream communitarianism, people with certain differences are sometimes marginalised or erased (see Chapter 5). The communitarian notion of the 'active citizen' was well developed amongst many of the people I interviewed, especially those at the more mainstream end of the trans communities. As noted above, people contributed to wider society, as well as the trans – and in some cases the feminist, lesbian, gay and bisexual – communities. Narratives concerning parenthood, artistic and academic achievements, and contributions

to the political process were all evident. However, as with sexuality, the contributions of these citizens may remain unrecognised if they are marginalised or face discrimination. In addition, there is perhaps a danger of constructing a 'nice trans person' model which then excludes the 'less nice' trans people: lesbian, gay and bisexual or polysexual trans people, sex workers, gender ambiguous and gender queer people, trans people with disabilities and mental health problems, trans people in custody and others. Also, there is a problem with overlooking contributions to the communities that do not fit the moral frameworks imposed by the mainstream, for example trans people taking part in gay and lesbian activism. So, whilst the notions of responsibility and community embodied in communitarianism are important for trans citizenship, there is a need to broaden out the dominant moral framework, and to also ensure that appeals to the mainstream do not ride roughshod over the needs of less 'respectable' trans people.

Trans, Intersex, and Sexual Citizenships

Some of the authors working in the field of sexual citizenship, especially Evans (1993) and Plummer (1995), have addressed certain forms of trans. Whilst useful, their discussions have mostly taken place in relation to sexuality. Although there are important overlaps between trans people's concerns and experiences and those of sexual minorities (see Chapter 5) there are obvious differences between most forms of trans and sexuality issues, because trans is primarily concerned with gender rather than desire (the only real exception is fetishistic cross-dressing, which I have discussed above). In addition, as argued in Chapter 2, trans and intersex scramble sexual orientation categories, provoking the broadening out of sexual orientation categories to include gender diversity, and/or the creation of new types of sexual orientation. Despite these issues, sexual citizenship provides a rich territory for gender diverse citizenship in its concerns with rights, transgression, morality, and the public–private divide. Notions such as Plummer's idea of intimate citizenship (1995) are particularly relevant, and Plummer explicitly includes self-determination concerning gender identity in his model of sexual citizenship. Some of the debates raised by sexual citizenship theorists can be transferred to trans citizenship, and this is what I will now attempt to do.

Richardson's (2000c) distinction between rights-oriented models of lesbian citizenship and models that broaden out the concept of citizenship itself is a useful one in relation to trans. Trans and intersex citizenships are frequently framed in terms of rights (see Chapters 4, 6 and 8). As noted previously, the problem with rights claims is that they may simply mean a replication of the dominant order, or assimilation of marginalised groups into the mainstream. This issue is particularly pronounced for trans people, as the majority of transsexuals wish to assimilate and would see no conflict between their interests and mainstream models of citizenship as based on the gender binary system, except insofar as the mainstream models need expanding to include transsexuals. The majority, mainstream approach tends, however, to erase the concerns of trans and intersex people who do not fit male and female categories. In addition, reform within the gender binary system involves convoluted legislative change, which is linked with homophobic processes in which lesbian, gay and bisexual rights are denied (see Sharpe 2002). A minority of transsexuals, and other trans people, wish to disrupt the dominant gender order and would not seek to frame their interests in terms of citizenship (see Chapter 8). These people would be more likely to build alliances with sexual dissidents, and to build their communities and power loci away from the mainstream.

Do trans and intersex citizenships broaden out mainstream citizenship? As described above, many transsexuals wish to fit into the mainstream, but this 'fitting in' does in itself widen the mainstream to an extent. Equal rights for transsexuals increase choice generally (people are perhaps more likely to see gender reassignment as a viable option) and they scramble non-trans people's assumptions about gender. Intersex, third sex/gender and androgyne rights would involve a very significant broadening out of mainstream models of citizenship (see Chapter 4). Cross-dresser's rights would entail changes to dress codes and for fetishistic cross-dressers, and alterations to the public–private divide (as described above).

CONCLUSION

This chapter has outlined some aspects of mainstream models of citizenship and analysed them in relation to feminist, sexual minority, and trans citizenships. I have used mainstream, feminist, and sexual citizenships as a basis for beginning to develop models of bisexual, SM/fetishist, and trans and intersex citizenship.

Feminist and sexual models of citizenship have developed in response to the inadequacies of mainstream models of citizenship, which overlook or marginalise women and sexual minorities, and foreground the male, heterosexual, white, able-bodied subject. However, feminist models of citizenship are themselves limited, in that they serve to erase subjects with identities that do not fit into male or female, or gay and straight, categories. Bisexual, SM/fetish-oriented, and trans people challenge the binaries on which feminist citizenship are based – but feminist models of citizenship remain important in supporting the rights of trans and non-trans women, as well as highlighting issues such as the public–private divide. There is a wide range of approaches to sexual citizenship, but there has been little analysis of bisexual citizenship, and existing work on fetishism and SM is limited. Bisexual citizenship focuses on concerns such as increasing bisexual visibility, creating support for same-sex relationships in a way that does not produce rigid categories, and polyamory. SM and fetish citizenships are concerned with equal rights for adults to participate in consensual fetish and SM activities, including group activities in semi-public places. Issues concerning morality are of particular importance to those interested in sexual citizenship; these concerns are shared across gender and sexual orientation categories, leading to calls for an expansion in mainstream notions of morality, underpinned by self-determination, consent, and care. Similarly, there has been a limited amount of work on trans and intersex citizenship. Central concerns are with rights claims and managing the destabilisation of gender and sexual orientation binaries that trans and intersex involve. These areas of citizenship can all be analysed using mainstream notions of citizenship. To summarise, civic republicanism supports those actors who wish to engage with public reform – but it fails to address the structural inequalities that affect people's ability to participate in the political process. Liberalism is important in providing a basis for rights claims and self-determination, but the separation of the public and private spheres that is central to liberalism is problematic in relation to gender and sexuality. Lastly, communitarianism is helpful in that it moves away from the individualism of the first two approaches, focusing on the interdependence of communities. This interdependence is a feature of some sections of the sexual and gender minority communities. Notions of contributing positively to society are also evident in these communities, but unfortunately communitarianism, with its narrow models of morality, often serves to exclude these groups.

8
Gender and Democracy

Democracy, in fact almost *any* government or politics, doesn't include me for the simple reason that I keep trying to change who and what I am every day of my life, and Democracy seeks to govern by the representation of some clearly (to them) defined 'average identity'.

Bornstein 1998: 270

Equality and self-determination are crucial for trans and bisexual politics. These concepts underpin democracy: 'Its basic premise is the idea of equal human worth or dignity, and its core value is that of human self determination or autonomy' (Beetham 1999: 7). However, mainstream models of democracy do not always support genuine equality. They are deeply gendered, foreground heterosexual men's lives and interests, and erase gender and sexual diversity. Mainstream approaches to democracy usually assume a male subject, or, as Carver (1998: 24, 25) notes, a neutral or de-gendered subject into which various characteristics of dominant masculinities (for example rationalism and individualism) are smuggled. Gender diversity is absent from both mainstream and feminist literatures on democracy, both of which tend to reiterate gender binaries, for example 'Democracy is government without heroes; ordinary women and men doing extraordinary things on a regular and continued basis' (Barber 1996: 155). Similarly, the democratic concerns of people with fluid sexualities tend to be overlooked – where sexuality is discussed, it is usually in terms of heterosexual, or, much less frequently, lesbian and gay, subjects.

It is tempting, in a discussion concerning gender and sexual diversity and democracy, to take feminist approaches as a starting point. This chapter, after all, aims to critique models of democracy in relation to gender, and to explore models of democracy that support the equality of people with diverse genders and sexualities (focusing on trans). Feminist theorists have ploughed a well-worn path through the rather turgid debates concerning democracy, developing analysis that can be used as a basis for theorising democracy in relation to trans and bisexuality. However, before looking at the feminist approaches to democracy, I would like to briefly outline mainstream positions, as discussions concerning mainstream models of democracy, particularly the advantages of representative versus direct, or participative democracy, are relevant to theorising gender diverse politics. The divisions between mainstream theorists and feminist ones are somewhat arbitrary; here, my objective is to provide an overview of some of the key concepts relevant to both, and to analyse the ways in which these concepts can be applied to gender diversity and sexual/gender fluidity.

This chapter addresses liberal, representative, direct, and participative models of democracy, before discussing them in relation to gender and sexual diversity, looking mostly at trans but including bisexuality to some extent. I then move on to discuss some of the key themes from the feminist literature on democracy, and the ways in which these might be used in theorising gender diverse democracy. It is important to point out that although I have found the academic discussions concerning democracy useful for understanding gender and sexual minority politics, some contributors to research project (d) felt that trans and bisexual politics were insufficiently developed to enable analysis in relation to different models of democracy. For instance, Giles suggested that

> bisexual politics is at such an early stage that it's hard to differentiate from campaigns for other rights, and I'm not sure that a differentiation between electoral or liberal democracy and participatory democracy is necessary – it is not an issue yet.

It is also worth noting that there are several bodies of literature that are relevant to discussions about gender diversity and democracy which I will not have space to include here, in particular, writing on democracy and globalisation (see for example Held 1995, Giddens 2001); sexuality, gender and the state (see for instance Mouffe 1992, Cooper 1995, and Waylen 1998); and governance (including Rhodes 1997 and Wilkinson and Hughes 2002). Lastly, it is important to contextualise this discussion, which is limited to the Western (specifically UK) situation. 'In 1975 at least 68 per cent of countries in the world were authoritarian; by the end of 1995 about 26 per cent were authoritarian' (Potter 1997: 1). Whilst many authoritarian countries have poor human rights records with respect to gender and sexual minorities (see Baird 2001), the existence of a democracy does not necessarily mean that rights will be in place. As journalist Chua (2004) argues, the export of Western-style capitalist democracy can have a very damaging effect on the rights of women and minority groups in poorer countries in which democracies have not been able to develop over time.

DEMOCRACY: AN OVERVIEW

The notion of democracy has undergone a considerable amount of construction and deconstruction since it was invented by the ancient Greeks (Parry and Moran 1994: 2). Beetham acknowledges the multiple definitions of the term, and provides a useful mainstream interpretation. He sees 'democracy' as concerning the space in which collectively binding decisions are made, with popular control and political equality forming the key principles of democracy (1999: 5). There are a wide range of different (overlapping) forms of democracy: associative democracy (Hirst 1993), deliberative democracy (Miller 1993) and strong democracy (Barber 1984) as well as others (see Phillips 1991, 1993). There are various ways of classifying them. Held (1995), for instance, identifies the conflict within democratic theory between popular power and participation versus electoral representation, suggesting that this has given rise to three models of democracy – direct or participatory democracy, liberal or representative democracy, and one-party democracy. I will focus on only some models of democracy (representative and liberal, participatory and direct), using the representative–participative continuum as a means of plotting out some of the key characteristics of mainstream models of democracy. I would like to acknowledge here the difficulties with placing diverse writers and theories within such a broad typology, as well as the limitations associated with dividing concepts of democracy up in this way (see Phillips 1991: 12).[1] I would also like to note that although I will not discuss deliberative democracy (in which space for discussion and deliberation forms a central part of democracy) in any depth here, findings indicate its importance to gender and sexual minority politics – for instance contributor Ann Goodley said that 'I think we should have a dialogue with legislators as they make terrible mistakes. Communication is the name of the game.'

Representative and Liberal Democracy

> Representative democracy constituted the key institutional innovation to overcome the problem of balancing coercive power and liberty. The liberal concern with reason, lawful government and freedom of choice could only be upheld properly by recognising the political equality of all mature individuals. Such equality would ensure not only a secure social environment in which people would be free to pursue their private activities and interests, but also a state which, under the watchful eye of political representatives accountable to an electorate, would do what is best in the general or public interest.
>
> Held 1995: 9

Liberal or representative democracy is a means of rule in which elected individuals 'represent' the interests of citizens whilst maintaining the rule of law (Held 1995: 5).[2] Liberalism is defined by individualism (in which people are seen as self-interestedly pursuing their own separate goals), the protection of basic rights, a separation of the public and private realms, and a limited role for the state (Phillips 1991). Such principles as equal respect for persons, equality before the law, and equal civil and political rights of citizens are central to liberalism, and embodied in different degrees in the structures of all liberal-democratic states (Parekh 1994: 199). Elected governments and equal voting rights are seen as the minimum criteria for a liberal democracy (Phillips 1991: 10).

Liberalism can be seen as problematic for anyone who is not white, Western, male, able-bodied and heterosexual. For example, it overlooks the way in which some non-Western societies have communal, rather than individualistic, cultural norms. There are critiques of the way in which liberal democracy marginalises lesbian, gay and bisexual people – for instance Wilson (1995) analyses the way in which liberal democracy is based on notions of a heterosexual nuclear family (in which the man takes a public role and the family and sexuality are privatised). Liberalism has also been criticised for placing limits on governments, so that, whilst protecting individual freedoms, it sustains inequalities, as power and resources are unequally distributed (Phillips 1991: 15). Overall, as contributor Roz Kaveney says:

> Part of the problem is the liberal democracy has never entirely fulfilled its own prospectus – in theory it is all about bringing progressively larger

groups of minorities into public life, and inevitably there's always lack. Liberal democracy is an institution and a process – one of the problems is that in order to get in and tinker with the gears of liberal democracy, if you belong to a group that's excluded, you have to put yourself through shit.

There are strong approaches to liberal democracy which address some of the difficulties with liberalism. For example Parekh (1993, 1994) discusses cultural pluralism, which concerns the way in which culturally distinct groups, including immigrants, indigenous ethnic minorities and religious groups seek cultural space in which to live their lifestyles and make distinct contributions to communal life. He notes that demands for the acknowledgement of cultural diversity can come from groups with shared, self-chosen lifestyles, including lesbian and gay men (see Parekh 1993, 1994). He describes cultural pluralism as welcoming diversity because it broadens individuals' horizons and argues that this is valuable because it increases cultural richness, and our life choices, self-awareness and capacity for empathy. Parekh (1993, 1994) describes cultural pluralism as a collective good, which requires state support in order to protect and promote it – action to protect cultural minorities against discrimination, mitigate against the dominance of mainstream assumptions about identity and behaviour, and support minority cultures, for example the teaching of minority languages. Parekh also describes the limits to permissible diversity, which, for liberals, involve, first, individual autonomy and whether minority customs contravene this; second, non-harm – practices which harm others should be banned; and third, fundamental social values (1994: 214). He discusses the way in which the notion of core values is problematic – core values are hard to define and open to dispute. However, he suggests a set of 'operative public values' – values which society aims to live by, including equal respect, human dignity, freedom for dissent, secure spaces for self-determination, and the pursuit of collective self-interest. These discussions are important in dealing with the homogenising tendencies of liberalism, in which white male heterosexuality is assumed to be the norm.

To sum up, liberal and representative forms of democracy involve individualism, state protection of basic rights, a separation of the public and private spheres, and representation of the populace via elections. There are a number of difficulties with liberal and representative democracies, which can be dealt with to an extent by stronger forms of liberalism, which support diversity via increased state intervention.

Participatory Democracy

Modern participatory, strong and radical models of democracy developed as a critique of liberal models of democracy. Participatory democracy differs from liberal approaches in a number of ways. 'Direct or participatory democracy, [is] a system of decision-making about public affairs in which citizens are directly involved' (Held 1995: 5). Participatory democracy usually redefines the focus of democracy, challenging the public–private distinction, and extending beyond the traditional concern with party politics (Phillips 1991: 11, 16). In this respect, it overlaps with feminist approaches to democracy; feminists have traditionally questioned the public–private divide that is basic to liberal democracy. Mouffe, for instance, envisages the increasing extension of democratic principles into the realm of the social, so that more equality and liberty is achievable in all realms. She calls for democracy to be freed from 'the individualistic and rationalistic premises that have become fetters to democracy in its current form' (1992: 3). Participatory democracy entails greater citizen involvement in the political process, such as attendance at party meetings and participation in workplace management and government (Parry and Moyser 1994: 46).[3]

Needless to say, the extent to which democracy is participative varies between countries, with a greater emphasis on achieving social and economic equality present in Europe, and more emphasis on participation in the US (Phillips 1993: 3). In the UK, in recent years there has been a governmental drive towards democratic renewal which has combined aspects of both representative and participative democracy: proposals to improve electoral turnout as well as guidelines aimed at increased levels of citizen participation in local government (Leach and Wingfield 1999), although there is ambiguity concerning the extent to which citizen participation is supported. '[T]here is a world of difference between different forms of so-called citizen participation, which may range from tokenism, through information provision and consultation, to shared or delegated power over certain decisions' (Leach and Wingfield 1999: 47). Participation may be limited – an issue that may be compounded by issues concerning self-interest and parochialism amongst grass-roots activists (see Phillips 1993: 13).

Participatory and direct forms of democracy provide a vital alternative (or complement) to liberal and representative types of democracy. Electoral politics is limited in terms of citizen engagement, whereas there are various means of influencing the political process using the tools of participatory democracy. Notions of moving the remit of politics beyond the public sphere are also useful, although as I shall argue below, not without problems.

GENDER AND SEXUAL DIVERSITY AND DEMOCRACY

How useful are the different models of democracy for trans and bisexual politics? As we have already seen, trans activists span a wide political spectrum. One noticeable theme is the rejection of mainstream politics by some authors and activists, usually linked with the adoption of queer politics or anarchism. I will look at this type of approach first, as it is central to the 'transgressive' approach to gender politics, and then address liberal and participative approaches.

Anarchist and Queer

I have categorised anarchist and queer politics together in this section, because both involve disrupting mainstream categories and institutions. Queer and anarchist LGBT people include Bornstein, who argues that:

> The laws in this land [the US] in which I'm living now are derived democratically. That means they're made by other people who are supposed to have my best interests at heart. Well, the fact is that I cannot marry a woman in this country. The fact is that a transgendered child on the street is not going to be cared for by the social machinery created by the people who are supposed to have hir best interests at heart ... it boils down to this: democracy and outlaws of any stripe don't mix up very well together. (1998: 269)

Bornstein does not argue for a widespread flouting of all social rules, rather, for the disobeying of cultural rules concerning gender (1998: 272). As Whittle (1996: 211) says,

> Bornstein argues that the transgendered person as a gender outlaw causes the destruction of the gendered system of reality on which most people base major aspects of their lives ... she proposes a play with gender partitioning to ultimately make the partitions meaningless.

Bornstein also argues for a personal anarchy, which does not involve rules, regulations or constitutions, thereby rejecting the trappings of liberal, and some forms of participatory, democracy. Here, the force behind trans politics comes from the grass roots, rather than the top-down approach that is led by policy-makers or politicians, or political engagement moderated via fora and consultation mechanisms. As Stryker says:

> This new [transgender] visibility is attributable directly to the global, grassroots transgender political mobilization of the 1990s, which has made living a transgendered life more socially feasible. Consequently, self-proclaimed transgender voices increasingly participate in discussions of transgender phenomenon in any number of cultural contexts, often in ways that fundamentally affect the circulation of transgender discourses. (1998: 147)[4]

What are the advantages of anarchist and queer theories in relation to gender, sexuality, and democracy?

- an emphasis on autonomy and self-determination;
- enabling people to live (partially) outside of the institutions that shape our social reality;
- avoidance of co-option and assimilation, which can be a problem for community groups that engage with the mainstream political process;
- the ability to create alternative social spaces, for instance spaces where multiple or fluid genders and sexualities are welcome;
- community building, and the development of alliances with other 'outsider' groups.

Overall, within an already democratic society, Western transgressive gender politics act to shake up social institutions that perpetuate inequalities, forming a crucial plank in the movement for equality. However, there are a number of limitations to anarchist and queer approaches, including (1) their individualism; (2) a tendency to vanguardism; and (3) an apparent rejection of the political frameworks that enable self-determination and equality. I will address these in turn

(1) The individualism of some of the 'outlaw' discourses is demonstrated by the quotes and exercises in the section of Bornstein's book which concerns democracy, which emphasise individual gender role transgression, for instance 'I'm a lipstick lesbian [who uses] power tools and work boots' (Bornstein 1998: 270). This individualism translates into something that looks suspiciously like liberalism, and does not necessarily challenge structural inequalities. In addition, however, (as with much feminist and participative politics) the personal is the political – but this is likely to be a limited strategy

without proactive engagement with mainstream society. As trans woman Caroline <http://www.spunk.org/texts/pubs/lr/sp001714/gender.html> suggests, 'The transgender movement needs to broaden its analysis of oppression, while striking at the institutions that oppress us. A transgender "free space" is important. However, that space won't mean much if we don't become committed to challenging wider society.' In other words, the trans communities need to think beyond the individual's personal rights and freedoms, towards challenging socially embedded gender roles and the institutions that support them. Engagement with wider society is crucial, because transgender politics takes place within a much wider social, economic and cultural context.

(2) Anarchist and queer forms of trans politics risk valorising certain types of gender identity. Anarchist trans people are aware of this – for example Caroline (above) describes the way that 'For many anti-authoritarians there may be some temptation to "smash gender" or "destroy" gender roles ... I believe this too leads to an alternative form of authoritarianism' (as it is unrepresentative of the whole trans community).

(3) Western anarchist or queer trans (and other) people could be criticised for failing to acknowledge and support the liberal democratic system, which, however limited, does enable free speech and a certain level of autonomy and self-expression for trans people and sexual minorities.

Liberal

Trans and bisexual activist discourses often have a liberal flavour. For example, most trans activists seek to be treated equally to other citizens (see for instance Whittle 2002), whilst some of the research contributors explicitly appealed to liberal notions such as fairness and non-harm (projects (a), (b), and (d)). For instance:

> We need to participate in the struggle for comprehensive across-the-board anti-discrimination measures and ensure that any such laws specifically include us; we need to join in the struggle for all long-term partnerships to be recognized; we need to join in the struggle for an ethic of fair and just treatment for all in a just society. (Kaveney 1999: 157)

> What interests me about organisations like PFC [Press For Change] is that they are immanent. They represent people saying 'for us, in our circumstances, this won't do, and we are going to assert out reasonable

right to have a voice and to make arguments and be heard'. And if the arguments get smacked down then so be it, that is the nature of democracy. (Pamela Summers)

There are a number of other aspects of liberalism that are relevant to discussions of democracy and trans politics, including individualism, autonomy and self-determination. In addition, stronger approaches involve the recognition of cultural diversity as a collective good, and state intervention to support diversity. Liberalism also entails discussions about the limits to permissive diversity. I shall address these points in turn.

Individualism, Autonomy and Self-Determination

Calls for equality and self-determination are crucial for trans and bisexual politics. For example, a number of authors (including Dreger 2000 and Feinberg 1996) discuss the lack of autonomy and self-determination experienced by intersex people, because they are often operated on in infancy and sometimes also deceived about their condition. However, whilst self-determination is clearly crucial for sexual and gender minority politics, there are some difficulties with liberal notions of autonomy. First, liberal approaches ignore the historical and social conditions that produce particular preferences. Second, they may serve some people but not others (for example, transsexuals changing sex fully as opposed to those who are unsure or remain fluid), given a political context in which certain identities are recognised and others are not. Third, as contributor Roz Kaveney notes, communities such as the bisexual polyamorous and SM scenes involve a high level of interpersonal interdependence in terms of relationships, mutual support, and internal policing (for example ensuring that SM relationships are consensual). This means that the individualistic stance that characterises liberal democracy is problematic for some sections of the gender and sexual minority communities, because members operate in a less individualistic way than many mainstream actors. In addition, as Phillips (1991: 8) points out, liberalism can be criticised for assuming that individuals will pursue their own self-interest. Research with trans and LGB people showed that this is clearly not always the case. People showed, in some cases, considerable empathy with others and willingness to support the causes of others (all projects).

Representation

It is difficult to assess the extent to which elections serve the interests of trans people. As minorities, facing a substantial amount of prejudice from majority groups, elections are not necessarily going to serve their needs (although of course trans and bisexual people have interests other than those concerning gender and sexuality). However, some of the contributors did discuss the importance of elections, for instance:

> electoral politics has a role – two elections ago Paddy Ashdown was being questioned about equal rights and he said he supported the equal age of consent, and that is the sort of thing that makes you lean towards a particular party ... even if there are no bisexual people in parliament at least we can say there are gay ministers. (Giles)

Cowen and Daly (1999) argue that political representation is crucial in preventing the most articulate and powerful members of the public from dominating the political process, and as a means of preventing the marginalisation of social groups. Representation of sexual and gender minorities is particularly important because of the small numbers of individuals involved, and current levels of exclusion.

Strong Liberalism and Cultural Pluralism

Stronger approaches to liberalism, which support the autonomy and self-determination of excluded groups, are very compatible with the project of gender and sexual equality. For example, contributor Roz Kaveney argues for an expanded liberal democracy, in which people with fluid or mixed identities are seen as valued members of society because identity complexity is accepted. Strong approaches to democracy overlap with the pluralist models of democracy discussed below, as does cultural pluralism. Cultural pluralism provides one way of framing gender diversity within a liberal paradigm, because of its emphasis on valuing diversity, diversity as a common good, and state intervention to support diversity. However, cultural pluralism could risk reinforcing divisions between different cultural or social groups. It could also mean that transgender and sexual minority groups are separated away from the mainstream, so that any challenges they might pose are nullified (see Evans

1993), a problem endemic to multiculturalism. In addition, authors such as Parekh (1993, 1994) fail to address conflicts between the cultures of different minorities, a problem of great pertinence to transgender and sexual minority communities, given the fundamentalist Christian and Islamic assaults on sexual and gender diversity. In order to address this issue we need to fall back on some of the core tenets of liberalism. As Beetham (1999: 15) says, 'that capacity [to be different] also sets limits to the cultural practices of others that can be endorsed by the principles of equal respect, and would exclude, for example, the subordination of women'; principles of equal respect for others mean taking a critical approach to cultural practices that infringe on this.

Permissive Diversity

Issues concerning the limitations of strong liberalism and cultural pluralism are crystallised in discussions concerning permissiveness. The spectre of permissiveness remains a source of worry for people who are concerned about the deterioration of 'traditional values' concerning gender and sexuality. As noted above, Parekh (1993, 1994) outlines the limits to permissive diversity as concerning non-harm and individual autonomy. In other words, actions that could harm others or infringe on their processes of self-determination, for example forcing a boy to wear dresses, would be considered unacceptable within a strong liberal approach to democracy. In general, alternative forms of gender expression, such as gender fluid identities, are not harmful to others and could in fact be seen as contributing to the greater good, because they enrich the social landscape and provide a wider range of possibilities for self-expression. However, non-trans traditionalists might argue that any form of trans is threatening to the social order, whilst trans traditionalists might see gender ambiguous or fluid identities as similarly threatening. These debates are ongoing, the central tension being between the perceived well-being of minorities and the perceived well-being of majority groups. The best working solution appears to be one that supports diversity – both mainstream and other identities. As contributor Pamela Summers said, people will continue to engage in heterosexual reproduction but that does not mean that heterosexual and gender binaried identities are better than other ways of being.

Overall, there are a number of aspects of liberal models of democracy that are relevant to gender and sexual diversity. These include core values, such as equality, fairness, and autonomy, which are found in much trans and bisexual activist discourse. The form that liberal democracy takes, representation via elections, is useful to sexual and gender minorities, because it can be used to support a certain amount of inclusion and representation. In other words, sexual and gender minorities can express their concerns by voting for people who represent these – but voting is limited in its effects, especially if there are no politicians who represent the interests of gender and sexual minorities. Stronger approaches to liberalism, which actively support diversity and welcome the cultural richness that this allows, are of greater use to gender and sexual minorities, although there is a risk of encouraging factionalism if difference is overemphasised. Strong democracy provokes questions about permissiveness and conflicts between the interests of different communities, which can be addressed by reinstating the core values of liberalism, although debates will be ongoing.

Participatory Democracy

As I have shown, participatory democracy emphasises higher levels of citizen participation in the political process and increased state intervention in order to protect and support minorities. State intervention via legislative protection, support for anti-discriminatory measures such as anti-harassment strategies in the workplace and housing, and the resourcing of the transgender and LGB community sector are clearly important for transgender politics (see Chapter 4). However, higher levels of citizen participation, whilst a worthy goal, do involve some difficulties, including problems with achieving real participation and with ensuring that different sections of minority groups are adequately represented by the participatory process. Here, I will look briefly at some of the issues concerning trans and bisexual participation in the UK (see also Monro 2003) and some of the difficulties with participatory approaches to trans and bisexual democracy.

The traditional participatory model of democracy involves citizen participation via, for example, workplace organisation. For example Kirsch (2000: 120–1) lists a number of strategies for overcoming the oppression of queer and other peoples, including democracy in the workplace, and movements to include discussion of diversity, gender and sexuality within public curricula. Research indicates the existence of such structures. For instance, findings from project (b) showed that LGBT (or lesbian and gay or LGB) workers fora had been established in a few local authorities, and that these provided support for workers and a space for organising concerning equality, for example pension rights. The creation of fora that aim to feed directly into the policy process is also an important facet of participatory democracy. This has taken place in the UK at both national, and, to an extent, local levels. In the UK, central government established an Interdepartmental Working Group on Transsexual People in 1999 <http://www.lcd.gov.uk/constitution/transsex/tpeople.htm> and this body has representatives from a number of trans groups. An example of the type of participatory democracy espoused by New Labour, it has enabled trans people to achieve greater participation and influence on policy-making and implementation than was possible in the past. The network of organisations and support groups concerning trans, and also LGB, people in the UK is crucial for participatory democracy in this field, partly because it provides a space in which rights issues can be discussed, and partly because public fora and consultation mechanisms rely on the voluntary and community sector to provide community representatives.

There are some problems with participatory democracy for gender diverse people and sexual minorities. There is a severe lack of public investment in the trans and LGB community and voluntary sectors in the UK. Findings from project (b) indicated that a strong community sector was crucial for LG/LGBT representation – where the sector was weak, consultation mechanisms struggled. Structural inequalities may block engagement (see Chapter 2). In addition, there are problems with criticising the public–private divide and arguing that 'the personal is political', as many people, first, wish for much of their life to remain private, and second, do not want to engage in the public political realm. As contributor Roz Kaveney argues: 'I agree with the need for a public–private divide – what is necessary is a level playing field. It's oppressive to force everyone to take part in politics.' Although difficulties with dissolving the public–private divide are a general concern, they are particularly relevant to trans and LGB people because of the levels of discrimination these groups face, as well as the absence of viable social identities for people who wish to identify as other than male or female. Furthermore many cross-dressers and fetishists prefer to maintain these identities as private, in other words they are not 'out' about these identities and do not use them as a basis for activism. As contributor Roz Kaveney suggests:

Being an outlaw community is part of the SM community identity – this community would not want a breakdown of the public–private divide. It is even more the case for smaller minority communities ... the other thing about the public–private divide is that there are all sorts of private spheres that aren't really private. People tend to see the public–private divide as a divide between party politics and the nuclear family. There's a lot more to the private sphere – this also relates to the multicultural critique of individualism.

It seems therefore that simply arguing for dissolution of a perceived public–private divide is untenable. Perhaps, following Phillips (1993), what is needed is a revitalisation of the public sphere, for example investment in trans and LGB community organisations and an infrastructure to support them.

Other problems with participatory democracy, such as 'the conflict ... between raising levels of participation and ensuring that all groups have an equal say' (Phillips 1991: 18) are clearly relevant to the engagement of gender and sexual minorities. Most trans and LGB organisations aim to operate democratically – for instance, the UK organisation Press For Change has elected representatives. Many also seek to be representative of their diverse members – for instance bisexual contributor Kerry noted that 'the bi community is very disability aware, more than anywhere I've seen. It is probably because some people have been aware of things being needlessly difficult for them in the past.' However, problems achieving adequate representation of communities did seem to be a common theme (projects (b) and (d)). For instance:

It's so personal [bisexuality], so much of yourself is on the line, so that you end up with vocal, loud, confident people in the groups – you won't get the voices of those who feel less sure, or threatened. (Jane)

It certainly can be unrepresentative – we [the bisexual community] are unrepresentative of bisexual people, for example rural bisexuals or small town bisexuals. Our community groups are incredibly valuable but they generally happen once a month in cities ... there are elements – mental health issues, social skills issues, that don't fit the bisexual model ... there are certainly issues of 'coolness' in [a particular group]. (John)

Some contributors discussed ways of tackling problems of representation; for example the coordinator of a LGB infrastructure organisation discussed the way in which he does not claim to represent their members, but said 'what you can do is try to be representative'.

Overall, there are a number of approaches to politics concerning gender and sexual diversity, including anarchist and queer, liberal, and participative approaches. Anarchist and queer strategies are helpful in disrupting normative structures concerning gender, but risk individualism and a lack of political efficacy. Liberal approaches have a number of advantages, in particular the universal appeal of calls for equality, and strong forms of liberalism appear to provide a useful vehicle for gender and sexual minorities. However, weak liberalism is limited in clout, and, as with participatory and direct democracy, the particularism of strong liberalism could be divisive. Participatory and direct democracy are crucial for gender and sexual minority politics, but difficulties with achieving representativeness and with the erosion of the public–private divide are ongoing. Whilst some of the above models, especially anarchist/queer and liberal, are likely to conflict, there are also some substantial over-laps (for example anarchist/queer and liberal models all tend to reject state involvement in managing sexual/gender diversity). It is important to note that in practice many activist organisations utilise methods pertaining to different forms of democracy. For example, a representative of Stonewall (LGB rights organisation) said that:

> We try and harness the power of the communities when we run campaigns. We lobby MPs and the House of Lords members. But, for example, in the campaign to get rid of section 28 we went to nightclubs and gave out postcards ... we try and bridge the gap and give voice. We quite often go to consultations and can provide information from the community.

FEMINISM AND DEMOCRACY

Gender deconstruction and fluidity are central to trans and bisexual politics, as are concerns with the universalism–diversity debate. Feminist scholars have provided concepts that are relevant to dis-cussions of these areas. Here, I will draw on the work of feminists in order to begin to develop analysis of trans and bisexual democracy. This section begins with a brief overview of feminist writing con-cerning democracy, before addressing gender fluidity, multiplicity, and universalism versus diversity debates, which are important to trans and bisexual democracy.

Background to Feminist Notions of Democracy

As Phillips (1991) says, the traditions of feminism and democracy share an interest in equality, and early feminists recognised a link between democracy and feminism. However, there has also been a sustained feminist challenge concerning the gendering of models of democracy. In the early Western societies that are seen as the spawning ground of democracy, theorists of democracy acknowledged women, but they were constructed as second-class citizens belonging in the private sphere (Lister 1997). The models of democracy that developed appeared to have universal appeal, but in fact concentrated on the public sphere and the interests of men. So, 'many feminists now see sexual inequality as something built into the very foundations of both classical and contemporary thought' (Phillips 1991: 3) (see Chapter 7).

Feminist discussions about democracy have developed along a number of lines. One of these critiques liberal, universalist models of democracy as involving masculine values, for example 'a psychology of competitive self-interest in material things, rationality and individualism' (see Carver 1998: 24, 25). Here, feminist models of democracy foreground women's supposedly different notions of morality and subjectivity (see Phillips 1991: 4). However, the idea of 'women's values' is problematic, because values such as empathy are not restricted to women; arguably, naming them as 'women's values' reinforces gender binaries. It could be argued that the attachment of certain values to gender is too slippery to be of much use in modelling democracy.[5] The feminist notion of women's embodiment as being important for models of democracy (see Phillips 1991, 1993) is also problematic. Women's experiences of embodiment are diverse, and supposedly shared characteristics such as menstruation and childbirth are neither standard for all women nor restricted to women, as some trans men and intersex people experience these. Whilst embodiment and democracy are worthy topics of investigation, gendering this in a binaried way is somewhat untenable. Therefore, rather than addressing 'women's values' and embodiment here, I shall explore two themes: gender categorisation and fluidity, and universalism versus diversity, before moving on to a discussion of radical pluralism.

Gender Categorisation and Fluidity

As I have already shown, one of the key issues for understanding trans and bisexual equality concerns the tension between categories as prisons, which restrict people, and categories as necessary in order to enable people to develop their identities and identity politics. I have argued that feminist approaches often, in attempting to redress the imbalance caused by the mainstream exclusion of women, end up reifying gender divisions (see Chapter 2). Feminist authors such as Nash (1998) address the difficulties faced by theorists who seek to supersede gender categories but, by naming those categories, reinforce them, a theme that has played a central role in this book. This is a crucial issue for trans democracy, partly because it is the reinforcement of gender binaries that acts to exclude gender ambiguity and trans people, but also because the problem of naming a category and thereby reinforcing it is centrally relevant to trans politics. Do transsexuals take a public position as transsexual, thus reinforcing an identity that many seek to drop once they have transitioned? Do people who are gender ambiguous adopt third or other sexes/genders as social positions from which to make rights claims, or would this, first, lead to ghettoisation, and, second, act to reinforce gender categorisation in a way that some activists and theorists would reject? On the other hand, does failing to foreground transsexual, gender ambiguous, fluid, or multiple positions mean that masculinist universalism or assumptions about gender binarism continue?

Following discussions within feminism (as above), it is clear that the public adoption of identities that are visible and that form a basis for organisation is politically efficacious. As Carver says, 'working from the category of "women" has been and should continue to be successful' (1998: 27). Taking public identities is certainly crucial for transsexual politics; visibility has normalised trans (Whittle 1998a: 8–9). As Kaveney says, 'We cannot claim freedom from discrimination as transsexuals by denying that we are transsexuals. Disappearing into invisibility is escaping … it will fail as a defence from oppression' (1999: 150). Being 'out' as a transsexual man or woman, whilst problematic (given the level of discrimination that transsexuals face) is now a social possibility in some contexts. This is not generally true, however, of some other identities – gender fluid, gender ambiguous, or multiply gendered. As discussed previously, adoption of these identities is highly contentious within the trans communities, and practically unheard of within the mainstream in the UK. Whether fluid and multiple positions remain liminal and hidden, or become socially viable through visibility and activism, remains to be seen. Arguably, the latter would provide space for people of all genders to explore different gender identities – identities that are at present absent due to a lack of any categorisation at all, so that the gender binary system remains universal by default. The issue of whether non-categorisation and fluidity can be socially viable identities remains, but, arguably, it is impossible to make rights claims if a subject position is not taken (see Chapter 2). These issues also apply to bisexuality and other sexual orientations such as polysexuality, except insofar as some bisexuals and others move fluidly between different sexualities rather than having long-term identities with more serious social implications.

Universalism and Diversity

> The 'politics of universalism' aims at the equalisation of rights, entitlements and immunities for everyone, or, at least, for every citizen. The politics of difference, on the other hand, aims at recognizing the unique identity of concrete individuals and groups, their distinctness from everyone else.
>
> Axtman 1996: 92

Universalism versus diversity debates are important to exploring democracy in relation to gender and sexual minorities. This section builds on the discussions in Chapter 5 about universalism and particularism. I will focus here on universalism, discussing diversity more fully in the section on radical pluralism. According to Young, universalism entails citizens being defined by what they have in common, rather than differences, as well as universally binding rules and laws (see 1990: 114). 'It may signify the philosophical belief that there is a fundamental human nature or human essence that defines who we are as humans' (Benhabib 2002: 26). As Young (2001: 203) says, notions of universal humanity that override differences have been central to the struggle against social exclusion and status differentiation, making claims for equal rights possible.

In recent years, oppressed groups have rejected universalism and the assimilation that goes with it, and asserted separate group identities and interests that affirm difference as a positive thing (Young 2001). There are general difficulties with universalism. Insisting on a form of equality that ignores difference may perpetuate social exclusion. 'Blindness to difference disadvantages groups whose experience, culture, and socialized capacities differ from those of privileged groups' (Young 2001: 207); bringing marginalised groups into the mainstream means that they have to play by the rules already established by more powerful groups. The notion of universalism also allows privileged groups to ignore their own specificity, so that their values and norms appear to be neutral and universal (Young 2001: 208).

Universalism is problematic for conceptualising trans democracy because it masks the specificity of trans concerns, especially those that fall within the private sphere, such as health issues, partnership and reproduction, as well as the contributions of the trans community networks, some of which fall outside of the public sphere because people are closeted. Similarly, universalism overrides the interests of people who have same-sex desires and relationships, and overlooks issues that are especially relevant to bisexuals, such as visibility, sexual orientation fluidity, and polyamory. Universalism perpetuates the framing of political concerns in assimilationist terms, and risks the erasure of subjectivities that disrupt this. It allows discrete male and female categorisation to be normalised, because male and female categories are seen as universal and subsequently privileged. Similarly, monosexual orientations (predominantly heterosexuality) are framed as ordinary, with fluid or multiple orientations being stigmatised in a number of ways (see Chapter 5). Non-trans men and women and heterosexuals may continue to assume that their own gender and sexual identities are normal and universal, with anything else being seen as a deviation. Alternatives to the binary systems, such as polyamory, are usually framed as too radical for consideration. The more radical trans communities, and the queer and bisexual communities, break this cycle by affirming the possibility of gender and sexual fluidity and multiplicity. This is effective to an extent – as Young says,

> In a political struggle where oppressed groups insist on the positive value of their specific culture and experience, it becomes increasingly difficult for dominant groups to parade their norms as neutral and universal, and to construct the values and behaviour of the oppressed as deviant, perverted and inferior. (2001: 209)

Despite the difficulties with universalism, appeal to universal values such as equality is crucial for gender and sexual minorities. A universalism that is expanded to include gender and sexuality minorities in an equal way is one strategy for dealing with the tensions between universalism and particularism. As contributor Roz Kaveney argues:

> A particularist stance is problematic because it could lead, for example, to religious fundamentalists arguing for separate social space ... we need the

same rights universally applied. I think the standard Enlightenment model was right – there is a debate in the USA about how 'the forefathers couldn't have meant "x" groups being involved'. But the founding fathers didn't know anything.

Another, similar, way of addressing the limitations of universalism is to fuse universalist and particularist (diversity-based) approaches. Benhabib (2002: 33–7) suggests a global 'pluralistically enlightened ethical universalism', because norms of universal respect and egalitarian reciprocity provide guidelines for the process of managing cultural interdependencies. Mouffe (1993) argues for some level of universalism because democracy requires a certain amount of homogeneity – the acceptance of political principles by citizens. At the same time she maintains an anti-essentialist view of identity as contingent and shifting. Mouffe (1993) rejects notions of gender specific democratic citizenship – the idea that citizenship must be gendered in order to account for differences between the sexes. For Mouffe, this would mean essentialising identities and fixing notions of 'women'; although there is a certain amount of identity, particularism, and relational fixity involved in Mouffe's notion of radical politics – for example she does not see maternity rights as gender neutral. Political positions that balance diversity and universalism are also found amongst writers in the field of sexuality, in particular Weeks (1995), who discusses radical humanism as involving a balancing of diversity against common values (such as equality and care). Some mainstream theorists of democracy, for example Beetham (1999: 15), also argue that liberalism supports diversity, as 'the capacity for self-determination is precisely a capacity to be different, both individually and collectively, and a claim to have these differences respected by others'. Some of the research findings from project (d) supported the fusion of universalist and particularist approaches, for instance:

Interviewer: *What are the advantages of 'one size fits all' versus diversity oriented approaches?*

Contributor: My view would be that you need a bit of both. Just as we need the rights that heterosexuals have, but not all heterosexuals agree with marriage. It's about creating new approaches that might be relevant to heterosexuals and also to bisexual and trans people. But at the same time, it

> still needs to be about equality. Maybe there needs to be a
> minimal level of rights – something that is equivalent, not
> just the same. It is difficult, but, for example, me taking
> time off for childcare isn't relevant – but taking time off to
> care for older parents is. (Coordinator, LGB consortium)

Radical Pluralism

Broadly, radical pluralism offers an epistemological, ontological and normative perspective that straddles liberal individualism, communitarianism,
Gramscian Marxism, feminisms, post-colonialism, lesbian and gay studies and
poststructuralism.

Cooper 2000: 1063

Another way of resolving the dichotomy between universalism and
diversity is via radical pluralism. Radical pluralism draws an emphasis on notions such as privacy, consent, and state recognition of
diversity from liberalism, whilst the idea that people are part of communities is drawn from communitarianism. There is also a focus on
social meanings and power, and the possibilities offered by radical
pluralism for discursive change (Cooper 2000: 1063). So, drawing on
post-structuralism, authors such as McClure argue that ' "politics"
is not simply the projection of group "interests" onto the screen of
social policy, but indeed precedes this in the intricate processes of
articulation through which such identities, representations, and rights
claims are themselves constructed' (1992: 121). Subjectivity is also
problematised, so that there is an 'increased insistence on a multiplicity of perspectives and values: a growing recognition that, while
individuals may and do change their beliefs and values, there is noth-
ing that guarantees convergence over some basic or unifying concerns' (Phillips 1993: 142). Contingency, difference, and contestation
are foregrounded, and monolithic solutions viewed with suspicion.
Multiple avenues of democratic engagement are emphasised, and
there is increasing focus on the political importance of subgroups
defined by characteristics such as gender and sexuality.[6] However,
radical pluralism involves tensions between the 'liberal multicultural
paradigm of culturally diverse groups and the Marxist-Feminist
model of intersecting oppressions' (Cooper 2000: 1063). This type of
pluralism is more radical that mainstream pluralism, so that:

Far from ignoring systematic social inequality (as in the blander versions of
mainstream pluralism) such theorists treat social heterogeneity as both
necessary and positive. Such theorists will support the self-organisation of

women, of black people, of lesbians and gay men … [and] in the more
fully developed versions, have called for new democratic procedures that
will ensure additional representation for all oppressed groups. (Phillips
1993: 145–6)

This approach appears to be useful for trans and bisexual politics
because it foregrounds multiplicity, enables the challenging of structural inequalities, and emphasises multiple means of political
engagement. However, it is flawed in certain ways. The radical
pluralist approach could encourage fragmentation and division.
Groups often consolidate their identity via opposition to some
'other', sometimes excluding others; so that, for instance, tensions
over separatism and sexuality were a significant factor in the demise
of a unified women's movement in Britain (Phillips 1993: 148) (see
Chapter 5). Theorists such as Phillips avoid this problem by framing
particularist politics as necessary but temporary, stating that 'the
ultimate goal remains the forging of common cause across the
boundaries of difference' (1993: 161).[7] This type of approach is useful for trans and bisexual politics, as it allows for acknowledgement
of individual fluidity and also supports wider alliance building
because it avoids 'freezing' difference into rigid categories.

The fusion of universalism and diversity-based approaches is a
challenge in practice. Both universalism and a politics of difference
are based on ideals of equal respect, but they conflict because universalism entails the glossing over of distinctness, which means
that unique identities become subsumed under the dominant or
majority identity, whereas difference politics involves asserting non-
majority identities (see Axtman 1996: 92).[8] The balancing of the
diverse needs of the different groups against the good of the whole
community (or communities) – and the common good – is an
important theme for sexual and gender politics – for example the
trans campaigning organisation Press For Change (see 1997a, 1997b)
notes the importance of ensuring that civil rights activism for one
group does not destroy the rights of another.

CONCLUSION

The aims of this chapter have been to provide a review of different
models of democracy in relation to gender and sexual diversity, focusing on trans and, to a lesser extent, bisexuality. I began the chapter
by outlining some of the key aspects of liberal and representative,

and participative models of democracy. I argued that both of these approaches have advantages and disadvantages for gender and sexual minority politics. Liberal democracy provides crucial concepts, such as equality, autonomy and self-determination – ideas that are found in a lot of trans and bisexual activist discourse. Representative democracy also appears to play a part, as sexual and gender minorities are able to vote for representatives of their communities, and others who support their interests – although these may in practice be rather thin on the ground. The problems with liberal and representative forms of democracy include individualism, a reliance on a coherent subject, and a tendency to reinforce the interests of the majority, erasing those of minorities. Stronger forms of liberalism that support the interests of minorities via increased state intervention are one means of tackling such difficulties. I argued that participative and direct (strong) forms of democracy are also important in addressing the needs of gender and sexual minorities, which are often erased by representative politics. The difficulties with participatory democracy revolve around a lack of capacity in the LGB/LGBT community sector due (at least in part) to structural inequalities, and the related problems of achieving adequate representation of the communities. In this section I also discussed anarchist and queer stances on democracy, suggesting that their transgressive, individualistic approaches are useful in promoting autonomy and the establishment of alternative social spaces, as well as disrupting rigid norms, but that greater engagement in mainstream democratic processes is needed if widespread social change is to be achieved.

In the second part of the chapter I explored a number of debates in the feminist literature concerning democracy in relation to gender and sexual diversity, again focusing on trans. I argued that some concepts, such as the notion of 'women's values', are problematic because they rely on gender binarism. However, other themes, in particular discussions about fluidity and categorisation, and universalism and diversity, are important for beginning to theorise trans and bisexuality in relation to democracy. The tension between deconstructing identities – and the social erasure that this entails – and affirming identities as a strategic political move, has been central to this book. Drawing on the feminist literature, as well as research findings (all projects), I argued that asserting trans and bisexual identities is important in gaining social recognition and a political voice, even though ultimately these identities (and others) may be fictious. I also drew on the feminist literature about democracy in my discussions of the tensions between universalism and diversity. I suggested that certain aspects of universalism, such as appeals to universal human rights, are important for sexual and gender minority politics, but that universalism risks erasing difference. A fusion of approaches, in which particularism and universalism are balanced, seems to be the best approach. Radical pluralism provides a viable (and possibly stronger) alternative in which structural inequalities are addressed, identities are viewed as complex and contested, and multiple avenues for democratic engagement are utilised. This could, however, be problematic if it encouraged fragmentation and division, problems that could perhaps be countered by reinvoking notions of universal – if differentiated rights.

Glossary

With thanks to the Gender Trust. These definitions are intended as a rough guide only.

Androgyne: Individual who assumes characteristics that are not limited to either of the two traditionally accepted gender classifications, masculine and feminine.

Bisexual: Capable of desiring people of more than one gender, or a person who identifies as potentially desiring people of more than one gender. 'Bisexual' has also been given other meanings, such as someone who has two gender identities.

Butch: Masculine or macho dress and behaviour, regardless of sex or gender identity.

Camp: Exaggeration of feminine behaviours, usually for other's entertainment.

Cross-dressing: The adoption, fully or partially, of the clothes normally identified as belonging to the opposite sex.

Cross-dresser: One who, regardless of the motivation, wears the clothes, make-up, etc. assigned by society to the opposite sex. Generally, these persons do not alter their bodies.

Drag (DRessed As a Girl): Wearing clothes considered appropriate to the other sex.

Drag queen: Generally a gay cross-dresser, who often cross-dresses for other people's entertainment or appreciation.

FTM: Female-to-Male transsexual. Used to specify the direction of a change of sex or gender role.

Femme: Feminine or effeminate dress and behaviour, regardless of sex or gender identity (see Butch).

Female: One of the two main physical sexes.

Feminine: The gender role assigned to females (also woman).

Fetishistic transvestite: A transvestite whose primary cross-dressing motivation is erotic response.

Gay: Males who desire only other males, the characteristic of same-sex male attraction.

Gender Dysphoria (GD) or Gender Identity Disorder (GID): Dissatisfaction with one's gender (masculinity or femininity) which is in conflict with one's physical sex. The term is usually restricted to those who seek medical and surgical assistance to resolve their difficulty.

Gender fuck: Conflicting sex/gender signals.

Gender pluralism: Several different gendered personalities within one psyche.

Gender queer: Combinations of (usually oppositional) gender and sexual orientation characteristics.

Gender Reassignment Surgery (GRS): Term used in the UK for Sex Reassignment Surgery (from male to female or vice versa).

Gender Role: Interaction with society as a member of a specific gender (i.e. as a man or woman) by following arbitrary rules assigned by society that define what clothing, behaviours, thoughts, feelings, relationships, etc. are considered appropriate and inappropriate for members of each sex.

Hermaphroditism: Where the physiological sex is ambiguous. The situation may, or may not, be accompanied by various degrees of gender dysphoria.

Heterosexual: Someone who is attracted only to people of the opposite sex. The characteristic of opposite-sex attraction.

Intersex: Intersex people are born with a mixture of the physiological characteristics usually associated with females and males, or are born gender ambiguous. Intersex conditions include congenital adrenal hyperplasia, androgyn insensitivity syndrome, gonadal dysgenesis and hypospadias.

Lesbian: A woman who desires other women, the characteristic of people who are female desiring other females. Has also been used by some feminists to mean social/political affiliations with other women.

Male: One of the two main physical sexes.

Man: One who identifies with the masculine gender role, regardless of present sex or sexual identity.

Masculine: The gender role assigned to males (also men).

MTF: Male-to-Female transsexual.

Out: Being open about your sexual and/or gender orientation.

Passing: The opposite of 'Being Read'. A term often used to describe your ability to be accepted by most people as your preferred gender.

Polysexual: Desiring people with a range of gender identities, for example male, non-gendered, third gender.

Sex: Identifies the biological differences between women, men, and intersex people.

Sexual Orientation: A term which refers to whom one is affectionally and sexually attracted, usually based on gender and sex characteristics.

Trannie lover: Someone who desires cross-dressers.

Trans: An umbrella term covering transgender people.

Transgender: An umbrella term which includes cross-dressers, transsexuals, androgynes, drag artists, third and other gender people, and other people with gender identities that are more complex than simply 'male' or 'female'.

Transition: The period of time between when the individual first starts the sex-reassignment procedure and when the individual is living totally as a member of the opposite sex.

Transsexual (TS): A person who feels a consistent and overwhelming desire to transition and fulfil their lives as members of the opposite gender. Most transsexuals actively desire and complete Sexual Reassignment Surgery.

Notes

CHAPTER 1

1. The term 'trans' is a shortened form of the term 'transgender', which aims to move beyond the disputes concerning terminology that are currently taking place in the gender minority communities (in which the term 'transgender' is claimed by transsexuals and narrowed to exclude others).
2. Intersex people are those people who are born with a mixture of the physiological characteristics associated with women and men, or who are gender ambiguous. Intersex conditions include congenital adrenal hyperplasia, androgyn insensitivity syndrome, gonadal dysgenesis, hypospadias, and unusual chromosomal compositions such as XXY (Fausto-Sterling 2000).
3. This does not include any minorities engaged in abusive or non-consensual sexual arrangements, or those who are sexually involved with minors.
4. Equality is difficult to define because it represents a continuum of concepts. It can mean equality of opportunity, freedom from discrimination, equal treatment, equal benefit, equality of status or equality of results <http://canada.justice.gc.ca/en/dept/pub/guide/appendix_C.htm>. In this book I use the term to mean equality of opportunity, freedom from discrimination, and positive measures to ensure fair outcomes, so that people of all genders and sexual orientations contribute to, and benefit equally from, political, economic, and social development.
5. In addition, there are many subgroups within, for example the lesbian 'community'. I therefore use the term 'communities' rather than 'community', in order to represent the diversity and complexity of these social groupings.
6. There are an estimated 1,550–5,000 transsexual people in the UK (Home Office 2000) and intersex conditions vary, at 0.15 per cent (Dreger 2000), 1.7 per cent (Fausto-Sterling 2000), and 4 per cent (Nataf 1996, Rothblatt 1995) of the population.

CHAPTER 2

1. Following Beasley (1999: 105) I shall use 'race' and 'ethnicity' in conjunction whilst not assuming that they are either identical or separate. I shall use 'black' or 'minority ethnic' people to refer to people who are not white, or who come from ethnic groupings that are in the minority in the UK.
2. Gender fuck is extremely contentious within the trans communities because it is seen as radical and as potentially threatening to the campaign for equal rights and establishing a place in mainstream society. However, there is support in the literature for 'gender fuck' type stances, for example, Halberstam argues that gender performances within public spaces

produce radically reconfigured notions of 'proper' gender, and map new genders onto a utopian vision of radically different bodies and sexualities (2002).

3. See for example Carbido's (1999) discussion of sexism and homophobia within some sections of the black civil rights movement.

4. I use the 'discourse' definition of ideology: ideologies are sets of interrelated ideas that are both normative and descriptive (Heywood 1992).

5. Seabrook's material is taken from a newspaper cutting found in an archive in a library in Delhi, with no page numbers given.

6. Contributors emphasised the usefulness of terms such as 'gay' and 'transgender' in India – for example, one contributor said that the term 'transgender' is used by Kothis because it is destigmatising.

7. The situation appears to be similar for lesbians and trans people, and there are also other Western categories such as 'men who sleep with men' and 'metrosexual' (non-stereotypical man) in usage amongst educated English speakers.

8. Kothis regularly experience violence and abuse – including the extraction of monies, and rape, by the police. Newspaper coverage shows that Hijras are 'denied the most basic social rights because they refuse to be categorised as either male or female and wish to claim a third gender for themselves' (Doshi 2003: 5).

9. Some cultural feminists strongly reject androgyny, for example Daly argues that it is a ploy by men to appropriate what is best about women (see Tong 1998).

10. Unlike postmodern feminists, however, black and post-colonial feminists do not necessarily reject macro forms of analysis or embrace notions of plural identities.

11. I discuss post-structuralist feminist and transgender theory – and its problems – in greater depth in Monro (2004).

12. For example, Gutterman (1994) describes the strategic use of dominant masculinities by pro-feminist men who 'pass' as mainstream but openly support feminist aims.

13. However, these categories are themselves problematic – there is no single black or single working-class masculinity.

14. Development of this and other approaches relies of course on the choices of gender diverse people – many choose to assimilate, and ethical self-determination is central to any progressive political project.

CHAPTER 3

1. It is worth pointing out that there are exceptions – for example one transvestite contributor has been out dressed-up in broad daylight without experiencing harassment, but this was in an urban student environment.

2. A government consultation concerning partnership rights is taking place at the time of writing.

3. Legislative discrimination against gay men also affects trans women – both are subject to statute against gross indecency, (Evans 1993), meaning that, for instance, a trans prostitute was sent to jail for gross indecency

rather than being charged with the less serious offence of soliciting <http://www.pfc.org.uk/>.

4. I do not wish to argue that all gender stereotypical behaviour is oppressively imposed. Many trans people wish to adopt stereotypical roles, and, moreover, professionals are increasingly arguing for the support of gender and sexual diversity (see Watson and Hitchcock 2000).

5. The 2000 report from the Transsexual Working Group discussed sterilisation as a means of stopping transsexual men from bearing babies themselves, although this was not turned into statute, again illustrating the rigid, binaried approach taken by legislators (Home Office 2000).

6. Swan (1997) discusses the reality of the current crisis in morality, but argues that this is not solved by the silencing of sexual and gender minorities. He suggests that Christian values support tolerance and pluralism rather than the stigmatisation of socially marginalised groups.

7. An alternative analysis of transgender and capital focuses on the way in which capital appears to operate in a neutral fashion to some extent, with commodification enabling transgender expression, and the market forcing social change. There is some support for this in the findings. For example, the increase in private treatment of transsexuality appears to be putting pressure on NHS providers to release outdated, gender stereotypical treatment norms, and recreational transgender is linked with a liberalisation of public attitudes towards transgender.

8. Cosmetic surgery can be linked with excessive materialism, with identities being based on the physical, so that presentation becomes extremely important and people are categorised on the basis of their appearance. This links with critiques of the discourses of social exclusion – where these are based on the ability to participate in mainstream society, with its consumerist norms, they are problematic. There is an argument for 'breaking with the logic of exchange-values, which dictates that the only needs worth expressing are those that correspond to commodity equivalents' (Bowring 2000: 307).

9. For example, I met several transsexual people and cross-dressers in well-paid professional positions, who nonetheless faced certain types of social stigmatisation.

CHAPTER 4

1. See for example Hill (1997).

2. I use the terms 'equalities' and 'diversities' primarily when discussing initiatives concerning equality and diversity, to mirror developments within local and central government. I use the terms 'equality' and 'diversity' more generally, to refer to issues concerning gender and sexual equality and diversity.

3. There are various versions of each broad type: my intention here is to map their main characteristics.

4. See Butler (1997), who examines the ways in which childhood suppression of homosexual urges is linked with homophobia.

5. There are various approaches that aim for a middle ground between rational choice and incrementalist approaches (Hill 1997), which I will not examine here.

6. However, as Bagilhole (1997) notes, this definition is problematic, as it involves treating everybody equally, and equal opportunities can also entail differential treatment.

7. Liberal and radical approaches are conceptually distinct. However, as Jewson and Mason (1985: 309) found in their research on private and public sector organisations: 'in *practice* the adherents of each of the two conceptions needed or required, in certain circumstances and situations, to borrow some of the ideas and the rhetoric of the other.'

8. It is important to point out that the majority of bisexual contributors thought that polyamory was not a priority for policy reform, given the more important goals of attaining equality for people in same-sex relationships and increasing visibility and awareness concerning bisexuality (see also Chapter 6).

9. Chris Creegan and Sarah Lee, writing for Dialogue (2003) (with the Local Government Association, Stonewall, UNISON and the Association of London Government) provide an excellent guide to LGB work in local government in the UK.

10. As contributor Roz Kaveney says: 'everyone should have the equipment to participate in whatever sphere of life they prefer'.

11. I explore internecine conflicts in Chapter 5.

12. As well as those of, for example, the lesbian communities, which generally define 'butch' as female.

13. Ultimately, degendering may be the most appealing long-term strategy, but degendering at present is likely to marginalise gender diverse people and sexual minorities.

CHAPTER 5

1. Whilst I will not attempt to review the well-trodden field of community studies here, it is important to note that the notion of 'community' is problematic in this context – for example some of the contributors in my study of transgender said that they thought that there was no transgender community. The idea of 'community' implies a sense of cohesion and belonging, which may not necessarily be present.

2. Obviously, there is an overlap between lesbian and feminist politics – I have separated them here only as an analytical strategy.

3. FTM and MTF transsexuals have very different experiences of surgery. Many FTM people only have top surgery (a mastectomy), meaning that the distinction between pre- and post-operative is less relevant to them.

4. Califia was not trans at the time of writing *Transgender Politics*.

5. It is important to point out that some heterosexual feminists are also prejudiced against bisexuals, for similar reasons (perceived fence-sitting, dislike of the disruption of the gay–straight divide, for example).

6. There were also some bisexual-positive publications, such as Valverde's (1985) discussion of bisexuality as a challenge to the view that people are essentially either gay/lesbian or heterosexual.
7. Masculinity politics would be similarly problematic.
8. Brah (1996) discusses various definitions of 'difference': 'difference' as social relations constructed within the systems of power that underlie structures of class, racism, sexuality and gender, and 'difference' as experiential diversity – the variety of ways in which ideological and institutional practices affect our everyday lives, both as collective histories and as personal experiences. It is important to ascertain whether 'difference' is organised laterally or hierarchically, and whether it is asserted as a means of challenging domination, or used to legitimate domination.

CHAPTER 6

1. For example Obershall 1997 and Larana et al. 1994.
2. Resource mobilisation theory analysts have also emphasised the continuities between the institutional arrangements of conventional social life and those of collective protest, overlooking the discontinuities between the two types of behaviour and 'normalising' collective protest, for instance treating collective action as more organised than it actually is (Piven and Cloward 1995). For instance, whilst writing this chapter, I listened to the track 'In Yer Face' (by 808 State), which begins with the quote 'There are new forces in the world ... a powerful feeling that the American system is failing to deal with the real threats to life – the bomb, and the pollution.' The overlap between the diffuse underground and youth cultures and NSMs cannot be adequately dealt with by resource mobilisation theory.
3. Early political movements concerning women's rights are well documented in Rowbotham (1992), who discusses developments in the US and Europe, and some of the Southern nations such as India and China.
4. Some authors are critical of this men's movement – for example Ferber (2000) draws parallels between it and the white supremacist movement, and, as I noted in Chapter 2, it problematically essentialises masculinity. However, there are parallels with the work of African American pro-feminist male author Byrd (2001) who seeks to remodel black masculinity in a life affirming and non-hegemonic fashion; pro-feminist men also need a space in which to remodel themselves.
5. The only exception would be the Sisters of Perpetual Indulgence, a group mostly of gay men who drag as nuns, and who have demonstrated against the homophobic church – this group, however, is primarily gay identified rather than transgender identified.

CHAPTER 7

1. Others, such as Lister (1997), identify two mainstream forms of citizenship (liberal-social and republican).

2. Some critiques concern the limitations of citizenship itself. For example, Turner and Hamilton (1994) argue that the importance of citizenship may decline in favour of a more radical or universal view of human rights, which could draw on non-Western political traditions.
3. Bisexuals face discrimination from the lesbian and gay communities as well as the heterosexual mainstream. This raises questions about whether membership of the non-heterosexual communities can be seen as a citizenship issue. Are there citizenships within oppositional cultures? Decentring citizenship, away from the institution of heterosexuality and towards the sexual minorities, could broaden it out as a concept as well as providing a tool for resolving some of the difficulties between different subsections of the lesbian, gay and bisexual communities.
4. Although the bisexual communities are marked out by an acceptance of difference and self-identification which does form a basis for critiquing the heterosexual system.
5. Although Plummer (1995), in particular, addresses fetishism in some depth.
6. Although this is true of most commercial scenes.

CHAPTER 8

1. As Phillips (1991: 14) says, there is not a single either/or choice between models of democracy, and in addition issues concerning representative versus direct democracy do not translate smoothly into debates about liberal versus radical democracy.
2. Homogenising the different approaches to liberalism is problematic. As Held notes, 'There are distinctive liberal traditions which embody quite different conceptions from each other of the individual agent, of autonomy, of the rights and duties of subjects, and of the proper nature and form of community', and democracies that might vaguely appeal to liberal models take a number of different forms, also depending on the way in which national and international forces intersect in different contexts (1995: 4). In addition, representative and liberal democracy do not mean the same thing; here I have placed them together as a means of introducing core concepts.
3. Following the demise of state socialism radicals have been forced to re-evaluate participatory politics, and their focus has shifted to include the rights and freedoms of the individual and the importance of elections (see Phillips 1991: 13).
4. Needless to say, grass-roots activism is also associated with the participative and strong forms of democracy that I discuss elsewhere.
5. However, the notion of 'women's values' could perhaps be adapted to trans and bisexual democracy, as gender and sexual minorities, are likely to experience subjugation. Therefore, they might, like non-transgender women, be likely to develop values such as empathy and community orientation.
6. It is important in discussing gender diverse politics not to fall into the trap of assuming that diverse communities are homogeneous (see Axtman 1996).

7. Phillips (1993: 11) discusses the way in which particularist approaches – feminist, postmodern, and communitarian – have been criticised for incipient conservatism. In other words, focusing on particular standpoints in a way that lacks external reference points could prevent critical thinking. Celebrating difference could block comparisons and alliances; however, Phillips (1993: 12) argues that there is little risk of this amongst contemporary feminists.
8. Some male sexualities and reproductive roles are also marginalised by this process (see Carver 1998: 25).

Methodological Note

This book draws on empirical material from four research projects: (a) Transgender Politics; (b) Lesbian and Gay Equality in Local Government; (c) Gender and Sexual Diversity in India; and (d) LGBT research.

(a) Transgender Politics (1996–2000). This Economic and Social Research Council funded doctoral research utilised a participative, feminist standpoint approach with a range of transgender people. The methodology involved 24 in-depth interviews, over 50 informal interviews, a focus group and over 1,000 hours of participant observation with transsexuals, transvestites, cross-dressers, intersexes, an androgyne, a gender transient, drag kings and queens, other transgender people and related professionals. I aimed for representation across demographic variables such as age, ethnicity and class. Most of the contributors were white and middle class, but some were working class, two were from ethnic minority groups, and a range of ages were represented. Research contributors were involved in the research design and analysis as far as was possible, enabling a richer picture to be developed than would have been possible using traditional methodologies.

(b) Lesbian and Gay Equality in Local Government, 1990 and 2001 (2001–03). This project was funded by the Economic and Social Research Council (project number R000 239293), and I worked on it in collaboration with Davina Cooper (University of Kent) and Jean Carabine (Open University). After conducting literature work and scoping interviews, we did case studies of twelve local authorities in England, Scotland and Wales, interviewing approximately eight to ten officers, councillors, community members and workers in partner agencies in the different localities, as well as some national players (a total of 100 full interviews).

(c) Gender and Sexual Diversity in India (2003). This research was funded as part of a Leverhulme exchange project between the universities of Delhi, Keele and Leeds, on the subject of gender, sexuality and the law. It was a small project aiming to gain some insight into gender and sexual orientation categorisation in India. I conducted web and literature searches, did literature work (including documentary analysis of newspapers collected in India), and interviewed six Kothi and gay men living in Delhi.

(d) LGBT Research (2003). This project involved conducting interviews with sixteen bisexual, gay and trans people, in order to update earlier material and to gain more understanding of bisexual politics. I also attended a BiCon Bisexual conference and went to several workshops on issues such as gender diversity, bisexual activism and polyamory and parenting.

When I began this research I identified as female and lesbian (I was identified as female at birth but have not had chromosome testing). During the course of the research, and partially because of it, I came to re-examine my identity (see Monro 2000b). I explored male transgender identities to a degree, but eventually reconstructed myself as female and bisexual (or, more accurately, polysexual). I am privileged, white and middle class, but have experienced some social exclusion due to issues around illness, poverty and sexual orientation. During the first research project I took a very participative approach, working together with trans people as an activist, and this stance has continued to some extent, although I have pulled back into an 'academic activist' identity rather than a frontline activist one.

I am aware of the guidelines developed by Jacob Hale and Emi Koyama (see <http://www.isna.org/faq/writing-guidelines.html>) concerning non-trans and non-intersex people writing about trans and intersex. I hope that I have succeeded in meeting some of these guidelines – for example I have tried to avoid appropriating people's experiences for specific political ends, framing myself as an expert, constructing intersex people as being part of the LGBT communities, or masking diversity. Some aspects of the guidelines have, however, been difficult to follow, for example representing the multidimensionality of trans and intersex people – this book is about gender politics, and including material from people's lives that is not relevant to discussions is problematic, so I would like to emphasise here that intersex and trans people's lives are as full of non-gender-related interests, and as diverse, as everyone else's lives. Another difficulty has concerned being conversant with all the different debates taking place within the intersex and trans communities; as I said in introduction, this book is part of an ongoing process, and there will of course be issues that I am not currently aware of.

Some of the contributors to the research wished to be quoted by name or by pseudonym. I list these people here, together with the dates of the fieldwork with them. I have included some aspects of their identities, as a way of giving readers some idea about their standpoint with respect to gender and sexuality. Of course, they all have many other characteristics, for example ethnic, class, national and life interests.

CONTRIBUTORS WHO WISHED TO BE NAMED

Grant Denkinson	2003	Bisexual man
Simon Dessloch	1998	FTM transsexual
Christie Elan Cane	1996/8	Androgyne (now identifies as non-gendered)
James Green	1996	FTM transsexual
Graham Holmes	2003	Cross-dresser
Roz Kaveney	1996/2003	MTF transsexual
Phaedra Kelly	1998	Gender transient
Del LaGrace	1996	Hermaphrodyke at that time
Tracey Lee	2004	Not known
Hamish Macdonald	1998	FTM cross-dresser
John Marshall	1996	Transvestite
Jennifer Moore	2003	Bisexual woman/genderqueer
Kate More	1996	MTF transsexual
Zachary Nataf	1996	FTM transsexual
Mjka Scott	1998	MTF transsexual
Yvonne Sinclair	1996/8	Transvestite
Alex Whinnom	1996	FTM transsexual

Stephen Whittle	1996	FTM transsexual
Kate N' Ha Ysabet	1998	MTF transsexual
Giles	2003	Bisexual man
Jane	2003	Bisexual woman
John	2003	Bisexual man
Kerry	2003	Bisexual woman
Kim	2003	Bisexual woman
Mary	2003	Bisexual woman

CONTRIBUTORS WHO WISHED TO BE ANONYMISED

Justin Bannon	1996	Transvestite
Annie Cox	1996	MTF transsexual
Penny Gainsborough	1996	MTF transsexual
Ann Goodley	1996/8/2003	Initially intersexual, then MTF transsexual
Joanna/Dave Jones	1998	Transvestite, drag queen
Elizabeth Loxley	1996	MTF transsexual
Meredith Malek	1996	MTF transsexual
Salmacis	1998	Intersexual
Pamela Summers	1996	MTF transsexual
Craig	2003	Bisexual man
Mike	2004	Bisexual man

Bibliography

Aberdeen City Council (2003) *Lesbian, Gay, Bisexual and Transgender Action Plan*. Aberdeen: Aberdeen City Council.

Adam, B. (1987) *The Rise of the Gay and Lesbian Movement*. Boston: Twayne Publishers.

Alcoff, L. (1995) 'Cultural Feminism Versus Post-Structuralism: The Identity Crisis in Feminist Theory', in: N. Tuana and R. Tong (eds) *Feminism and Philosophy: Essential Readings in Theory, Reinterpretation and Application*. Boulder: Westview Press.

Ardill, S. and S. O'Sullivan (1993) 'Difference, Desires and Sadomasochism', in: S. Jackson et al. (eds) *Women's Studies: A Reader*. Hemel Hempstead: Harvester Wheatsheaf.

Axtman, R. (1996) *Liberal Democracy into the Twenty-First Century: Globalisation, Integration and the Nation-State*. Manchester: Manchester University Press.

Bacchi, C. (1999) *Women, Policy and Politics: The Construction of Policy Problems*. London: Sage.

Back, L. and J. Solomos (eds) (2000) *Theories of Race and Racism: A Reader*. London: Routledge.

Bagilhole, B. (1993) 'Managing to be Fair: Implementing Equal Opportunities in a Local Authority', *Local Government Studies*, 19(2): 163–75.

—— (1997) *Equal Opportunities and Social Policy Issues of Gender, Race and Disability*. London: Longman.

Baird, V. (2001) *The No-Nonsense Guide to Sexual Diversity*. Padstow, Cornwall: New Internationalist in association with Verso.

Barber, B. (1984) *Strong Democracy: Participatory Politics for a New Age*. Berkeley: University of California Press.

—— (1996) 'Three Challenges to Reinventing Democracy', in: P. Hirst and S. Khilnani (eds) *Reinventing Democracy*. Oxford: Blackwell Publishers.

Barnes, M. and S. Shaw (2000) 'Older People, Citizenship and Collective Action', in: A.M. Warnes, L. Warren and M. Nolan (eds) *Care Services for Later Life: Transformations and Critiques*. London: Jessica Kingsley.

Beasley, C. (1999) *What is Feminism? An Introduction to Feminist Theory*. London: Sage.

Beetham, D. (1993) 'Liberal Democracy and the Limits of Democratisation', in: D. Held (ed.) *Prospects for Democracy: North, South, East, West*. Cambridge: Polity Press.

—— (1999) *Democracy and Human Rights*. Cambridge: Polity Press.

Beh, H.G. and M. Diamond (2000) 'An Emerging Ethical and Medical Dilemma: Should Physicians Perform Sex Assignment Surgery on Infants with Ambiguous Genitalia?', *Michigan Journal of Gender and the Law*, 7 (on ISNA site).

Bell, D. and J. Binnie (2000) *The Sexual Citizen: Queer Politics and Beyond*. Cambridge: Polity Press.

Bem, S. (1976) 'Probing the Promise of Androgyny', in: A.G. Kaplan and J.P. Bean (eds) *Beyond Sex-Role Stereotypes: Reading Towards a Psychology of Androgyny*. New York: Alfred Knopf.

Benford, R.D. and S.A. Hunt (1992) 'Dramaturgy and Social Movements: The Social Construction and Communication of Power', *Sociological Inquirer*, 62(1): 36–55.

Benhabib, S. (2002) *The Claims of Culture: Equality and Diversity in the Global Era*. Princeton, New Jersey: Princeton University Press.

Bergling, T. (2001) *Sissyphobia: Gay Men and Effeminate Behaviour*. New York: Harrington Park Press.

Billings, D.B. and T. Urban (1982) 'The Socio-Medical Construction of Transsexualism: An Interpretation and Critique', *Social Problems*, 29: 266–82.

Blackburn, M. (2002) *Sexuality and Disability*. Oxford: Butterworth Heinemann.

Bland, J. (1994) *Transvestism: Four Monographs*. Derby: The Derby TV/TS Group.

Bloomfield, A. (1996) 'Discrimination in the Institution', *Gemsnews*, 25.

Blumer, H. (1995) 'Social Movements', in: S.M. Lyman (ed.) *Social Movements: Critiques, Concepts, Case-Studies*. New York: New York University Press. Reprinted from A.M. Lee (ed.) (1951) *New Outline of the Principles of Sociology*. New York: Barnes and Noble, Inc.

Bly, R. (1990) *Iron John: A Book about Men*. Reading, MA: Addison-Wesley.

Boris, E. (1995) 'The Racialized Gendered State: Constructions of Citizenship in the United States', *Social Politics*, Summer: 160–80.

Bornstein, K. (1994) *Gender Outlaw: On Men, Women and the Rest of us*. London: Routledge.

—— (1998) *My Gender Workbook*. London: Routledge.

Bower, T. (1995) 'Bisexual Women, Feminist Politics', in: N. Tucker (ed.) *Bisexual Politics: Theories, Queries and Visions*. New York: Harrington Park Press.

Bowring, F. (2000) 'Social Exclusion: Limitations of the Debate', *Critical Social Policy*, 64(20): 307–29.

Brah, A. (1996) *Cartographies of Diaspora: Contesting Identities*. London: Routledge.

Bulbeck, C. (1988) *One World Women's Movement*. London: Pluto Press.

Bullough, V. (1976) *Sexual Variance in Society and History*. New York: Wiley.

—— and B. Bullough (1993) *Cross Dressing, Sex and Gender*. Philadelphia: University of Philadelphia Press.

Burchardt, T., J. Le Grand and D. Piachaud (2002) 'Introduction', in: J. Hills, J. Le Grand and D. Piachaud, *Understanding Social Exclusion*. Oxford: Oxford University Press.

Bussemaker, J. and R. Voet (1998) 'Citizenship and Gender: Theoretical Approaches and Historical Legacies', *Critical Social Policy*, 18(3): 278–307.

Butler, J. (1990) *Gender Trouble: Feminism and the Subversion of Identity*. London: Routledge.

—— (1991) 'Imitation and Gender Insubordination', in: D. Fuss (ed.) *Inside/Out*. London: Routledge.

—— (1992) 'Contingent Foundations: Feminism and the Question of "Postmodernism" ', in: J. Butler and J. Scott (eds) *Feminists Theorise the Political*. London: Routledge.

—— (1993) *Bodies that Matter: On the Discursive Limits of 'Sex'*. London: Routledge.

—— (1997) *The Psychic Life of Power*. Stanford: Stanford University Press.

Byrd, R.P. (2001) 'Prologue: The Tradition of John: A Mode of Black Masculinity', in: R.P. Byrd and B. Guy-Sheftall (eds) *Traps: African American Men on Gender and Sexuality*. Bloomington: Indiana University Press.

—— and B. Guy-Sheftall (eds) (2001) *Traps: African American Men on Gender and Sexuality*. Bloomington USA: Indiana University Press.

Byrne, D. (1999) *Social Exclusion*. Oxford: Oxford University Press.

Byrne, P. (1997) *Social Movements in Britain*. London: Routledge.

Califia, P. (1997) *Sex Changes: The Politics of Transgenderism*. San Francisco: Cleis Press.

Campbell, J. and M. Oliver (1996) *Disability Politics: Understanding Our Past, Changing Our Future*. London: Routledge.

Cameron, L. (1996) *Body Alchemy: Transsexual Portraits*. USA: San Francisco: Cleis Press.

Carabine, J. (1995) 'Invisible Sexualities: Sexuality, Politics, and Influencing Policy-Making', in: A. Wilson (ed.) *A Simple Matter of Justice?* London: Cassell.

—— (1996a) 'Heterosexuality and Social Policy', in: D. Richardson (ed.) *Theorising Heterosexuality*. Buckingham: Open University Press.

—— (1996b) 'A Straight Playing Field of Queering the Pitch? Centring Sexuality in Social Policy', *Feminist Review*, 54: 31–64.

Carbado, D. (1999) *Black Men on Race, Gender, and Sexuality: A Critical Reader*. New York: New York University Press.

Carrigan, T., B. Connell and J. Lee (1987) 'Towards a New Sociology of Masculinity', in: H. Brod (ed.) *The Making of Masculinities: The New Men's Studies*. Winchester: Allen and Unwin.

Carver, T. (1998) 'A Political Theory of Gender: Perspectives on the "Universal Subject" ', in: V. Randall and G. Waylen (eds) *Gender, Politics and the State*. London: Routledge.

Chase, C. (1998) 'Affronting Reason', in: D. Atkins (ed.) *Looking Queer: Body Image and Identity in Lesbian, Bisexual, Gay and Transgender Communities*. New York: Harrington Park Press.

Chakraborty, T. (2002) 'Patna Eunuchs in Power Play', *Telegraph*, 6 March.

Chua, A. (2004) 'Our Most Dangerous Export', *Guardian*, 28 February.

Cole, C. and W.J. Meyer (1998) 'Transgender Behaviour and DSM IV', in: D. Denny (ed.) *Current Concepts in Transgender Identity*. London: Garland Publishing.

Connell, R.W. (2002) *Gender*. Cambridge: Polity Press.

Cooper, D. (1994) *Sexing the City*. London: Rivers Oram Press.

—— (1995) *Power in Struggle: Feminism, Sexuality and the State*. Buckingham: Open University Press.

—— (2000) 'Promoting Injury or Freedom: Radical Pluralism and Orthodox Jewish Symbolism', *Ethnic and Racial Studies*, 23(6): 1062–85.

Count Me In (2001) *Count Me In: Findings*. Brighton and Hove: Brighton and Hove City Council.

Cowen, H. and G. Daly (1999) 'Democracy and Citizenship in the New Millennium'. Paper presented at the British Sociological Association Annual Conference, Glasgow, 6–9 April.

Cromwell, J. (1999) 'Passing Women and Female-Bodied Men: (Re)claiming FTM History', in: K. More and S. Whittle (eds) *Reclaiming Genders: Transsexual Grammars at the Fin de Siecle*. London: Cassell.

Cruikshank, M. (1992) *The Gay and Lesbian Liberation Movement*. London: Routledge.

Dalton, R.J. and M. Kuechler (eds) (1990) *Challenging the Political Order: New Social and Political Movements in Western Democracies*. Cambridge: Polity Press.

Daly, G. and H. Cowen (2000) 'Redefining the Local Citizen', in: L. McKie and N. Watson (eds) *Organizing Bodies*. London: Macmillan.

Daly, M. (1984) *Pure Lust: Elemental Feminist Philosophy*. London: Women's Press.

Davis, A. (1981) *Women, Race and Class*. New York: Random House.

Dialogue (2003) *Sexuality – The New Agenda. A Guide for Local Authorities on Engaging with Lesbian, Gay and Bisexual Communities*. London: Employers' Organisation for Local Government, Local Government Association.

Doshi, T. (2003) 'Lessons in Transformation', *The Hindu*, 25 May.

Dreger, A.D. (ed.) (2000) *Intersex in the Age of Ethics*. Maryland: University Publishing Group.

Dunphy, R. (2000) *Sexual Politics: An Introduction*. Edinburgh: Edinburgh University Press.

Durham, M. (1995) 'The Public Management of Sexuality'. Paper presented at the New Sexual Agendas Conference, Middlesex University, July.

Eadie, J. (1994) 'Activating Bisexuality: Towards a Bi/Sexual Politics', in: J. Bristow and A.R. Wilson (eds) *Activating Theory; Lesbian, Gay and Bisexual Politics*. London: Lawrence and Wishart.

Ekins, R. (1997) *Male Femaling: A Grounded Theory Approach to Cross Dressing*. London: Routledge.

Elliott, B. (1991) 'Bisexuality: The Best Thing that Ever Happened to Lesbian Feminism', in: L. Hutchins and L. Kaahamanu (eds) *Bi Any Other Name: Bisexual People Speak Out*. Boston: Alyson Publications Inc.

Engel, S.M. (2001) *The Unfinished Revolution: Social Movement Theory and the Gay and Lesbian Movement*. Cambridge: Cambridge University Press.

Epstein, S. (1999) 'Gay and Lesbian Movements in the United States: Dilemmas of Identity, Diversity, and Political Strategy', in: B.D. Adam, J.W. Duyvendak and A. Krouwel (eds) *The Global Emergence of Gay and Lesbian Politics: National Imprints of a Worldwide Movement*. Philadelphia: Temple University Press.

Escott, F. and D. Whitfield (2002) *Promoting Gender Equality in the Public Sector*. London: Equal Opportunities Commission.

Evans, D. (1993) *Sexual Citizenship: The Material Construction of Sexualities*. London: Routledge.

Faludi, S. (1992) *Backlash: The Undeclared War Against American Women*. New York: Anchor.

Farajaje-Jones, E. (1995) 'Fluid Desire: Race, HIV/AIDS, and Bisexual Politics', in: N. Tucker (ed.) *Bisexual Politics: Theories, Queries and Visions*. New York: Harrington Park Press.

Fausto-Sterling, A. (2000) *Sexing the Body*. New York: Basic Books.

Feinberg, L. (1996) *Transgender Warriors: Making History from Joan of Arc to Dennis Rodman*. Boston: Beacon Press.

Ferber, A.L. (2000) 'Racial Warriors and Weekend Warriors: The Construction of Masculinity in Mythopoetic and White Supremacist Discourse', *Men and Masculinities*, 3(1): 30–56.

Firestein, B. (ed.) (1996) *Bisexuality: The Psychology and Politics of an Invisible Minority*. London: Sage.

Firestone, S. (1970) *The Dialectic of Sex*. New York: Bantam Books.

Foucault, M. (1979) *The History of Sexuality. Vol. 1: An Introduction*. London: Allen Lane.

Fox, R.L. (1997) *Gender Dynamics in Congressional Elections*. London: Sage.

Freeman, J. (1975) *The Politics of Women's Liberation*. New York: David Mackay.

Gamson, W.A. (1990) *The Strategy of Social Protest*. Belmont: Wadsworth.

Garber, M. (1992) *Vested Interests: Cross-Dressing and Cultural Anxiety*. London: Penguin.

George, S. (1993) *Women and Bisexuality*. London: Scarlet Press.

Giddens, A. (ed.) (2001) *The Global Third Way Debate*. Cambridge: Polity Press.

Greer, G. (1999) *The Whole Woman*. New York: Alfred A. Knopf.

Gupta, A. (2002) 'Transgender Law and Civil Rights', *The Lawyers Collective*, Mumbai.

Gutterman, D.S. (1994) 'Postmodernism and the Interrogation of Masculinity', in: H. Brod and M. Kaufman (eds) *Theorizing Masculinities*. London: Sage.

—— (2001) 'Postmodernism and the Interrogation of Masculinity', in: S.M. Whitehead and F.J. Barrett (eds) *The Masculinities Reader*. Cambridge: Polity Press.

Halberstam, J. (2002) 'An Introduction to Female Masculinity: Masculinity Without Men', in: R. Adams and D. Savran (eds) *The Masculinity Studies Reader*. Oxford: Blackwell Publishers.

Haraway, D. (1991) *Symians, Cyborgs and Women*. London: Free Association Books.

Hearn, J. and D.L. Collinson (1994) 'Theorizing Unities and Differences Between Men and Between Masculinities', in: H. Brod and M. Kaufman (eds) *Theorizing Masculinities*. London: Sage.

Hearn, J. and D. Morgan (1990) *Men, Masculinities and Social Theory*. London: Unwin Hyman.

Held, D. (1995) *Democracy and the Global Order: From the Modern State to Cosmopolitan Governance*. Cambridge: Polity Press.

Hemmings, C. (2002) *Bisexual Spaces: A Geography of Sexuality and Gender*. London: Routledge.

Herdt, G. (ed.) (1994) *Third Sex Third Gender: Beyond Sexual Dimorphism in Culture and History*. New York: Zone Books.

Heywood, A. (1992) *Political Ideologies: An Introduction*. London: Macmillan.

Hill, M. (1997) *Understanding Social Policy*. Oxford: Blackwell Publishers.

Hill Collins, P. (1990) *Black Feminist Thought: Knowledge, Consciousness, and the Politics of Empowerment*. London: Unwin Hyman.

Hirst, P. (1993) 'Associational Democracy', in: D. Held (ed.) *Prospects for Democracy: North, South, East, West*. Cambridge: Polity Press.

Hohler, E. (1996) 'When Girls are Made of Boys', *Sunday Telegraph*, 18 February.

Holmes, G. (2003) 'Is that a Blank Sheet of Paper, or a List of Crossdressers' Achievements?' Unpublished, see <http://totalclothingrights.org>.

Holmes, M. (1998) 'In(to) Visibility: Intersexuality in the Field of Queer', in: D. Atkins (ed.) *Looking Queer: Body Image and Identity in Lesbian, Bisexual, Gay and Transgender Communities*. New York: Harrington Park Press.

Home Office (2000) Report on the Interdepartmental Working Group on Transsexual People. London: Home Office.

hooks, b. (1984) *Feminist Theory: From Margin to Centre*. Boston: South End Press.

Hugill, B. (1998) 'In Ancient Greece She'd Have Been a God. In Wales They Spit on Her', *Observer*, 24 May: 7.

Hutchins, L. (1996) 'Bisexuality: Politics and Community', in: B. Firestein (ed.) *Bisexuality: The Psychology and Politics of an Invisible Minority*. London: Sage.

—— and L. Kaahamanu (eds) (1991) *Bi any other Name: Bisexual People Speak Out*. Boston: Alyson Publications Inc.

International Congress on Transgender Law and Employment Policy, Inc. (1993) *The International Bill of Gender Rights*. As adopted on 28 August 1993 at the International Conference on Transgender Law and Employment Policy, Houston, US.

Irigaray, L. (1985) *This Sex which is not the One*. Trans. C. Porter, Ithaca: Cornell University Press.

Israel, G.E. and D.E. Tarver (1997) *Transgender Care: Recommended Guidelines, Practical Information and Personal Accounts*. Philadelphia: Temple University Press.

Jackson, S. et al. (eds) (1993) *Women's Studies: A Reader*. Hemel Hempstead: Harvester Wheatsheaf.

Jaffrey, Z. (1996) *The Invisibles: A Tale of the Eunuchs of India*. New York: Vintage Books.

Jeffreys, S. (1996) 'Heterosexuality and the Desire for Gender', in: D. Richardson (ed.) *Theorising Heterosexuality: Telling it Straight*. Buckingham: Open University Press.

—— (1999) 'Bisexual Politics: A Superior Form of Feminism?', *Women's Studies International Forum*, 22(3): 273–85.

Jewson, N. and D. Mason (1985) 'The Theory and Practice of Equal Opportunities Policies: Liberal and Radical Approaches', *Sociological Review*, 34(2): 307–34.

Kaldera, R. (1998) ' "Agdistis" Children: Living Bi-Gendered in a Single-Gendered World', in: D. Atkins (ed.) *Looking Queer: Body Image and Identity in Lesbian, Bisexual, Gay and Transgender Communities*. New York: Harrington Park Press.

Kaveney, R. (1999) 'Talking Transgender Politics', in: K. More and S. Whittle (eds) *Reclaiming Genders: Transsexual Grammars at the Fin de Siecle*. London: Cassell.

Kessler, S. (1998) *Lessons from the Intersexed*. New Brunswick: Rutgers University Press.

King, D. (1986) 'The Transvestite and the Transsexual: A Case Study of Public Categories and Private Identities'. Unpublished PhD thesis, University of Essex.

—— (1993) *The Transvestite and the Transsexual: A Case Study of Public Categories and Private Identities.* Aldershot: Avebury.

Kirby, M. (1995) *Investigating Political Sociology.* London: Collins.

Kirk, K. and E. Heath (1984) *Men In Frocks.* London: Gay Men's Press.

Kirsch, M.H. (2000) *Queer Theory and Social Change.* London: Routledge.

Kristeva, J. (1982) *Desire in Language.* Trans. L. Roudiez, New York: Columbia University Press.

Kymlicka, W. (1995) *Multicultural Citizenship: A Liberal Theory of Minority Rights.* Oxford: Clarendon Press.

Lacey, H. (1999) 'The Beautiful and the Damned', *Independent on Sunday*, 14 March.

Lano, K. and C. Parry (eds) (1995) *Breaking the Barriers to Desire: New Approaches to Multiple Relationships.* Nottinghám: Five Leaves Publications.

Larana, E., H. Johnston and J. Gusfield (eds) (1994) *New Social Movements: From Ideology to Identity.* Philadelphia: Temple University Press.

Leach, S. and M. Wingfield (1999) 'Public Participation and the Democratic Renewal Agenda: Prioritisation or Marginalisation?', *Local Government Studies*, 25(4): 46–59.

Lechte, J. (1994) *Fifty Key Contemporary Thinkers: From Structuralism to Postmodernity.* London: Routledge.

Lemons, G.L. (2001) 'When and Where (We) Enter. In Search of a Feminist Forefather – Reclaiming the *Womanist* Legacy of W.E.B. Du Bois', in: R.P. Byrd and B. Guy-Sheftall (eds) *Traps: African American Men on Gender and Sexuality.* Bloomington: Indiana University Press.

Levitas, R. (1998) *The Inclusive Society? Social Exclusion and New Labour.* London: Macmillan.

Lewis, G. (1998) 'Coming Apart at the Seams: The Crisis of the Welfare State', in: G. Hughes and G. Lewis (eds) *Rethinking Social Policy.* London: Routledge.

—— (2000) 'Introduction: Expanding the Social Policy Imaginary', in: G. Lewis, G. Gerwirtz and J. Clarke (eds) *Rethinking Social Policy.* London: The Open University in association with Sage.

Lindblom, C.E. (1959) 'The Science of Muddling Through', *Public Administration Review*, 19: 79–88.

Lister, R. (1997) *Citizenship: Feminist Perspectives.* London: Macmillan.

—— (2000) 'Gender and the Analysis of Social Policy', in: G. Lewis, G. Gerwirtz and J. Clarke (eds) *Rethinking Social Policy.* London: The Open University in association with Sage.

Llamas, R. and F. Vila (1999) 'Passion for Life: A History of the Lesbian and Gay Movement in Spain', in: B. Adam, J.W. Duyvendak and A. Krouwel (eds) *The Global Emergence of Gay and Lesbian Politics.* Philadelphia: Temple University Press.

Lorber, J. (1994) *Paradoxes of Gender.* New Haven: Yale University Press.

MacInnes, J. (1998) *The End of Masculinity.* Buckingham: Open University Press.

MacKenzie, G. (1994) *Transgender Nation*. Ohio: Bowling Green State University Popular Press.

Marshall, T.H. (1950) *Citizenship and Social Class and Other Essays*. Cambridge: Cambridge University Press.

Mattesson, D. (1991) 'Bisexual Feminist Man', in: L. Hutchins and L. Kaahumanu (eds) *Bi any other name: Bisexual People Speak Out*. Boston: Alyson Publications Inc.

Mayes, D.G., J. Berghman and R. Salais (eds) (2001) *Social Exclusion and European Policy*. Cheltenham: Edward Elgar Publishing Ltd.

McAdam, D. (1986) 'Recruitment to High-Risk Activism: The Case of Freedom Summer', *American Journal of Sociology*, 92: 64–90.

McClinton, A. (1995) *Imperial Leather: Race, Gender and Sexuality in the Colonial Contest*. London: Routledge.

McClure, K. (1992) 'On the Subject of Rights: Pluralism, Plurality, and Political Identity', in: C. Mouffe (ed.) *Dimensions of Radical Democracy: Pluralism, Citizenship and Community*. London: Verso.

McMullen, M. and S. Whittle (1994) *Transvestism, Transsexualism and the Law*. London: The Beaumont Trust.

Miller, D. (1993) 'Deliberative Democracy and Social Change', in: D. Held (ed.) *Prospects for Democracy: North, South, East, West*. Cambridge: Polity Press.

Millet, K. (1970) *Sexual Politics*. New York: Doubleday.

Mohanty, C.T., A. Russo and L. Torres (eds) (1991) *Third World Women and the Politics of Feminism*. Bloomington: Indiana University Press.

Monro, S. (2000a) 'Theorizing Transgender Diversity: Towards a Social Model of Health', *Sexual and Relationship Therapy*, 15(1): 33–45.

—— (2000b) *Transgender Politics*. Unpublished thesis, University of Sheffield.

—— (2003) 'Transgender Politics in the UK', *Critical Social Policy*, 23(4): 433–52.

—— (2004) 'Poststructuralism and the Spectrum of Gender', *International Journal of Transgender Studies*.

—— (unpublished) 'Evaluating Local Government Equalities Work: The Case of Sexuality Initiatives in the UK'.

—— and L. Warren (2004) 'Transgendering Citizenship', *Sexualities*.

More, K. (1996) 'Let(TS)sbigay Together', *Radical Deviance: A Journal of Transgendered Politics*, 2(2): 50–3.

—— (1999) 'Newer Mind the Bollocks: 1. Trans Theory in the UK', in: K. More and S. Whittle (eds) *Reclaiming Genders: Transsexual Grammars at the Fin de Siecle*. London: Cassell.

—— and S. Whittle (eds) (1999) *Reclaiming Genders: Transsexual Grammars at the Fin de Siecle*. London: Cassell.

More, S.D. (1998) 'The Pregnant Man – An Oxymoron?', *Journal of Gender Studies*, 7(3): 319–29.

Morris, E. (2004) 'The Self I will Never Know', *New Internationalist*, 364, January/February: 25–7.

Morris, A.D. and C. McClurg (eds) (1992) *Frontiers in New Social Movement Theory*. New Haven: Yale University Press.

Mouffe, C. (1992) 'Feminism, Citizenship and Radical Democratic Politics', in: J. Butler and J.W. Scott (eds) *Feminists Theorize the Political*. London: Routledge.

—— (1993) *Return of the Political*. London: Verso.

Mueller, C.M. (1992) 'Building New Social Movement Theory', in: A.D. Morris and C. McClurg (eds) *Frontiers in New Social Movement Theory*. New Haven: Yale University Press.

—— (2000) *Gender Diversity: Crosscultural Variations*. Prospect Heights: Waveland Press Inc.

—— and A.D. Morris (1992) *Frontiers in Social Movement Theory*. New Haven: Yale University Press.

Nangle, J. (1995) 'Framing Radical Bisexuality: Toward a Gender Agenda', in: N. Tucker (ed.) *Bisexual Politics: Theories, Queries, and Visions*. New York: Harrington Park Press.

Nash, K. (1998) 'Beyond Liberalism: Feminist Theories of Democracy', in: V. Randall and G. Waylen (eds) *Gender, Politics and the State*. London: Routledge.

Nataf, Z. (1996) *Lesbians Talk Transgender*. London: Scarlett Press.

Obershall, A. (1997) *Social Movements: Ideologies, Interests and Identities*. New Brunswick: Transaction Publishers.

Ochs, R. (1996) 'Biphobia: It Goes More than Two Ways', in: B.A. Firestein (ed.) *Bisexuality: The Psychology and Politics of an Invisible Minority*. London: Sage.

Parekh, B. (1993) 'The Cultural Particularity of Liberal Democracy', in: D. Held (ed.) *Prospects for Democracy: North, South, East, West*. Cambridge: Polity.

—— (1994) 'Cultural Diversity and Liberal Democracy', in: G. Parry and M. Moran (eds) *Democracy and Democratization*. London: Routledge.

Parry, G. and M. Moran (1994) 'Introduction: Problems of Democracy and Democratization', in: G. Parry and M. Moran (eds) *Democracy and Democratization*. London: Routledge.

Parry, G. and G. Moyser (1994) 'More Participation, More Democracy?', in: D. Beetham (ed.) *Defining and Measuring Democracy*. London: Sage.

Pateman, C. (1989) *The Disorder of Women: Disorder, Feminism, and Political Theory*. Cambridge: Polity Press.

Penrose, W. (2001) 'Hidden in History: Female Homoeroticism and Women of a "Third Nature" in the South Asian Past', *Journal of the History of Sexuality*, 10(1): 3–39.

Perez, L.M. (1995) 'Go Ahead: Make my Movement', in: N. Tucker (ed.) *Bisexual Politics: Theories, Queries, and Visions*. New York: Harrington Park Press.

Phillips, A. (1991) *Engendering Democracy*. Cambridge: Polity Press.

—— (1993) *Democracy and Difference*. Cambridge: Polity Press.

Pink Paper (2000) 'Catholic School Backs Sex Change', 3 March: 4.

Piven, F.F and R.A. Cloward (1995) 'Collective Protest: A Critique of Resource Mobilization Theory', in: S.M. Lyman (ed.) *Social Movements: Critiques, Concepts, Case-Studies*. New York: New York University Press.

Plant, M., B. Mason and C. Thornton (1999) *Experiences and Perceptions of Violence and Intimidation of the Lesbian, Gay, Bisexual and Transgender Communities in Edinburgh*. Edinburgh: City of Edinburgh Council.

Plummer, K. (1995) *Telling Sexual Stories: Power, Change and Social Worlds.* London: Routledge.

Potter, D. (1997) 'Explaining Democratization', in: D. Potter, D. Goldblatt, M. Kiloh and P. Lewis (eds) *Democratization.* Cambridge: Polity Press in association with The Open University.

Prabhudas, Y. (1999) 'Bisexuals and People of Mixed-Race: Arbiters of Change', in: M. Storr (ed.) *Bisexuality: A Critical Reader.* London: Routledge.

Press For Change (1997a) *Legislating For Equality: Five Principles for the Evaluation of Legislative Proposals Covering Transsexual and Transgender People in the United Kingdom.* London: Press For Change.

—— (1997b) *Where do We Go from Here, What do We do Now?* Consultation Document 23, London: Press For Change.

Prieur, A. (1998) *Mema's House, Mexico City: On Transvestites, Queens and Machos.* Chicago: The University of Chicago Press.

Prosser, J. (1998) *Second Skins: The Body Narratives of Transsexuality.* New York: Columbia University Press.

PUCL-K (2003) *Human Rights Violations against the Transgender Community: A Study of Kothi and Hijra Sex Workers in Bangalore, India.* Bangalore: People's Union for Civil Liberties, Karnataka.

Purnell, A. (1998) 'Exceptional People whose Greatest Aspiration is to Be Seen as Ordinary: A Counsellor's View', *Gendys Journal*, 1: 8–14.

Queen, C. and L. Schimel (eds) (1997) *Pomosexuals: Challenging Assumptions about Gender and Sexuality.* San Francisco: Cleis Press.

Ramet, S. (1997) *Gender Reversals and Gender Cultures: Anthropological and Historical Perspectives.* London: Routledge.

Raymond, J. (1980) *The Transsexual Empire: The Making of the She-Male.* London: The Women's Press.

—— (1994) 'The Politics of Transgender', *Feminism and Psychology*, 4(4): 628–33.

Raymond, K. (1997) 'Confessions of a Second-Generation ... Dyke?: Reflections on Sexual Non-Identity', in: C. Queen and L. Schimel (eds) *Pomosexuals: Challenging Assumptions about Gender and Sexuality.* San Francisco: Cleis Press.

Reinharz, S. (1992) *Feminist Methods in Social Research.* Oxford: Oxford University Press.

Rhodes, R.A.W. (1997) *Understanding Governance Policy Networks: Governance, Reflexivity, and Accountability.* Buckingham: Open University Press.

Richardson, D. (1996) 'Heterosexuality and Social Theory', in: D. Richardson (ed.) *Theorising Heterosexuality: Telling it Straight.* Buckingham: Open University Press.

—— (2000a) 'Extending Citizenship: Cultural Citizenship and Sexuality', in: N. Stevenson (ed.) *Culture and Citizenship.* London: Sage.

—— (2000b) 'Extending Citizenship: Cultural Citizenship and Sexuality', in: N. Stevenson (ed.) *Culture and Citizenship.* London: Sage.

—— (2000c) 'Claiming Citizenship? Sexuality, Citizenship and Lesbian/ Feminist Theory', *Sexualities*, 3(2): 255–72.

—— (2000d) *Rethinking Sexuality.* London: Sage.

Roche, M. (1992) *Rethinking Citizenship: Welfare, Ideology and Change in Modern Society.* Cambridge: Polity Press.

Roen, K. (2001) 'Transgender Theory and Embodiment: The Risk of Racial Marginalisation', *Journal of Gender Studies*, 10(3): 253–63.

Rosario, V. (1996) 'Trans (Homo) Sexuality? Double Inversion, Psychiatric Confusion, and Hetero-Hegemony', in: B. Beemyn and M. Eliason (eds) *Queer Studies: A Lesbian, Gay, Bisexual and Transgender Anthology*. New York: New York University Press.

Rothblatt, M. (1995) *The Apartheid of Sex: A Manifesto for the Freedom of Gender*. New York: Crown.

Rowbotham, S. (1992) *Women in Movement: Feminism and Social Action*. London: Routledge.

Rubin, G. (1984) 'Thinking Sex: Notes for a Radical Theory of the Politics of Sexuality', in: H. Abelove, M. Barale and D. Halperin (eds) *The Lesbian and Gay Studies Reader*. London: Routledge.

Rubin, H. (1999) 'Transstudies: Between a Metaphysics of Presence and Absence', in: K. More and S. Whittle (eds) *Reclaiming Genders: Transsexual Grammars at the Fin de Siecle*. London: Cassell.

Rust, P. (1995) *Bisexuality and the Challenge to Lesbian Politics: Sex, Loyalty and Revolution*. New York: New York University Press.

—— (1996) 'Monogamy and Polyamory: Relationship Issues for Bisexuals', in: B. Firestein (ed.) *Bisexuality*. London: Sage.

Sampath, N. (2001) 'Crabs in a Bucket: Reforming Male Identities in Trinidad', in: S.M. Whitehead and F.J. Barrett (eds) *The Masculinities Reader*. Cambridge: Polity Press.

Sawicki, J. (1991) *Disciplining Foucault: Feminism, Power and the Body*. London: Routledge.

Seabrook, J. (1997) 'Not "Straight", not Gay', *Pioneer*, 30 September.

Sedgewick, E. (1991) *Epistemology of the Closet*. Hemel Hempstead: Harvester Wheatsheaf.

Shapiro, J. (1991) 'Transsexualism: Reflections on the Persistence of Gender and the Mutability of Sex', in: J. Epstein and K. Straub (eds) *Body Guards: The Cultural Politics of Gender Ambiguity*. London: Routledge.

Sharpe, A.N. (2002) *Transgender Jurisprudence: Dysphoric Bodies of Law*. London: Cavendish Publishing Limited.

Sibley, D. (1995) *Geographies of Exclusion: Society and Difference in the West*. London: Routledge.

Simpson, M. (1994) *Male Impersonators*. London: Cassell.

Slater, D. (1992) 'Theories of Development and Politics of the Post-Modern – Exploring a Border Zone', *Development and Change*, 23(3): 283–319.

Smart, C. (1995) *Law, Crime, and Sexuality: Essays in Feminism*. London: Sage.

Socarides, C.W. (1970) 'A Psychoanalytic Study of the Desire for Sexual Transformation ("Transsexualism"): The Plaster-of Paris Man', *International Journal of Psychoanalysis*, 51: 341.

—— (ed.) (1991) *The Homosexualities and the Therapeutic Process*. Madison: International Universities Press.

Somers, C. and F. Haynes (2001) 'Intersex: Beyond the Hidden A-genders', in: F. Haynes and T. McKenna (eds) *Unseen Genders: Beyond the Binaries*. New York: Peter Lang Publishers.

Spivak, G. (1987) *In Other Worlds: Essays in Cultural Politics*. London: Methuen.

Stacey, J. (1993) 'Untangling Feminist Theory', in: D. Richardson and V. Robinson (eds) *Introducing Women's Studies*. London: Macmillan.

Stevenson, N. (ed.) (2000) *Culture and Citizenship*. London: Sage.

Storr, M. (ed.) (1999) *Bisexuality: A Critical Reader*. London: Routledge.

Stone, S. (1991) 'The Empire Strikes Back: A Posttransexual Manifesto', in: J. Epstein and K. Straub (eds) *Body Guards: The Cultural Politics of Gender Ambiguity*. London: Routledge.

Stryker, S. (1998) 'The Transgender Issue: An Introduction', in: S. Stryker (ed.) *The Transgender Issue*. GLQ: A Journal of Lesbian and Gay Studies: 4(2), Duke University Press.

Sturgis, S.M. (1996) 'Bisexual Feminism: Challenging the Splits', in: S. Rose, C. Stevens et al. (eds) *Bisexual Horizons: Politics, Histories, Lives*. London: Lawrence and Wishart.

Swan, W.K. (ed.) (1997) *Gay/Lesbian/Bisexual/Transgender Public Issues: A Citizen's Guide to the New Cultural Struggle*. New York: Harrington Park Press.

Swaab, D.F. and M.A. Hofman (1995) 'Sexual Differentiation and the Human Hypothalamus in Relation to Gender and Sexual Orientation', *Trends in Neurosciences*, 18(6): 264–70.

Swain, J., V. Finkelstein, S. French and M. Oliver (eds) (1993) *Disabling Barriers – Enabling Environments*. London: Sage.

Tarrow, S. (1998) *Power in Movement*. Cambridge: Cambridge University Press.

Tauchert, A. (1998) 'Beyond the Binary: Fuzzy Gender and the Radical Centre'. Paper presented at The Third International Conference on Gender and Sexuality: TrAnsGENDER AGENDA for the New Millenium, Exeter College, Oxford University, September 17–20.

Taylor, V. (1999) 'Gender and Social Movements: Gender Processes in Women's Self-Help Movements', *Gender and Society*, 13(1): 8–33.

—— and N.E. Whittier (1992) 'Collective Identity in Social Movement Communities: Lesbian Feminist Mobilization', in: A.D. Morris and C. McClurg (eds) *Frontiers in New Social Movement Theory*. New Haven: Yale University Press.

Taylor-Gooby, P. (1994) 'Postmodernism and Social Policy: A Great Leap Backwards?', *Journal of Social Policy*, 23(3): 387–403.

Thompson, B. (1994) *Sadomasochism: Painful Perversion of Pleasurable Play?* London: Cassell.

Tilly, C. (1978) *From Mobilisation to Revolution*. Reading: Addison-Wesley.

Tong, R.P. (1998) *Feminist Thought: A More Comprehensive Introduction*. Boulder: Westview Press.

Tucker, K.H. (1991) 'How New are the New Social Movements?', *Theory, Culture and Society*, 8: 75–98.

Turner, B. and P. Hamilton (eds) (1994) *Citizenship: Critical Concepts*. London: Routledge.

Valverde, M. (1985) *Sex, Power and Pleasure*. London: The Women's Press.

Vance, C. (ed.) (1984) *Pleasure and Danger: Exploring Female Sexuality*. London: Routledge.

Wajcman, J. (1991) *Feminism Confronts Technology*. Cambridge: Polity Press.

Wakeford, N. (2000) 'Gender and the Landscapes of Computing in an Internet Cafe', in: G. Kirkup, L. Janes, K. Woodward and F. Hovenden (eds)

The Gendered Cyborg: A Reader. London: Routledge in association with The Open University.

Walby, S. (1994) 'Is Citizenship Gendered?', *Sociology*, 28(2): 379–95.

Watson, J. and R. Hitchcock (2000) 'Correspondence: Theorizing Transgender Diversity: Towards a Social Model of Health', *Sexual and Relationship Therapy*, 15(4): 417–18.

Waylen, G. (1998) 'Gender, Feminism and the State: An Overview', in: V. Randall and G. Waylen (eds) *Gender, Politics and the State*. London: Routledge.

Webb, J. (1997) 'The Politics of Equal Opportunity', *Gender, Work and Organisation*, 4(3): 159–69.

Weber, L. (2001) *Race, Gender, Class and Sexuality: A Conceptual Framework*. New York: McGraw-Hill Higher Education.

Weedon, C. (1994) 'Feminism and the Principles of Poststructuralism', in: J. Storey (ed.) *Cultural Theory and Popular Culture*. Hemel Hempstead: Harvester Wheatsheaf.

—— (1999) *Feminism, Theory, and the Politics of Difference*. Oxford: Blackwell Publishers.

Weeks, J. (1985) *Sexuality and its Discontents: Meanings, Myths and Modern Sexualities*. London: Routledge.

—— (1995) *Invented Moralities: Sexual Values in an Age of Uncertainty*. Cambridge: Polity Press.

—— (1998) 'The Sexual Citizen', *Theory, Culture and Society*, 15(3–4): 35–52.

Weinberg, G. (1972) *Society and the Healthy Homosexual*. New York: St Martins.

Weise, E.R. (ed.) (1992) *Closer to Home: Bisexuality and Feminism*. New York: Seal Press.

Wheelwright, J. (1995) 'I'm just a Sweet Transgenderist: Forget Drag Kings and Men in Skirts: A Third Sex is now Emerging, neither Male nor Female but something in the Middle', *Independent*, 27 March.

Whittle, S. (1996) 'Gender Fucking or Fucking Gender? Current Contributions to Theories of Gender Blending', in: R. Ekins and D. King (eds) *Blending Genders; Social Aspects of Cross-Dressing and Sex-Changing*. London: Routledge.

—— (1998a) 'Guest Editorial', *Journal of Gender Studies*, 7(3): 269–71.

—— (1998b) 'The Trans-Cyberian Mail Way', *Social and Legal Studies*, 7(3): 398–408.

—— (2002) *Respect and Equality: Transsexual and Transgender Rights*. London: Cavendish.

—— and P. Stephens 'A Pilot Study of Provision for Transsexual and Transgender People in the Criminal Justice System, and the Information Needs of their Probation Officers'. <http://www.pfc.org.uk>; last visited 30 October 2003.

Wilchins, R.A. (1997) *Read My Lips: Sexual Subversion and the End of Gender*. Ann Arbor: Firebrand Books.

—— , E. Lombardi, D. Preising and D. Malouf (1997) *First National Survey of Transgender Violence*. <http://www.gpac.org/violence/HateCrimes Survey97>; last visited 10 April 2000.

Wilkinson, R. and S. Hughes (eds) (2002) *Global Governance: Critical Perspectives*. London: Routledge.

Wilson, A.R. (1995) 'Their Justice: Heterosexism in *A Theory of Justice*', in: A.R. Wilson (ed.) *A Simple Matter of Justice?* London: Cassell.

Wilson, A. (1997) 'Social Policy and Sexuality', in: M. Lavalette and A. Pratt (eds) *Social Policy: A Conceptual and Theoretical Introduction*. London: Sage.

Woodward, K. (1997) 'Feminist Critiques of Social Policy', in: M. Lavalette and A. Pratt (eds) *Social Policy: A Conceptual and Theoretical Introduction*. London: Sage.

—— (2002) 'Concepts of Identity and Difference', in: I. Grewal and C. Kaplan (eds) *An Introduction to Women's Studies: Gender in a Transnational World*. New York: McGraw-Hill Higher Education.

Young, B. (1993) 'Feminisms and Masculinism: A Backlash Response', in: T. Haddad (ed.) *Men and Masculinities: A Critical Anthology*. Toronto: Canadian Scholars' Press.

Young, I.M. (1990) 'Impartiality and the Civic Public: Some Implications of Feminist Critiques of Moral and Political Theory', in: I.M. Young (ed.) *Throwing Like a Girl and other Essays in Feminist Philosophy and Social Theory*. Bloomington: Indiana University Press.

—— (2001) 'Justice and the Politics of Difference', in: S. Seidman and J.C. Alexander (eds) *The New Social Theory Reader*. London: Routledge.

Young, L. (1996) 'Sometimes it's Hard to be a Woman', *Guardian*, 29 July: 6.

Young, S. (1995) 'Bisexuality, Lesbian and Gay Communities, and the Limits of Identity Politics', in: N. Tucker (ed.) *Bisexual Politics: Theories, Queries, and Visions*. New York: Harrington Park Press.

Zandvliet, T. (2000) 'Transgender Issues in Therapy', in: C. Neal and D. Davies (eds) *Issues in Therapy with Lesbian, Gay, Bisexual, and Transgender Clients*. Buckingham: Open University Press.

Zhou, J., M. Hofman, L. Gooren and D. Swaab (1995) 'A Sex Difference in the Human Brain and its Relation to Transsexuality', *Nature*, 378: 68–70.

Zirakzadeh, C.E. (1997) *Social Movements in Politics: A Comparative Study*. London: Longman.

WEBSITES

http://canada.justice.gc.ca/en/dept/pub/guide/appendix_C.htm (last visited 12 March 2004).

http://www//bitheway.org/Bi/History/htm (last visited 30 April 2003).

http://www.bmeworld.com/smooth/ (last visited 15 March 2004).

http://www//dmoz.org/society/Transgendered/Intersexed/Activism (last visited 10 November 2003).

http://www.gendertrust.org.uk/index/htm (last visited 30 October 2003).

http://www.isna.org/drupal/index. php (last visited 29 July 2004).

http://www.isna.org/taq/writing-guidelines.html (last visited 27 July 2004).

http://www//lcd.gov.uk/constitution/transsex/tpeople/htm (last visited 10 November 2003).

http://www.pfc.org.uk/ (last visited 30 October 2003).

http://prostrate-help.org/caeunuc.htm (last visited 15 March 2004).

http://www//spunk.org/texts/pubs/lr/spool1714/gender.html (last visited 07 June 2003).

http://www.stonewall.org.uk/stonewall/ (last visited 30 October 2003).
http://www.tgforum.com (last visited 27 July 2004).
http://www.transhistory.org (last visited 01 March 2003).
http://www//ukia.co.uk (last visited 20 November 2003).
http://www//whatexit.org/tal/mywritings/bipolitics.html (last visited 10 April 2003).

Index

Compiled by Stephanie Johnson